ELEMENTARY TEACHER'S COMPLETE IDEAS HANDBOOK

ELEMENTARY TEACHER'S COMPLETE

by

Dr. Sidney W. Tiedt

and

Iris M. Tiedt

IDEAS HANDBOOK

PRENTICE-HALL, INC.
Englewood Cliffs, N.J.

Elementary Teacher's Complete Ideas Handbook,
by Dr. Sidney W. Tiedt and Iris M. Tiedt

PRENTICE-HALL, INC.

ENGLEWOOD CLIFFS, N.J.

LIBRARY OF CONGRESS
CATALOG CARD NUMBER: 65–16586

PRINTED IN THE UNITED STATES OF AMERICA
26075—B & P

TO THE CLASSROOM TEACHER

"How can I get those boys interested in poetry?"
"Where can I find new ideas for bulletin boards?"
"What do you do about recess on a rainy day?"

These are but a few of the many questions we've been asked by elementary school teachers and student teachers with whom we worked. It was questions like these which prompted us to begin collecting specific ideas to help teachers solve these problems and others which daily present themselves in the busy elementary school classroom.

Elementary Teacher's Complete Ideas Handbook provides suggestions which explain How, Where, What—How to maintain discipline, Where to find ideas about creative writing, What to do with the gifted child. Here is a collection of teacher-tested techniques that are readily understood and easily put into practice in the classroom. The purpose of this book is clearly that of assisting the elementary school teacher in doing a more effective job of teaching.

Every effort has been made to present this material in a functional manner which means that the reader will not find himself lost in a maze of educational jargon. He will find instead a clear, provocative style of presentation as he reads the ten chapters which are organized according to the areas of study in the elementary school program.

The first chapter, "Organizing for Learning," is a collection of techniques for helping the teacher get off to a good start. Suggestions are given for learning names, establishing control of the classroom, collecting instructional materials, evaluating students, and making effective displays. An interesting feature of this chapter is "The Teacher's Calendar," a unique list of important dates which occur during the school year—birthdays, holidays, flag days, historic events, and weeks set aside for special observance—a real help in planning displays and classroom activities.

The other nine chapters deal with specific subject areas of the elementary school curriculum such as Reading, Mathematics, and Social Studies. In each of these chapters scores of interesting ideas are described concisely with examples given which can be used immediately by the teacher. At the end of the book is a section which explains how you can continue to find new ideas so that your "repertoire of teaching techniques" will remain fresh, effective, and stimulating.

The activities described have been placed in the chapters for which they seem most appropriate. Because subject areas are usually integrated in the elementary school classroom, the teacher will need to check chapters dealing with related areas when searching for teaching ideas in a specific field. Listening skills, for example, are directly involved in the teaching of spelling and reading. Art and music activities often help develop social studies understandings. At times, too, teachers will modify ideas suggested, for instance, in the reading chapter to adapt them for use in another area such as social studies.

Every teacher is continually searching for new ideas for teaching children. The ideas, techniques, and activities included in this comprehensive collection cover a wide variety of skills that are taught in the elementary school. They provide for wide differences in ability as well as differences in grade level. Although these ideas can be used exactly as described, the teacher can also adapt and expand them according to the needs and purposes of the individual classroom. Good teaching ideas are not limited to any specified grade level; they are simply interpreted by the maturity level of the students themselves. We would like to feel that these suggestions will serve as a launching pad for the creative teacher who will develop variations and continue to think of new activities to add to this collection noting variations directly in this book as it is put to use.

Teaching techniques such as those described in this book are not greatly affected by the passage of time. *Elementary Teacher's*

Complete Ideas Handbook will not, therefore, quickly become outdated, but will prove a helpful collection of ideas, a good investment for many years. We look forward to being in your classroom and welcome questions or comments from you as you use these ideas with students.

SIDNEY AND IRIS TIEDT

To Ryan and Pamela who may benefit from these ideas

TABLE OF CONTENTS

One must learn by doing the thing; for though you think you know it, you have no certainty until you try.

—Sophocles

1

ORGANIZING FOR LEARNING

In this chapter we shall consider aspects of teaching which do not pertain to any one subject area—discipline, getting acquainted with students, the development of an Instructional Materials File, effective display techniques, and maintaining good parent-teacher relationships. Although these subjects are not learning areas, efficient and effective classroom management will lead to a better learning situation.

An interesting feature at the end of the chapter is the Teacher's Calendar which lists significant dates—famous birthdays, historical events, holidays—information which is helpful as you plan activities for the next month. These dates suggest ideas for displays, ways of motivating student interest, and topics for discussion.

Classroom Control

Effective classroom management and good discipline begin from the moment the first child enters your classroom. It is much easier to establish the standards of good behavior, the understanding that the classroom is a workshop, a place for study, if this attitude is clear from the beginning. Once a class develops poor work habits or a few students are permitted to misbehave it is far more difficult to correct the problem than it is to avoid it from the start. It is toward this end that we aim the following suggestions.

Before school begins

The time actually spent in the classroom should justifiably be planned as a busy time for each student as he moves ahead at his rate of ability to learn. Plan an activity to occupy students the minute they enter the classroom which sets the tone for the entire day. (This is particularly necessary if you have busses which bring children to school early.) Here are several ideas for activities appropriate for this period of time:

1. Develop (with student assistance) a box of CHALLENGES from which each student can take a sheet as soon as he has hung up his coat. Include a variety of Crossword Puzzles, Magic Squares, Synonym Studies, Word Quizzes, as described in Chapter 3. As other children enter, they can take a sheet and begin working independently. The sheet can be completed in free time or at home. As a child completes a sheet, let him check his own paper against your Answer Sheet (some activities allow for a variety of possible answers).
2. Designate this time as Exploring Time during which a student may work on a research project (see Chapters 3 and 5). Some students may be interested in continuing creative writing activities, a story not yet completed or a poem they have in mind. Permit free use of available reference tools.
3. Assign specific use of this time for reviewing knowledge not yet learned such as Mathematics Facts. One student may be *requested* (permit refusal if an able student has work he wishes to do) to assist several others in using flashcards to review the multiplication facts or in reviewing spelling words. Or let students needing review rotate the position of teacher, for much is learned as each teaches the others.

4. Young students can use this time to sort pictures according to the initial consonant. A leader can call up students (several at a time) to print a word on the board that begins with a specified letter.
5. Print five or six consonants (or blends) on the board. Each student folds a lined sheet of paper in fourths lengthwise. At the top of each column he writes one of the consonants or blends. He then tries to write as many words beginning with each initial sound as possible. Rhymes can be used in this manner also with the teacher supplying words which have many rhymes—pat, fan, fall, told, sweet, and so on.

Short periods between scheduled activities

Frequently in the elementary classroom one activity is completed a few minutes before another is scheduled, for example, before recess, the lunch hour, or dismissal time. This period of time is not suitable for introducing a new project, but the teacher does not, on the other hand, want to waste the time or to permit the class to become unruly as it may with nothing to do. Here are suggestions for using these Five Minute Periods:

1. Mental Math—"Take the number 5; add 6; multiply by 3; subtract 3; divide by 5. What's your answer?" Include those processes known by your class. Speak slowly at first until your class becomes adept at solving these mental problems; then speak more quickly. It is advisable for each student to jot his answer on a slip of paper before someone gives the answer so each one has made a decision about the answer.
2. Singing of Favorites—"We have time for two songs. Who would like to choose the first one?" After the class has learned a number of songs together there will be many that they enjoy repeating. These odd moments give the teacher an opportunity to encourage the enjoyment of music.
3. Word Games—"I'm thinking of a word. Who can guess a letter in it?" Play HANGMAN, the word game that is the favorite in many classrooms. Select a word, perhaps GHOST.

Without revealing the word draw five spaces on the board to indicate the number of letters in the word chosen. Let class members take turns guessing letters which are in the word. Each right letter is printed above the correct space. Each wrong letter is printed above the game on the board so that all will know which letters have been guessed already. Each wrong letter adds one part to the body being hung on the gallows—head, neck, body, two arms, two legs—seven wrong guesses hang the man. The class tries to beat the Hangman by guessing the word.

Establishing a routine

If you establish certain classroom routines, children soon know what you expect of them. If they know, for example, that you usually (no routine is absolutely inflexible) read a story immediately after recess, the students will expect to enter the room quietly, hang up their coats, and take their seats quickly so they do not waste any story-time. A particular incentive is the reading of a longer book which the children are eager to continue such as *Charlotte's Web* by E. B. White, for younger children and Mark Twain's *Tom Sawyer* or Robert McCloskey's *Homer Price* for the upper grades.

1. Establish a *consistent form for heading papers,* so this question is not asked repeatedly. If this detail is "routinized," you will have more time for the content. When you say, "Head a paper for Reading," each student immediately knows what to do. A simple usable form for the elementary school is the following:

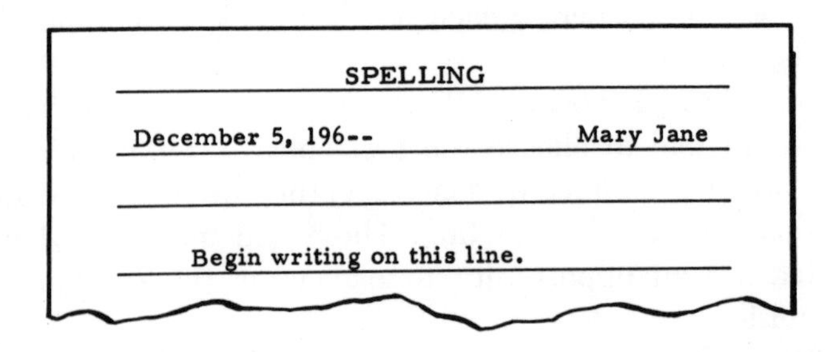
SPELLING

December 5, 196-- Mary Jane

Begin writing on this line.

2. Have a *copy of the class schedule* on a chart which is mounted in full view of the students. Although this schedule will

be changed as necessary, the students will know in general what is to be done and when their work should be completed. Write specific lesson assignments on the chalkboard so students can follow them without undue questioning.

Routines of this nature lend an element of security to the classroom proceduries. Children become accustomed to doing things in certain ways; they know what is expected of them.

Students require understanding

1. Discipline problems often occur because the child is striving for attention which he may not get at home. Try to give each student some measure of attention each day; make him a real part of the classroom and its activities. NEVER DO SOMETHING WHICH A CHILD CAN DO is a maxim which many teachers stress. The child who is asked to help the teacher even in some small way is usually pleased and will tend to be cooperative in the classroom.

2. Here is *an interesting experiment* which we wholeheartedly recommend to all teachers. Toward the end of the day read through the names of your students. Can you remember speaking directly to each student at some time during the day other than calling the roll or calling on him to answer a question? Most of the children will have talked with you about something, but often there will be a few who have had no direct warm contact with you during the day.

A walk around the classroom will provide you the opportunity to stop by the desks of these children, to perhaps pat a shoulder saying, "My, we certainly have worked hard today, haven't we, Joe?" or "Don't forget to tell your mother about our new reading words, Mary." This technique should lead to a feeling of greater security for each child, a feeling of belonging.

3. To encourage students to get to work on an assignment which has been made, begin walking around the room writing a number in ink on the corner of the students' papers. Write the number 1 on the papers of those who get started immediately (one minute), the number 2 for those who take a little longer (two minutes), and so forth.

Some teachers use the MAGIC TOUCH for designating those students who are working well. The teacher walks around the room touching the shoulders of those who are busily completing their assignment. The children get to know these techniques and respond accordingly.

Quieting the disturber

Often merely *looking directly at the student* who is causing the disturbance is sufficient to make him be quiet. *Walking around the room* as students work on a written assignment will usually quell students who are inclined to talk unnecessarily; it also makes you readily available for answering questions and giving help where needed. *Sitting at the back of the room* while students write is an excellent strategy, for students cannot see you without turning completely around which leaves them uncertain whether you are watching them. If a student, however, repeatedly disturbs the class, you may need to employ one of the following measures:

1. Have his desk removed completely apart from those of the other students. Be certain he is in a position where he cannot gain satisfaction from showing off.
2. Stop all work while you announce that the disturber has something important to say. Have him come to the front of the room to give his "speech." Even if he says nothing, have him stand before the class several minutes before dismissing him to return to his work.
3. Call the student to your desk where you can talk to him quietly. Have him show you the work he has done, and *determine his reason for being noisy*. It may be that he is confused about the work he has been assigned. If you feel this child simply needs attention, make a point of giving it to him at another time.

Varying types of activities

Children tend to become restless when they are tired or bored with what they are doing. The attention span of young children is rather short, so they should not be expected to focus attention on a reading job which involves numerous pages. Even older children will be better motivated if assignments are not unduly long and tedious.

After a period of working quietly at their desks with a written assignment have a music period during which you can include motion songs such as "Did You Ever See a Lassie?" or "Three

Blind Mice ." (See Chapter 9.) Or simply have the class stand up for the "Seventh Inning Stretch." They can do a few exercises or play a short game such as "Simon Says." (See Chapter 10.)

The room temperature and ventilation affect students' restlessness, too. Keep the room cool rather than warm by opening a window or door to avoid stuffiness.

Giving directions

Perhaps one of the most important aspects of teaching is the giving of clear directions which will not lead to confusion and misunderstanding. Good directions can save the teacher much time and effort in repeating instructions and clarifying what was meant. Here are some KEYS TO GIVING DIRECTIONS:

1. Be sure *you* understand the process being described. Rarely begin an art project, for example, without having tried the process or produced the object yourself.
2. Do not begin speaking until everyone is listening. Having students clear their desks before beginning explanations helps to remove distracting elements.
3. Speak clearly and loudly enough so all can hear.
4. Use understandable language, that which is familiar to your students. Carefully explain any unknown terms.
5. Tell the children the object of the lesson. Show them the finished product they are trying to produce, if possible.
6. Don't try to cover too much with one set of directions. If the project is complicated, work in stages. You may wish to duplicate instructions so that each student will have a guide or outline to follow as he works.
7. Have children repeat the directions. Ask them questions to see if they understand—"What do you do after you complete the sentences on the board?"—and so forth.
8. Ask students if they have any questions about the work before they begin. Discouraging questions after work has commenced will teach children to listen carefully while directions are being given.

Practice in following directions

The bulletin board used to demonstrate the development of a project gives students practice in following directions. Number

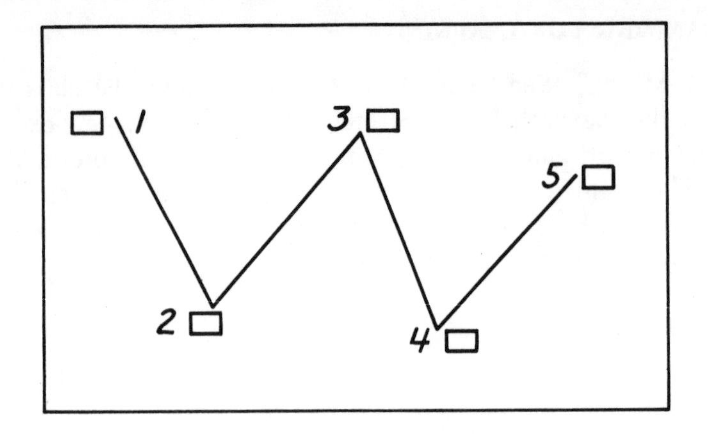

the Steps to be followed showing the results at each stage, if possible. Use this technique, for example, to show the class how to fold a paper snowflake including a large folded paper sample at each stage until the finished product is shown.

Let students try to produce snowflakes by reading and following directions. Those who are confused and cannot complete a snowflake can then be assisted in a small group with the teacher going over the directions and guiding their progress.

For further practice direct other tasks in the same manner, for we use this skill of following directions so much that it well warrants teaching. Duplicate simple directions which each child is to follow to produce a booklet. Mental arithmetic is also a good technique which teaches number facts as well as listening skills.

Don't talk too much

1. Sometimes we teachers talk too much when we would be more effective if we said less with greater emphasis. When you do speak, be sure that all students listen if you wish to address the entire class. Many teachers find that flicking the light switch, ringing a small bell, or playing a chord on the piano are more effective techniques for getting attention than speaking. Above all DON'T SHOUT.

2. An interesting technique is the designating of a period of time, perhaps thirty minutes or an hour according to the grade level, as a period of NO TALKING. During this time no one talks, not even the teacher. All should be working on an assignment independently which they will have to handle by themselves.

This technique works well in combination with the following of directions.

3. In order to avoid the impression of being the OGRE who is always correcting the wayward student, transfer some of this task to a puppet or a stuffed toy which becomes a sort of mascot who can give the class messages about their behavior or supply reminders. The teacher can speak for this mascot or print messages which the students will read. The mascot quickly becomes part of the class. He scolds the children, but he praises them, too. You can prepare (with a felt pen) several strips of tagboard with stock messages written such as: "I'm proud of you, my friends." or "Let's have a little quiet, please."

4. Students soon become accustomed to the use of signs or signals which direct them to do something. SSS written on the chalkboard means STAND, STRETCH, SIT in many classrooms. A big D tells the class they may have drinks of water if they go quietly in turn to the fountain. C U is the signal for cleaning up after an art period. It is surprising how quickly these signals pass around the room although the teacher has said nothing at all. You can develop those signals which you need for your own classroom.

Getting to Know Your Students

In order to teach effectively the teacher must know the students with whom she is working. Knowing them includes far more than scores on tests and results of physical examinations. The teacher must probe deeper to find reasons for a student's behavior, for the feelings and reactions of a child may have far-reaching effects on his classroom attitudes.

The first step in getting acquainted is learning the first names of students in a new class. Described here are several simple techniques for identifying students by name from the first day. Knowing the names of students is also the first step toward good classroom control.

Name tags

Leaf-shaped name tags can be cut from construction paper. These leaves can be displayed on a real branch which is held erect in a coffee can filled with sand or gravel. As each child's name is called, he can find his tag which is then pinned on him to assist you in addressing him during the first day. If the tags are returned to the tree before students leave in the afternoon, they can be used again for the second day.

Name games

To help both you and the class become familiar with the names of students in the room play NAMO which is played with sheets of construction paper on which a form has been dittoed (thinner paper can be used) similar to the sample shown. To play the game have each child in turn stand before the class. If a child can identify this person by name, he finds the correct name on the NAMO card. That name is covered with a square of colored con-

N	A	M	O
Mary	Charles	Susan	Ryan
Shirley	John	Rose	Don
Ralph	Pam	Earl	Linda
Bill	Helen	Robert	Roxanne

struction paper. A student with four names in a row calls NAMO, reading the names so the teacher can check his accuracy.

Creative writing reveals experiences

Often students reveal helpful information about their home relationships, their feelings, and their desires as they write reactions to a subject suggested by the teacher. Open-ended topics are especially conducive to the confiding of inner feelings. You might try some of these:

1. The only thing I could think of was . . .
2. One night I woke up so scared that . . .
3. Sometimes I have strange feelings about . . .
4. I am never so happy as when . . .
5. I was so angry I . . .

Talk to students individually

Are you approachable? Students often need to talk to someone. They want to tell you things that are happening to them, perhaps to ask questions, to seek reassurance. The individual conference used in conjunction with creative writing offers a good opportunity for the teacher to establish rapport with each individual student (see Chapter 3) and to demonstrate interest and concern for each one's thoughts and ideas and the work they are doing. Children often, too, like to share experiences with the teacher at recess time or before and after school. Individually the shy child will discuss things with the teacher which would never be revealed in a class discussion.

The case incident

Descriptions of case incidents can be duplicated or read aloud to the class. The students' written reactions to these incidents often provide much insight into the backgrounds of the children you have in your room. After the students write about an incident you may wish to have a discussion of the problem described. Here are several sample incidents which may be used:

> Pete's father is always yelling at him. If Mr. Harmon sees Pete reading a book, he gives the boy a job to do so he won't waste his time. When Pete is working for his father, the work is never right. No matter what Pete does, Mr. Harmon always finds something wrong. What can Pete do?

> Margaret is a new girl in the Townsend School. She is very quiet. No one is unkind to her, but the girls ignore her and leave her alone most of the time. What would you do if you were Margaret?

> Dave's class is being tested on the states and their capitals (or some other appropriate subject). He notices that his best friend is referring to a slip of paper which obviously has answers on it. Should Dave tell the teacher?

You can write brief descriptions of situations which may be helpful in working with your class. Use this approach to focus attention on a problem which has arisen. Always use anonymous names to disguise any individuals involved.

Letting students assume responsibilities

Students learn much by assuming responsibility for tasks which assist the teacher in smooth classroom operation. They also acquire a proprietary interest in *their* classroom as they help *their* teacher. Here are a number of areas which provide opportunity for student assistance:

1. Passing paper for art and language activities
2. Returning corrected work
3. Leading the Pledge of Allegiance and opening song
4. Care for chalkboards and erasers
5. Official pencil sharpener at specific time
6. Host and Hostess as guests arrive
7. Messenger
8. Windows and shades
9. Feeding pets
10. Watering flowers
11. Arranging displays (committee)
12. Filing material in Instructional Materials File (committee)
13. Friends for new students
14. Wastebasket
15. Leading students en route to lunch, etc.
16. Classroom librarian; working in central library
17. Checking attendance
18. Officers of class
19. Keeping routine records (milk money, charity contributions)
20. Student editors; assistant teachers

Care must be exercised to see that no one student is spending too much time on these activities. The gifted student should not, for example, be expected to busy himself with these activities in lieu of doing challenging research at his level of ability.

Rotate these positions each week so that all have an opportunity to participate. A chart can hold book pockets for each student, so that a symbol of his assigned duty can be inserted—perhaps a flower for the gardener, a musical note for the song leader, or simply a strip of tagboard with the name of the position lettered on it. Tongue depressors can hold a colored flag decorated with an appropriate word or symbol.

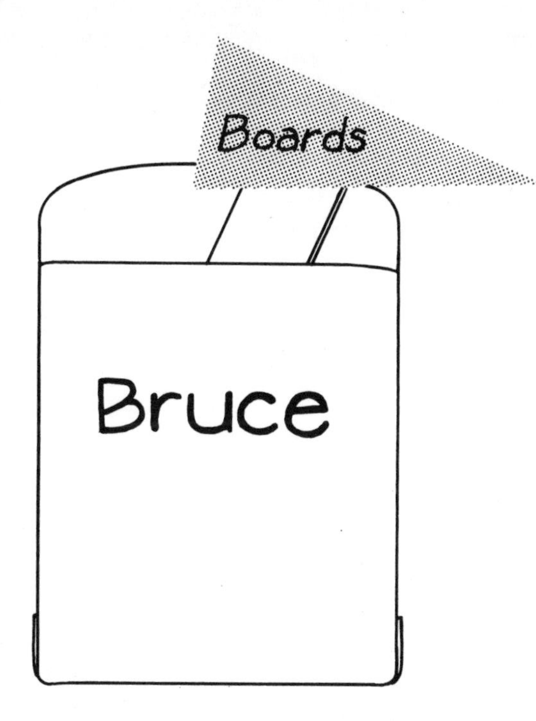

The Instructional Materials File

The experienced teacher soon collects a varied assortment of instructional materials which can be used year after year. These materials are invaluable because they lend *spice* to the learning situation and assist the teacher in teaching effectively. An INSTRUCTIONAL MATERIALS FILE is not, however, "built in a day." It is developed over a period of years; in fact, it never ceases to grow from the time you decide to become a teacher.

What makes up this valuable collection? We could not begin to name all the possible contents of a well-developed materials file, but here are general categories of materials which are often included:

Pictures to motivate writing, to illustrate science and social science units, to make the room attractive
Posters related to social science, health, science
Clippings related to any topic studied
Bulletin board displays—letters, motifs, backgrounds, ideas
Ditto masters and copies of seatwork, supplementary learning aids
Charts to illustrate concepts in language, science, mathematics

Pamphlets and leaflets providing supplementary, up-to-date information
Samples of art ideas

Sending for free instructional aids

Sometimes teachers will purchase charts or pictures which they feel warrant the expense, but there are many other sources of excellent materials which cost the teacher very little actual money —posters, pamphlets, maps, pictures, and other informational materials.

One source of such materials is the embassy or the industry which publishes good FREE teaching aids in an effort to promote public relations and to disseminate information. Here is a list of recommended books and pamphlets which present the names and addresses of sources which a teacher can contact to request free materials for use in her classroom:

Educators Progress Service. (Randolph, Wisconsin)
Educators Guide to Free Social Studies Materials ($6.95)
Elementary Teachers Guide to Free Curriculum Materials

Field Enterprises, Inc. (Educational Division, Merchandise Mart Plaza. Chicago 54, Illinois).
Sources of Free and Inexpensive Teaching Materials.

George Peabody College for Teachers. (Division of Surveys and Field Services. Nashville 5, Tennessee).
Free and Inexpensive Learning Materials. ($2.00)

Contemporary Press. (Box 1524, San Jose, California).
Selected Free Materials. ($1.00)

Magazine material

Magazines, too, provide an excellent source of worthwhile pictures and information. Let students assist you in trimming pictures and filing the material after it is collected. Look for pictures of animals, people in the news, neighbors in foreign lands, and other topics of general interest. Save pictures which show activities which might be used for motivating the writing of stories and poetry. Collect appropriate articles about life in other countries, scientific subjects, and so forth.

You don't have to rely on your own magazine subscriptions alone for these pictures and articles because parents will often contribute their magazines for this purpose. Have a MAGAZINE SHOWER to obtain a wealth of periodicals which can be sorted and clipped. This is particularly worthwhile if the school is developing a Central Instructional Materials File to be used by all the teachers in the school. Magazines which you might list as being specifically desirable include:

Life	*Holiday*
Sunset	*National Geographic*
Look	*Arizona Highways*
Travel	*Saturday Evening Post*

Organizing the file

Unless the materials you collect are organized, it is impossible to find the picture you need when it is appropriate. The majority of the materials to be included in the file will fit in manila folders. These folders can be kept in file drawers, if available, or in large cartons or wooden boxes. Compile a list of headings which you require such as BIRDS, ANIMALS, FAMOUS PEOPLE, COUNTRIES (by name), STATES (by name), HOLIDAYS, SCHOOL SUBJECTS (by name), MONTHS and SEASONS. Others will occur to you as you begin to file your various items. Wide pictures and charts can be rolled and kept in shipping tubes or in large cardboard folders if sufficient drawer space is not available.

Some schools have found it advantageous to pool teacher efforts by maintaining one extensive file in the school office, the library, or the teachers' room. This cooperative approach eliminates much duplication of effort and time. It means, also, that each teacher can benefit from a much more extensive collection of teaching aids than if she relied on herself alone. Clerical assistance is often supplied for the development of the central file.

Teacher-Parent Relationships

Parents are interested in knowing what their children are doing in school, but it is often difficult for them to find out this information from the student. Their picture of school activities is at best distorted. Here are a number of suggestions for improving the dissemination of information to the parent which at the same time should provide a desirable image of the workings of the school and its staff and lead to better understanding of school affairs.

Parent observations

Invite parents to come to school to observe a normal hour of class activities. They will be especially interested in watching you guide the children through reading groups, number activities, or a lesson in social studies. If you set one specific time to invite all parents to come, the observation will not disrupt classroom work unduly. Select an hour which immediately precedes a break in your schedule such as recess or lunch. In this way the observation is clearly ended as you leave the room with the children. The invitation to observe might be extended during EDUCATION WEEK.

Parent-teacher conferences

The conference is an excellent method for becoming acquainted with parents and provides them with a chance to ask questions specific to their child. Begin preparing for these conferences from the first day of school. In each child's folder save representative papers to give the parent an idea of the student's progress.

Parents have no means of comparison, so they usually have no accurate picture of appropriate standards for work their child is doing. An effective way of showing them how their child's work compares with the work of others in the same class is to prepare a set of papers (Handwriting, Stories on one topic, Social Studies reports) from which you have removed the names. You may number the papers so that you can identify each student's work. You can prepare a bulletin board display for Open House for this same purpose. Each child can identify his own writing, and the parent can compare the work with other student work both better and worse.

Folders of student work

It is a good idea to send completed work home daily with primary children. This work provides a clear picture for interested parents. They can note, for example, the reading vocabulary, the skill with numbers, and can help the child where necessary. Sending the papers home daily is practical from the teacher's viewpoint also for quantities of papers do not accumulate to be handled at one time.

Students in upper grades can collect their papers for a week, placing them in a colored paper folder (12 x 18 inch construction paper folded) which can be decorated. This folder is taken home on Friday so that parents have an indication of the quality of the work being done and also know what areas of knowledge are being studied. If you wish to make certain that a parent sees the student's work, require students to have their parents sign a specified paper which is to be returned to you.

Open house

OPEN HOUSE offers an excellent opportunity to show the parents what students are doing during school. For this reason don't clear away all the teaching aids, audio-visual equipment, supplementary materials which you use with the class. Parents, who know little about the modern educative process, will be much enlightened and genuinely interested in seeing the materials of teaching. A mural in progress or students who are working on a science project during the Open House will give the parent a more real impression of the classroom activities.

An unusual, yet effective, device for providing the parents with a chance to hear their child participating in class work is the TAPE which is played while parents are visiting the classroom. You can record any type of short language activity—reading, original poetry, speeches, short reports, other creative writing. If each student says his name before recording, parents can easily identify their child. This tape can be repeated several times in one corner of the room during the hour.

Letters to parents

A monthly one-page flyer or letter can be prepared by the class to inform parents of the activities that have taken place during the previous month—descriptions of projects completed, a listing of concepts studied, information acquired. Activities which are to begin can be introduced, and the aid of parents can be solicited—old magazines, realia from a country being studied, scrap cloth for collages, and so forth.

Informative notices of this nature make the parent feel a part of the activities that involve his child. He will be better able to help his child and will better understand what you are trying to accomplish.

Effective Display Techniques

Displays not only lend to the attractiveness of a classroom but also serve to motivate student interest in subjects being studied. Displays can also add to the knowledge of the class as they present new material. Display techniques encompass more than the bulletin board although that is the more common type of display and certainly an essential part of any classroom. We shall begin, therefore, with suggestions for the bulletin board before moving on to other interesting ideas for mobiles, hall displays, and wall hangings.

Bulletin board assistance

Let students help you in preparing bulletin board displays. They can learn much as they work on a team to develop an idea which may have originated with them or with you. Here are some general rules which can be printed on a chart for BULLETIN BOARD HELPERS:

1. Try to express just one idea in one display. Use only a few words.
2. Use contrasting colors, but use no more than three colors on one bulletin board.
3. Pin pictures and letters in place. Then step to the opposite side of the room to see if everything is well arranged and can be seen at a distance. Can letters be read?
4. Do not use too many different items on one board. Avoid a cluttery effect.
5. To line up letters, measure with the yardstick to make a light guideline on which to place the bottom edge of each letter.

Display captions

Often a stimulating caption will suggest the whole idea for an effective display. Here are some useful captions which can be adapted to a number of different topics:

SEEING FRANCE (feature a large eye in upper left-hand corner)
FOCUS ON DIVISION (three lines of yarn lead to center of focus)
KEY TO SUCCESS (use key shape)
SCENES OF NEW ENGLAND (group of pictures)
INTRODUCING NEW BOOKS (use book jackets)
TRAVEL TIPS (feature any country or area)
TICKET TO LONDON (feature large ticket)
TIME TO READ BIOGRAPHY (feature clock face)
THIS IS OUR BEST (can feature any type of work)

The words emphasized in the above captions can be changed to any topic you wish to feature. INTRODUCING, for example, might be followed by POETRY, BIOGRAPHY, NIGERIA, BRAZIL, BENJAMIN FRANKLIN, NEW FRIENDS, and so on.

Keep a notebook or packet of file cards to record ideas for the Bulletin Board Caption. You will find ideas in magazine advertisements, in displays seen in other rooms, and in books on this subject. A book which provides numerous captions for use on bulletin boards in the classroom is *Bulletin Board Captions* from Contemporary Press (Box 1524, San Jose, California) for one dollar.

Materials for displaying

Your Instructional Materials File will, of course, supply you with pictures, charts, posters, and other items which can be used on the bulletin board. Book jackets and student work are useful as display materials. Realia (real items) from geographic areas being studied add much to a display also. Small items can be attached directly to the board while larger items are arranged on a table below the bulletin board area.

Lettering

Remember that lettering should be easily read at a distance. The simplest variety to make is the block letter which students can cut out from construction paper. Use graph paper to construct a set of patterns like these:

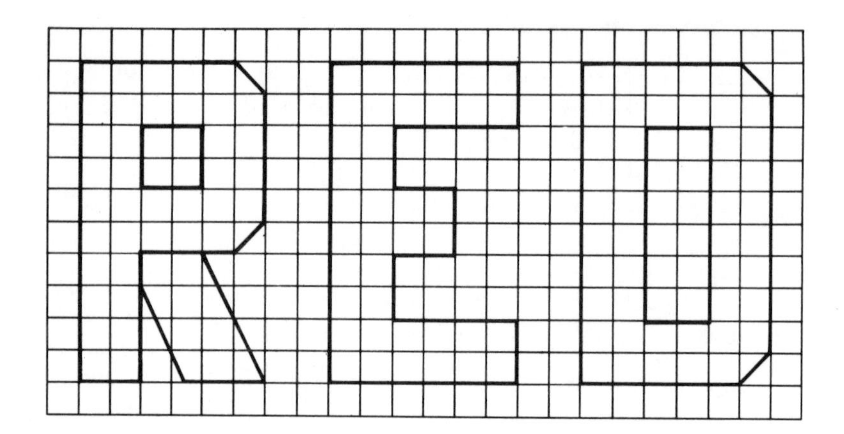

One set of letters can be constructed from each of these colors —black, white, red—to supply you with letters for any display. Other colors can be used also as desired. A set of letters should include the following numbers of each letter:

10	E, I, A, O, S
6	B, C, D, G, H, L, M, N, P, R, T, U, Y
2	F, J, K, Q, V, W, X, Z

Another simple and quick type of sign or label is that lettered by hand using the felt pen with varied colors of ink. Cut strips of paper three inches wide for this purpose. You can quickly print manuscript letters or for older children write the sign in script for a change.

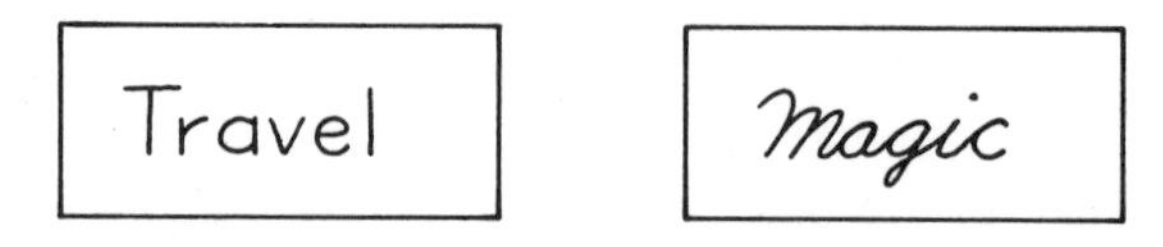

For special bulletin boards you may wish to experiment with unusual letters from a variety of materials. On a board featuring current events cut letters from newspaper to spell NEWS. Use yarn to write a caption like MYSTERY YARNS; pins will anchor the yarn in shape of the letters written in script. Letters can be fashioned from twigs, pipe cleaners, ribbon, wire or rope. Students will enjoy experimenting with different media when producing short captions.

Interesting backgrounds

Often the brown cork of the bulletin board serves as an effective background for a display, but for the sake of variety try other colors and textures. To avoid the task of pinning numerous small sheets of colored construction paper on a board obtain several large sheets of paper or cloth which will cover the board in one operation. There are many possibilities which can be explored. Listed here are but a few:

1. Colored burlap (interesting texture and color)
2. Discarded drapes, tablecloths
3. Wrapping papers, grasscloth, rice paper, crepe paper
4. Upholstery, drapery remnants
5. Patterned cloth (stripes, small figures, flowers)
6. Colored corrugated cardboard (lightweight, colored, in rolls)
7. Net or mesh (either cloth or screening)
8. Newspaper (travel or communications theme)

There are several distinct advantages to the use of these types of large coverings. The chief one is that you can cover the board quickly by inserting a few strategic pins or staples. The cloth has another advantage which is that of storage; it can be used repeatedly, stored easily, and pin or staple marks don't show.

Mobiles

It is fun and exciting to experiment with other types of display media. One which is really intriguing and uses formerly unused space in the classroom is the Mobile. Suspend single articles which children have made such as Halloween masks or hand puppets. There are many folded paper forms which lend themselves to this type of exhibition. (See Chapter 8.) An excellent book which will supply more ideas along this line is Pauline Johnson's *Creating with Paper* (University of Washington Press, 1958).

Students will enjoy, too, the construction of Mobiles which depict life in another country. When studying Russia, for example, a student might cut out pictures of famous Russians and symbols of this country to hang on a Mobile.

Book jackets, stapled together to resemble a closed book, can also be displayed in this manner. A Mobile can be constructed to feature the characters and setting of a book which a student has read to create a stimulating form for a Book Report.

A tree display

An effective device for displaying a variety of materials is a branch of a tree. A small branch can be fastened to the bulletin board or suspended mobile fashion. A large branch can be anchored erect in a can of sand or gravel to resemble a real tree. From the bare branches suspend light articles or fasten things directly on the small twigs.

This method is an attractive way to display marcaroni jewelry, paper leis or other work of this nature. Large colored leaves bearing words of interest to the class (words about a country being studied, new reading vocabulary, words in a foreign language, interesting synonyms) can be attached directly on the branches.

Suspend decorated Easter eggs (blown or papier-mâché) to make a lovely egg tree or hang valentines on the branch in February. Use the branch in its natural color or spray it white or any color that suits the purpose. Bird shapes, airplanes, and flowers can also be used to display short poems and interesting phrases which have appeared in student writing.

Wall hangings

The wall hanging is an attractive method of increasing display space. You can hang any interesting material such as a split bamboo drape, a woven rug, or a strip of heavy-weight cloth. Pins can be used to fasten pictures, writing, designs, or other decorations to the backdrop creating an unusually attractive display. Wall hangings can be of any size according to the space available.

Displays in the hall

Make a point of displaying student work in the hall. Here it can be seen by visiting parents and shared by members of other classes. If there are no display cases in your school hall, you can improvise with large pieces of beaver board. Mount beaver board on an easel to stand in the entry to the school where art work presents a bright welcome to anyone entering the school.

The Teacher's Calendar

Included here are dates of significance to the teacher in the classroom. Birthdates of famous people, dates of historical importance, and holidays are noted here so that the teacher can use this information in preparing displays and in planning learning experiences. Unless otherwise indicated, dates noted for famous people are birthdays.

How can you use this information? One of the most obvious ways is to *construct a calendar each month on a bulletin board* where those dates of significance to your class can be noted. As part of this display you might include a poem or speech by a person born during that month. You could also include pictures of famous people such as presidents or pictures typical of a state which was admitted to the Union during the month.

Prepare a bulletin board display featuring one important date such as September 17th which is Constitution Day, the day when our Constitution was officially adopted in 1787. For this display you could include a copy of the Constitution. Students could write brief information about signers of the Constitution. They could also list the states which originally ratified the Constitution and a list of the states which were later admitted. Amendments to the Constitution can also be featured. Let able students assist in planning displays for these special days.

Read poems, stories, even books written by famous authors. You can, for example, begin reading *Tom Sawyer* on November 30th, the birthday of one of our most famous writers, Mark Twain. On January 19th read Poe's best-known poem, "The Raven," or one of his short stories. Read a fairy tale by Hans Christian Andersen on his birthdate, April 2nd.

During the music period *feature a song appropriate to the date.* Make a point of discussing and singing the "Star-Spangled Banner" on September 14th, the day when Francis Scott Key completed this verse. Play a record of *Finlandia* by Jan Sibelius on December 8th. Sing the "Battle Hymn of the Republic" on Julia Ward Howe's birthday, May 27th.

Have small groups of students *prepare skits, puppet plays, or pantomimes depicting historical events.* On January 17th Benjamin Franklin was born; there are many interesting stories to tell about his life. Daniel Boone and Thomas Edison, both born on February 11th, also provide excellent dramatic material. Early American history can be featured with a story about the Boston Tea Party on December 16th or the Fall of the Alamo on March 6th. These activities are especially good for talented students who have time for independent exploration of such events and the preparation of a short drama to present to the class.

Feature the reading of books by the students. During Book Week in November you may devote time to discussing books of interest to your grade level. Let each student read an exciting portion of a book he would like to recommend. Introduce biographies of famous men and women which make good reading for young people—Buffalo Bill (February 26th), Kit Carson (December 24th), Louisa May Alcott (November 29th), and Theodore Roosevelt (October 27th).

Assign reports to be given by individual students on the appropriate date. Brief reports can be incorporated in the Opening Exercises or presented as part of a subject lesson. A girl could tell the class about the life of Florence Nightingale on May 12th. Another student could talk about the life of Robert Louis Stevenson on November 13th. Plan these reports so not more than one is presented on any one day. Encourage students to include recorded music or to display books which will add to the interest of their presentation. The report could be successfully united with a bulletin board display.

Center an art lesson or activity around events on the calendar. The anniversary of the Chicago fire (October 9th) provides excellent motivation for the painting of pictures depicting this event. It also ties in with Fire Prevention Week (second week in October). Holidays and famous birthdays supply a theme for a variety of cut paper work which decorates the room. Pictures can be drawn to depict scenes from the lives of famous Americans such as presidents, inventors, and writers. Boys would especially enjoy drawings featuring the first flights of the Wright Brothers on Wilbur Wright's birthday in April (Orville was born in August) or on the anniversary of that first flight at Kitty Hawk, December 17th.

Focus creative writing on these events, too. May 5th is Bird Day, which can provide an excellent stimulus for the writing of poetry about different birds. The class might compose a poem together to commemorate an event such as the assassination of Lincoln on April 15th. The discovery of gold in California on January 24th may produce imaginative stories entitled, "I Was There" or "My Name Is Sutter." Have students bring a figure from the past into our present year as they imagine "What Would George Washington Think?" or "What Would Martha Washington Say?"

SEPTEMBER

1 Child Labor Act 1916
1 Commercial Television authorized 1940
2 V-J Day (surrender of Japan) 1945
2 Eugene Field (poet) 1850–1895
First Monday—Labor Day
6 Jane Addams (social worker) 1860–1935
6 Lafayette (French patriot) 1757–1834
9 California (31st State) 1850
11 William Sydney Porter (O. Henry) 1862–1910
13 Dr. Walter Reed (yellow fever) 1851–1902
14 Francis Scott Key wrote "The Star-Spangled Banner" 1814
15 James Fenimore Cooper (author) 1789–1851
15 William H. Taft (27th President) 1857–1930
16 Pilgrims sailed from England 1620
17 Constitution Day; Constitution officially adopted 1787
17 Citizenship Day FLAG*
19 Washington's "Farewell Address" 1796
21 First day of FALL
25 Balboa first saw the Pacific Ocean 1513
28 American Indian Day (Fourth Friday)

OCTOBER

First Week—Religious Education Week
Second Week—Fire Presention Week, National Picture Week
Third Week—National Bible Week

* The word FLAG denotes a Flag Day.

OCTOBER

2 Pan-American Union first met 1889
4 Rutherford B. Hayes (19th President) 1822–1893
5 Chester A. Arthur (21st President) 1830–1886
7 James Whitcomb Riley (poet) 1849–1916
9 Chicago Fire 1871
12 Columbus Day, Discovery of America 1492 FLAG
13 White House begun 1792
14 William Penn (statesman) 1644–1718
14 Dwight D. Eisenhower (34th President) 1890–1969
16 Noah Webster 1758–1843
24 United Nations Day
27 Theodore Roosevelt (26th President) 1858–1919
27 Navy Day FLAG
28 Statue of Liberty unveiled 1886
29 John Keats (poet) 1795–1821
30 John Adams (2nd President) 1735–1826
31 Halloween
31 Nevada (36th State) 1864
31 Juliette Low (Founder of American Girl Scouts) 1860–1927

NOVEMBER

Second Week—Education Week
Material available from: National Education Association
1201 Sixteenth Street, N.W.
Washington 6, D.C.

Third Week—Book Week
Material available from: American Library Association
50 E. Huron Street
Chicago 11, Illinois

Tuesday after first Monday—Election Day
2 James Polk (11th President) 1795–1849
2 Warren Harding (29th President) 1865–1923
2 South Dakota (40th State) 1889
2 North Dakota (39th State) 1889
3 William C. Bryant (poet) 1794–1878
8 Montana (41st State) 1889
11 Mayflower Compact signed 1620

NOVEMBER

11 Washington (42nd State) 1889
11 Armistice Day, Veterans' Day FLAG
11 Unknown Soldier buried in Arlington Cemetery 1921
13 Robert Louis Stevenson (author, *Treasure Island*) 1850–1894
14 Freedom for Philippine Islands 1935
14 Robert Fulton (steam engine) 1765–1815
16 Oklahoma (46th State) 1907
17 Congress first used Capitol 1800
19 Gettysburg Address 1863
19 James Garfield (20th President) 1831–1881
21 North Carolina (ratified Constitution) 1789
22 Assassination of John F. Kennedy 1963
23 Franklin Pierce (14th President) 1804–1869
24 Zachary Taylor (12th President) 1784–1850
26 First Official Thanksgiving 1789 (Now fourth Thursday) FLAG
29 Louisa May Alcott (*Little Women*) 1832–1888
30 Samuel L. Clemens (Mark Twain) 1835–1910
30 Winston Churchill (Br. statesman) 1874–1965

DECEMBER

2 Monroe Doctrine 1823
3 Illinois (21st State) 1818
5 Martin Van Buren (8th President) 1782–1862
5 Walt Disney (film producer) 1901–
7 Pearl Harbor attacked 1941
7 Delaware (1st state to ratify Constitution) 1787
8 Eli Whitney (cotton gin) 1765–1825
9 Joel Chandler Harris (Uncle Remus stories) 1848–1908
10 Mississippi (20th State) 1817
10 U.S. acquired Cuba, Guam, Puerto Rico, Philippine Islands from Spain 1898
11 Indiana (19th State) 1816
12 Pennsylvania (ratified Constitution) 1787
12 National Capitol Day—Washington, D.C. 1800
14 George Washington's death 1799
14 Alabama (22nd State) 1819

DECEMBER

15 Bill of Rights 1791
16 Ludwig von Beethoven (composer) 1770–1827
16 Boston Tea Party 1773
17 First Flight at Kitty Hawk, N.C. by Wright brothers 1903
17 John Greenleaf Whittier (poet) 1807–1892
18 New Jersey (ratified Constitution) 1787
18 Atlas missile in orbit 1958
21 First day of WINTER
21 Pilgrims landed at Plymouth 1620
24 Christopher (Kit) Carson (scout) 1809–1868
25 Christmas Day FLAG
28 Woodrow Wilson (28th President) 1856–1924
28 Iowa (29th State) 1846
29 Andrew Johnson (17th President) 1808–1875
29 Texas (28th State) 1845

JANUARY

1 New Year's Day FLAG
1 Paul Revere (patriot) 1735–1818
1 Emancipation Proclamation 1863
1 Betsy Ross (American flag) 1752–1836
2 Georgia (ratified Constitution) 1788
3 Alaska (49th State) 1959
4 Utah (45th State) 1896
4 Louis Braille (blind teacher) 1809–1852
6 Twelfth Day—Epiphany
6 New Mexico (47th State) 1912
6 Demonstration of Telegraph 1844
6 Carl Sandburg (poet) 1878–
7 First National Election 1789
7 Millard Fillmore (13th President) 1800–1874
9 Connecticut (ratified Constitution) 1788
11 Alexander Hamilton (statesman) 1757–1804
17 Benjamin Franklin (inventor, statesman) 1706–1790
18 Daniel Webster (statesman) 1782–1852
19 Robert E. Lee (leader of Confederate Army) 1807–1870
19 Edgar Allan Poe (poet, "The Raven") 1809–1849

JANUARY

20 Inauguration Day FLAG
24 Gold discovered in California 1848
25 Robert Burns (poet, "Auld Lang Syne") 1759–1796
26 Michigan (26th State) 1837
26 Mary Mapes Dodge (author, *Hans Brinker*) 1838–1905
27 Lewis Carroll (author, *Alice in Wonderland*) 1832–1898
29 Kansas (34th State) 1961
29 William McKinley (25th President) 1843–1901
30 Franklin D. Roosevelt (32nd President) 1882–1945
31 Explorer I launched 1958

FEBRUARY

Second Week—Boy Scout Week, Negro History Week
1 Victor Herbert (composer) 1859–1924
2 Groundhog's Day
4 Charles Lindbergh (aviator) 1902–
6 George H. (Babe) Ruth (baseball player) 1895–1948
6 Massachusetts (ratified Constitution) 1788
7 Charles Dickens (author, *The Christmas Carol*) 1812–1870
8 Boy Scouts of America founded 1910
8 Jules Verne (author, *20,000 Leagues under the Sea*) 1828–1905
9 William H. Harrison (9th President) 1773–1841
9 U.S. Weather Service established 1870
11 Thomas A. Edison (inventor) 1847–1931
12 Abraham Lincoln (16th President) 1809–1865 FLAG
14 Saint Valentine's Day
14 Oregon (33rd State) 1859
14 Arizona (48th State) 1912
15 Galileo Galilei (scientist) 1564–1642
19 Nicolaus Copernicus (scientist) 1473–1543
19 Ohio (17th State) 1803
22 James Russell Lowell (poet) 1819–1891
22 George Washington (1st President) 1732–1799 FLAG
23 Johannes Gutenberg (German printer) Death, 1468
26 William Cody (Buffalo Bill) 1846–1917
27 Henry W. Longfellow (poet) 1807–1882

MARCH

Second Week—Girl Scout Week
Third Week—Hobby Week, Third Friday—Arbor Day
Last Week—Health Week
1 Nebraska (37th State) 1867
2 Sam Houston (soldier) 1793–1863
2 U.S. Post Office established 1799
3 Alexander Graham Bell (inventor) 1847–1922
3 Florida (27th State) 1845
3 "Star-Spangled Banner" adopted as National Anthem 1931
4 Vermont (14th State) 1791
6 Elizabeth B. Browning (poet) 1806–1861
6 Fall of the Alamo 1836
7 Luther Burbank (scientist) 1849–1926
8 Oliver Wendell Holmes (U.S. Supreme Court Justice) 1841–1935
10 First telephone message 1876
12 Girl Scouts of America formed 1912
15 Maine (23rd State) 1820
15 Andrew Jackson (7th President) 1767–1845
15 Ides of March
16 James Madison (4th President) 1751–1836
17 St. Patrick's Day
17 Kate Greenaway (illustrator) 1846–1901
18 Hawaii (50th State) 1959
20 Harriet Beecher Stowe's *Uncle Tom's Cabin* published 1852
22 Randolph Caldecott (illustrator, Caldecott Medal) 1846–1886
29 John Tyler (10th President) 1790–1862
30 Purchase of Alaska 1867

APRIL

Third Week—National Garden Week, National Forestry Week
Last Week—Humane Week
Easter—Changeable FLAG
1 April Fools' Day
2 Hans Christian Andersen (fairy tales) 1805–1875
2 U.S. Mint established 1792
3 First Pony Express 1860

APRIL

3 Washington Irving (author) 1783–1859
6 Army Day FLAG
6 War against Germany 1917
9 Surrender of Confederate Army 1865
10 Joseph Pulitzer (publisher) 1847–1911
12 Henry Clay (statesman) 1777–1852
13 Thomas Jefferson (3rd President) 1743–1826
14 Dictionary Day, Webster's Dictionary first published 1828
14 Pan-American Day
15 Death of Lincoln 1865
16 Wilbur Wright (Orville, August 19, 1871) 1867–1912
18 Paul Revere's ride, 1775
19 Battle of Lexington and Concord 1775
21 Queen Elizabeth II (Queen of England) 1926–
23 James Buchanan (15th President) 1791–1868
23 William Shakespeare (dramatist) 1564–1616
24 Library of Congress established 1800
25 Guglielmo Marconi (radio) 1874–1937
26 John J. Audubon (naturalist) 1785–1851
27 Samuel F. Morse (telegraph) 1791–1872
27 Ulysses S. Grant (18th President) 1822–1885
28 Maryland (ratified Constitution) 1788
28 James Monroe (5th President) 1758–1831
30 Louisiana Purchase 1803
30 Louisiana (18th State) 1812

MAY

First Week—Child Health Day, Boys and Girls Week
Second Week—National Music Week, National Family Week
  Second Sunday—Mother's Day FLAG
Third Week—Spring Book Festival
  Third Sunday—Citizenship Recognition Day
Fourth Week—National Poetry Week
1 May Day
4 Horace Mann (educator) 1796–1859
5 Bird Day, Arbor Day
8 V-E Day 1945
8 Harry S. Truman (33rd President) 1884–

MAY

9 James Barrie (author, *Peter Pan*) 1860–1937
10 Meeting of transcontinental railroads at Promontory, Utah 1869
11 Minnesota (32nd State) 1858
12 Edward Lear (poet) 1812–1888
12 Florence Nightingale (nurse) 1820–1910
13 Jamestown settled 1607
16 Joan of Arc canonized
17 I Am an American Day (3rd Sunday)
18 Peace Day—World Good Will Day
21 Lindbergh's flight across the Atlantic 1927
21 Red Cross founded 1881
23 South Carolina (ratified Constitution) 1788
25 Ralph Waldo Emerson (poet) 1803–1882
27 Julia Ward Howe (reformer, "Battle Hymn of the Republic") 1819–1910
29 Patrick Henry (patriot) 1736–1799
29 Rhode Island (ratified Constitution) 1790
29 John F. Kennedy (35th President) 1917–1963
29 Wisconsin (30th State) 1848
30 Memorial Day (Flag half-staff until noon) FLAG
31 Walt Whitman (poet, *Leaves of Grass*) 1819–1892

JUNE

Second Sunday—Children's Day
Third Sunday—Father's Day
1 Kentucky (15th State) 1792
1 Tennessee (16th State) 1796
2 Martha Washington (wife of first President) 1732–1802
3 Jefferson Davis (President of Confederate States) 1808–1889
6 Nathan Hale (patriot) 1755–1776
7 YMCA organized 1854
9 John Payne ("Home, Sweet Home") 1791–1852
14 Stars and Stripes officially adopted 1777
14 Flag Day FLAG
14 Bastille Day (France)
15 Arkansas (25th State) 1836

JUNE

15 Magna Carta signed 1215
16 Alaskan Gold Rush 1897
18 War of 1812 against Great Britain
20 Great Seal of United States adopted 1782
20 West Virginia (35th State) 1863
21 First day of SUMMER
26 United Nations Charter signed 1945
26 Virginia (ratified Constitution) 1788
27 Helen Keller 1880–

SOURCES:

Douglas, George W. *The American Book of Days.* New York: H. W. Wilson Co., 1937.

Hazeltine, Mary E. *Anniversaries and Holidays.* Chicago: American Library Assn., 1944.

World Almanac. New York World-Telegram, 1964.

If we encounter a man of rare intellect, we should ask him what books he has read.

—*Ralph Waldo Emerson*

2

IMPROVING THE READING PROGRAM

Few teachers would deny Reading its rightful designation as the *most important subject* taught in the elementary school, for reading is basic to every other subject the child learns. It is essential, therefore, that reading experiences be successful, pleasurable experiences from the very first moment.

Described in this chapter are suggestions for varying the routine of teaching the child to read, ideas for providing practice in using beginning skills without drudgery. Presented also are teacher-tested techniques for motivating continued interest in reading, encouraging the child to read with enjoyment so that he will continue to read and to read well.

The last section of this chapter discusses ideas for stimulating the growth of the able student, the student who needs no boost along the Reading Road. The able reader is ready to *use* reading, to *do something* with reading. Here are suggestions for projects which assist these students in developing advanced abilities.

Learning to Read

The process of learning to read is usually associated with entrance into first grade. A child may, however, be learning to read at any level. The ideas included in this section will, therefore, prove helpful to any person teaching a student to read whether he is an advanced kindergartener or a student in the fifth grade who needs remedial assistance.

Learning to read the first day

Every first grader expects (and his parents share this expectation) to read on the first day of school, for that is what first grade has come to mean. In order to avoid disappointment, therefore, we recommend teaching the children some words which are especially useful. You may feature some of the color words—Red, Yellow, Blue—on a bulletin board with the words mounted on balloons. (Number words—One, Two, Three—are also often used.) With the words identified before him on the board each child can begin reading by completing a simple worksheet like this one:

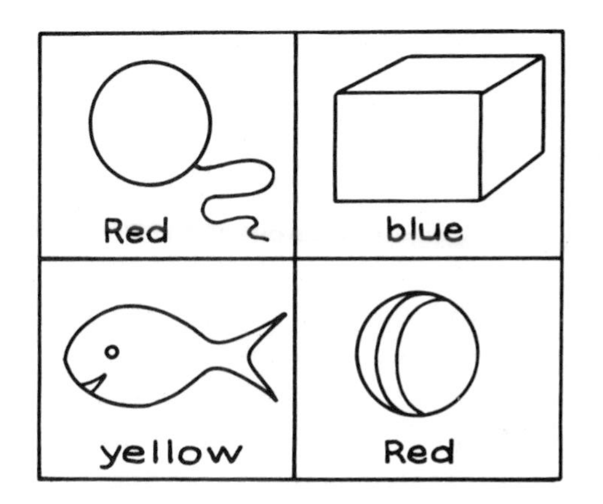

Recognition of letters

When children are learning to identify the shapes of letters, give them exercises such as the following in which they are to draw an X with a crayon on the boxes which are the same:

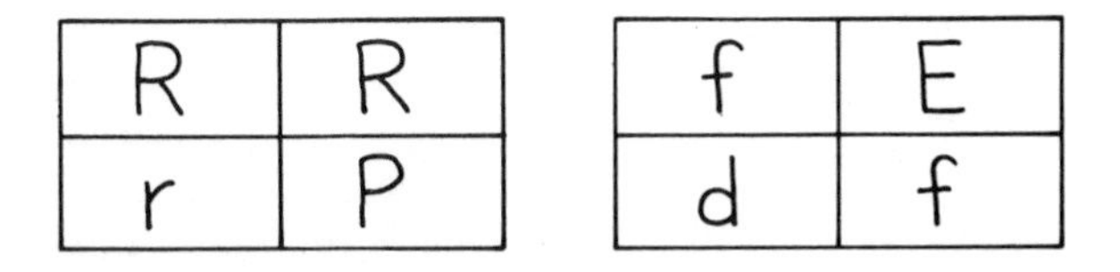

Encourage the children to construct similar boxes, for they will learn by this process also as they print letters which they have learned. They can exchange the boxes with others to see whether their friends can identify the letters which match.

Use large cardboard letter shapes which students can handle to illustrate the difference in letters which are often confused.

The alphabet

As children are learning the letters of the alphabet in order, there are a variety of activities which give practice in using this knowledge.

A Place two sets of Alphabet Cards in the chalk tray. Let two students see who can arrange the letters in alphabetical order the quickest. Permit others to challenge the winner to determine the ABC CHAMPION of your room.

B Call out one letter of the alphabet. Then call a child who must name the next three letters in order.

C Hold up an Alphabet Card. The child named must supply the letter which immediately precedes the given letter.

D An effective display connected with the learning of the Alphabet and the sounds each letter makes might feature interesting words using the common sound for each letter. Mount each letter and the word with a picture illustrating the word. Here are some words which can be used:

a	apron	i	ice cream	q	quack
b	bear	j	jumping	r	rose
c	coat	k	kite	s	soap
d	dog	l	lamp	t	towel
e	easel	m	map	u	uniform
f	fairy	n	nose	v	vase
g	ghost	o	orange	w	wall
h	house	p	pencil	x	xylophone
				y	yellow
				z	zebra

E Have the class line up for recess in Alphabetical Order.

Use either first or last names. Call out A with all those students whose names begin with A getting in line; then B, and so on. If anyone still remains in his seat after the alphabet is completed, help him discover his place.

F Have each child compile a BOOK OF SOUNDS which should contain a page for each letter of the alphabet. Using old copies of magazines let each cut pictures of objects which begin with the various letters pasting them on the appropriate pages. As their collection of pictures grows for each letter, students can exchange their books or work together to identify the objects included. (Stress the long vowel sounds for this beginning activity.) This book can be developed into a PICTURE DICTIONARY as the children learn words and learn to print. Let them print the words appropriate to each picture in their individual books.

Word recognition

- Each child makes two flashcards (3 x 5 inch cards) on which he prints the words YES and NO. As you hold up word cards, ask questions about the word; students will answer your questions by holding up the proper answer YES or NO.

Show the word WATER, for example, as you ask the class, "Is it something to wear?" (They show their NO cards.) "Is is something to drink?" (They flash YES.) "Who can say the word?" (Be sure everyone identifies the word which is then placed on the bottom of the pile.) Use this activity to review new vocabulary.

- Have each child search for a given word on a certain page of a story his group is reading. "Let's see who can find the word, ROBIN." If someone has difficulty, have a child near him point out the word or ask the child, "What letter do you hear at the beginning of the word ROBIN?"

> **Encourage pupils to work with words by having sets of letters which they can use to spell words they know or try to spell ones they have heard. The flannel board can be used for this purpose or words can be written on the chalkboard or paper.**

- Teach beginning readers the difference in appearance of

words by using this type of exercise in which they are to underline the two words which look alike:

Tom	Tom	yellow
red	street	street

Vowel sounds

Children love a game which combines new sounds they are learning and also involves a chance to wiggle a bit. As you say one syllable words containing either a LONG or a SHORT vowel sound, have the students raise both their arms up high if the vowel is long. If the vowel sound is short, they must fold their hands on the desk.

If, for example, you say the word PLAY, they should raise their arms as they identify the long A sound. When you say the word, NUT, however, they must fold their hands. (Always have someone identify the vowel heard.) After students become skilled in identifying LONG and SHORT sounds you may add the category NEITHER LONG NOR SHORT (indicated by hanging hands at sides) to make them aware of vowel sounds which are neither the long nor the short sound (ar, aw, er, oo, and so on).

Here is a chart we have used in teaching the basic vowel sounds to students—LONG, SHORT, and R.

	LONG	SHORT	R
A	ate	apple	star
E	eat	hen	her
I	ice	it	sir
O	no	hot	for
U	music	nut	spur

Notes on teaching vowels: We recommend teaching only the five vowels above and Y (which has no Long or Short sound, but at times substitutes for the long sounds of I and E). We question the advisability of calling W and X vowels, for they only influence the sound of the vowel which precedes them as is true of many other letters like R and L.

Initial consonants

The beginning consonant sounds are among the first to be learned by the young reader. Here are a number of activities which provide the much needed practice in identifying these sounds:

• Have students cut out numerous pictures of easily identifiable objects, animals, or people. Mount each picture on a square of construction paper or a 3 x 5 inch card for easy handling.

Students can sort the pictures according to the initial consonant (b, d, n, t, and so on) placing each picture in a shoe box labelled with that letter. Pictures of Tiger, Tree, Tepee, Turtle, Ticket, Tire would, for example, be placed in the T box. Have students check each other. It is also wise to have the student say the word for each picture as he sorts the cards, for different students may associate different words with the same pictured object. One may identify part of a tree as TREE while another says BRANCH, BARK or LIMB.

Mix the cards again for repeated use. Include a few foolers —objects which start with a letter other than those being studied; it is important that students realize that there are other sounds than those being emphasized. This same activity can later be used with blends of consonants—BL, CL, PR, SM, TR, and so forth.

• NOW CONCENTRATE is an activity which features consonant sounds and memory. You may begin by saying, "I am going to Paul's house and I'm going to take along a pear. What will you [take, Mary?" Mary responds, "I am going to Paul's house and I'm going to] take along a pear and a pencil." Each person adds one more item beginning with the same sound. For young children you may have them repeat only the last item or each child can simply name one new item to be taken. This activity can be used to focus attention on the blends, too, as the group visits Brenda, Trudy, Sharon, Charles, or Fred.

• FIND THE WORD Say three words aloud—Baby, Book, Cake or Trim, Trick, Crowd. Students must identify the one word which does not begin with the same sound as the other two.

• I SEE SOMETHING Here is an old favorite which children can use for indoor recess. The leader begins, "I see something that begins with B." Children raise their hands to guess—Blackboard, Bulletin Board, Ball, until the correct word is guessed. The one who guesses the right word then stands in front of the class to be the leader, and so on.

• THE LINE-UP Let children get in line for recess or going home by sounds. "All those whose first names begin like tangerine may get in line." "All those whose last names begin like lemon may line up." (If time runs short, simply say, "All those who have a vowel in their first names may get in line." That should take care of everyone else.)

• THE WORD HUNT Let each child search through a book (for a specified length of time) to find words beginning with a given sound. At the end of the time have the words named and listed on the board.

Consonant blends

In studying the initial blends you can use many of the same techniques as are used with the single consonants described above. Here are several additional ideas which have been found especially effective with the study of blends:

• WHAT ARE THE FIRST TWO LETTERS? Even young children are intrigued by "big words." Pronounce words for them letting them take turns in identifying the first two letters—Planet, Grasshopper, Glaring, Precious. The answers can be printed or written with each student correcting his answer as the correct one is given.

• HOW MANY WORDS? Ask the class, "How many words can we name that start like BLUE?" Orally the children will suggest any words which begin with the same sound—Black, Blouse, Bloom, Blossom, Blood. When that sound appears to be exhausted, move to another Blend. When incorrect words are suggested, repeat the sound you are using in order to help the students hear the sound correctly.

• MIND READING "What word do I have in mind?" Primary children enjoy trying to "read your mind" as you give them hints about the word you want them to guess as in this example:

> I grow outside. You can stand under me. I start like Trouble. What word do I have in mind?

• RIDDLES Type examples like those above for students to

read and to find the right answer. Multiple choice answers can be supplied to avoid spelling difficulty as in this example:

I am black; I come from a fire; I rhyme with Poke.
broke smoke flea

This is a *house* for a *horse*. It rhymes with Table.
fable gravel stable

• SHOW THE ANSWER Each child needs a set of cards on which are printed the consonants being studied (each card may contain one blend such as BL, CR, GL). As you call out a word, each child selects the two letter cards which designate the first two letters beginning that word. The cards are held up to face you so that you can quickly check their cards. Be sure to include words which the children cannot spell, even words they may never have heard before so they are not afraid of unknown words when they meet them in reading.

• RELAYS Divide the group into teams of five or six players for a review in the third or fourth grades. Each team is given a different blend—BL, BR, CR, CL, GR, GL, SP, ST, TR, and so on. When the leader says, "Go!" the first team member walks to the board and writes a word beginning with that blend on the board. He then returns to his seat, and the second player does the same thing. If a player cannot think of a word, he goes to the board and draws a straight line (which loses time for his side). Players continue taking turns until TIME is called.

Score by adding *1 point for each letter in every correctly spelled word*. Add 2 *points only for a word which was misspelled. Deduct 2 points for each straight line* drawn. This relay can be adapted to individual participation on sheets of paper with all students using the same given Blend. Exchange papers for scoring.

• PACKING PROBLEMS "I'm packing a box for Aunt Priscilla (Uncle Charlie, Grandpa, Aunt Stella, etc.). What shall I put in the box?" Answers must begin with PR (like the name specified)—primroses, precious jewels, prizes, priceless cloth, presents, pressing cloth, printing set, or a projector.

• DISCOVERY Mount a large picture on the bulletin board. Each child lists words in columns as he discovers objects in the picture which begin with sounds you specify, for example, CH, W, PL. See who can find the most words in ten minutes; then discuss the lists made noting any unusual words. Discuss the spelling of certain words.

• WHEEL OF SOUNDS Construct a Wheel of Sounds which students can manipulate as they use blends (or single consonants) in combination with common endings. Here is an example which can be made from tagboard or other heavy paper:

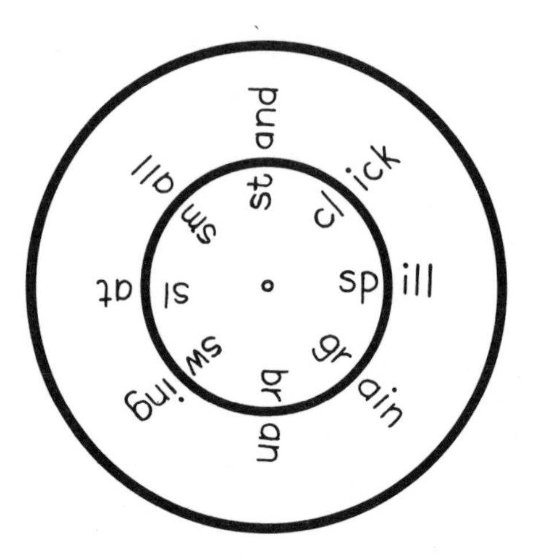

Increasing vocabulary

All of the activities focusing on words will help increase the student's vocabulary. Described here are more ideas which are directly related to vocabulary study.

• WORD FAMILIES Make posters for groups of words containing common endings such as AIN—rain, gain, grain, drain, chain, lain, main, pain, fain, train, slain, sprain, strain, brain, plain, vain. Let students collect a list of words for one sound for which they will make a poster to present to the rest of the class.

> **Have you ever tried hanging long wordlists from coat hangers? Print words with a felt pen so they can be read easily by students in their seats. Store these lists in a closet for repeated use.**

• WORDLISTS Duplicate sets of word lists appropriate for each reading group; these lists can be typed directly from lists in reading texts. The number of words on each list will vary according to the level of ability. For beginning readers each list may consist of only twenty-five words typed on the primary typewriter.

As an incentive to learning the words on each list, have each child cut an airplane shape from colored construction paper on which he prints his first name. On a long bulletin board designate various cities in the United States or around the world starting with your own town or city. All airplanes begin at the home airport flying to another city as a wordlist is learned. Appointing two checkers in each reading group will provide assistance in hearing students say the lists of words when they are ready.

Around the World With Words

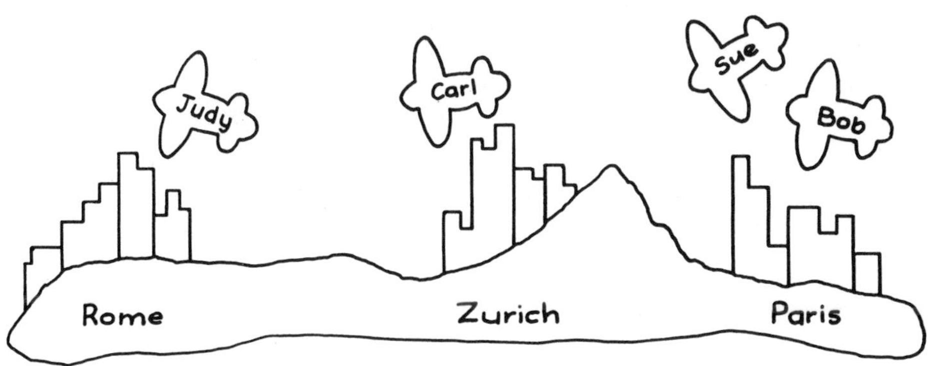

• FORMS OF WORDS To acquaint students with the varied forms of a word use exercises like this:

> I like to—reader, read, reading.
> That boy is—swing, swings, swinging.
> She started to—jumping, jumped, jump.
> I hear the baby—cried, crying, cried.

• WORDS IN THE ROOM As an introduction to many familiar words, print signs, name tags, and directions so that students see many words. Have children print some of the signs or tags for objects like the globe, table, bookshelf, window, bulletin board, door, desk, closet, or picture. Make use of these words as you teach, saying perhaps, to the student who requests help with spelling the word HOARD, "Here is the word BOARD; hoard rhymes with board. How would you spell hoard?" Have the children write a story using as many of these words as possible.

• FINDING WORDS Prepare a dittoed sheet containing various letters of the alphabet (be sure to include many vowels). Each student uses crayons (different color for each word) to connect letters which spell a word. The student may move only one space at a time vertically, horizontally, or diagonally as in the example:

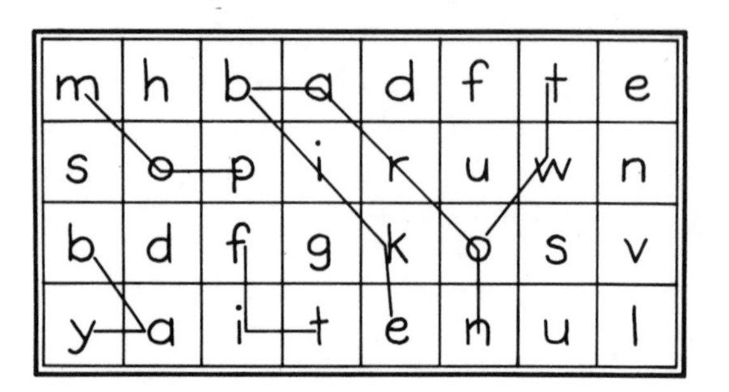

• MAKING WORDS Prepare charts for providing practice in using consonant beginnings with common endings. Let students take turns pronouncing the words made.

S	and	C	ake
H	ay	T	all
B	at	F	ame
	it		at
	ail		ore

• ADDING PREFIXES AND SUFFIXES Shallow boxes or lids of boxes can be made into simple tachistoscopes (devices which expose only one word at a time for practice in word recognition) through which strips of tagboard or heavy paper can be pulled as the student pronounces the word with the prefix or suffix added. You can use two different prefixes or suffixes with the same box by turning it around and using another wordlist.

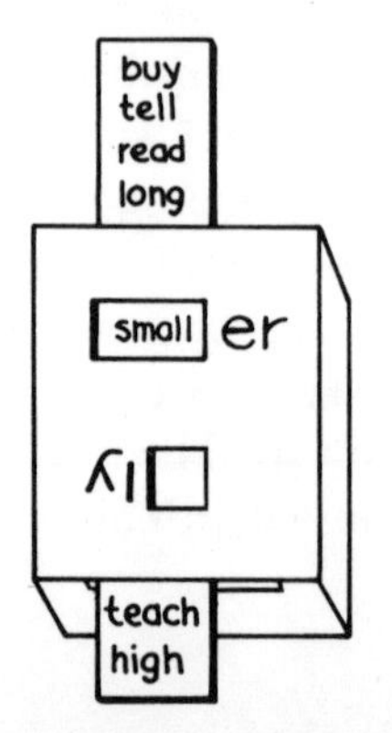

Dividing words into syllables

Syllabication is intriguing to students as long as you do not give them long lists of words to divide. More learning will take place if only short exercises are used at any one time. Here are several varieties of activities to provide the needed practice in using rules of syllabication:

• WHAT IS THE FIRST SYLLABLE? Say a word such as flutter. Ask students to spell the first syllable (they will be getting additional practice in the use of blends and vowel sounds). This exercise can be entirely oral or you can ask students to write the first syllable. Answers should be supplied immediately so students understand any mistakes made. Other examples which work well with this type of review are: perhaps, napping, helpless, detour, happy, spoken, ladle, between, spoon (this will catch some students), lightning, bubble, balloon, stop.

• COMBINING SYLLABICATION WITH VOCABULARY STUDY As you are reviewing lists of words, ask the group questions about the correct division of words which they are learning. Or as a student finishes reading a page aloud, ask questions about the division of several words which appeared on that page.

• BOOKLETS As children learn the rules for dividing words have them prepare a sheet for their notebooks or a booklet called DIVIDING WORDS. Include these rules with examples contributed by students:

If a word has only one syllable, it *cannot be divided.*
should goat book have light
A word which contains a double consonant should be divided between the double consonants.
mut/ter wig/gle lap/ping ad/dition
Compound words should be divided between the two smaller words.
high/way side/walk fire/side
When a word contains a prefix or suffix, divide after the prefix or before the suffix.
un/til re/turn sad/ness play/ful
If two unlike consonants are between two vowels, divide between the consonants.
mon/key ser/vant ig/nite

If a single consonant falls between two vowels, divide after the first vowel or after the consonant.

cam/el ti/ger li/ly bro/ken py/thon

If the final syllable ends in *le*, the consonant before the *le* is included in the final syllable.

cra/dle sta/ble bri/dle ea/gle

Digraphs (kn, gn, th) and blends (fl, sl, tr) are treated as single letters.

en/trance al/though tre/men/dous un/known

Oral and written practice of vowel and consonant sounds, syllabication rules, and so forth are excellent fillers for those few minutes which remain before dismissal.

• WHICH RULE TELLS YOU HOW? As students refer to their lists of numbered rules for syllabication, have them take turns in dividing words orally. Write the word *wayside,* for example; have someone read it and tell you the rule which tells them to divide this word between Y and S. (No. 3 in the preceding list.)

Demonstration to parents

Use an invented alphabet to illustrate to parents at Open House the difficulty of reading for the beginner. Write a paragraph or two in this alphabet to be duplicated and distributed to parents who attempt to "read" as you teach them the meaning of the different symbols used. Invent letters like these:

A = △ B = ⊥ C = ⦶ D = ▭ E = ⧅

For a free booklet which will help you with this demonstration request a copy of *Primer for Parents* from:

Houghton Mifflin Publishing Co.
2 Park Street
Boston 7, Massachusetts

Motivating Growth in Reading

Upon entering first grade the student is highly motivated to learn to read, but as he progresses the novelty may diminish. It is this stage which may account for the failure of some students to learn to read well and to consider reading pleasurable. For this reason it is essential that the reading program be kept stimulating and not permitted to deteriorate to deadening drill. Included in this section are described a number of ideas we have found successful in varying the teaching approaches in reading during this period when the student must be developing reading skills and facility with words.

Class Motto: The more we read the better we read.

Books written by the class

In primary grades students enjoy dictating stories to the teacher which can be compiled in a book from which students read in their free time. BIG BOOKS can be constructed with only a sentence or two printed on a page with a picture. Students enjoy collecting pictures to be included in books entitled SIGNS OF SPRING, GAMES, ONE DAY I SAW . . . which may contain one page done by each member of a reading group or the whole class. Each student prints a one or two line story with his picture.

Written directions

Write brief directions which can be covered by a map until you are ready for their use. When the directions are uncovered, let the class see how quickly they can read the directions and follow them exactly. Directions might read thus:

> Take out 1 sheet of paper. Sign your name at the bottom of the page. Number from 1 to 10 on the back of the sheet. Beside each number write a pair of homonyms (or a spelling word or a word that begins like Blade). Fold your paper in fourths when you have finished and place it on the right side of your desk. You may read a library book until everyone is ready.

When all have finished the page, discuss the directions. See how many followed the directions. Repeat this type of activity for better attention to directions which students read.

Keeping a reading diary

Have each child record (in a notebook containing one sheet per child) any time he spends reading either at home or at school. Every child will spend some time in school so all will make an entry each day thus:

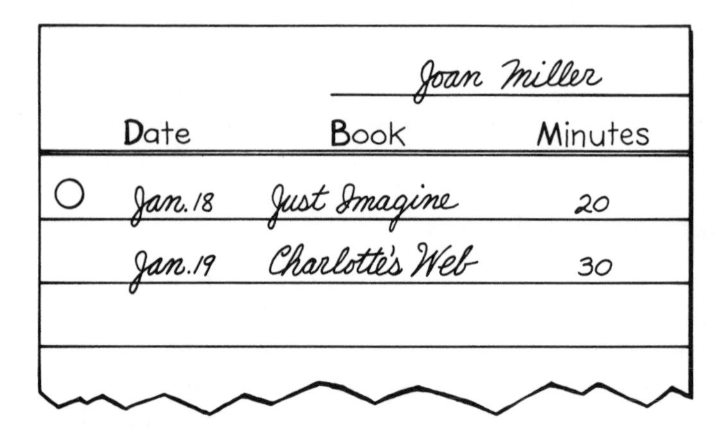

The reading table

An abundance of easy material should be available to supplement the daily reading lesson. Here are suggestions of materials which can be prepared as supplementary reading material other than library books and additional texts.

STORY FOLDERS A folded sheet of 12 x 18 inch construction paper can form the cover for an attractive booklet. On one side of the paper paste an attractive picture; opposite the picture mount a one-page article or story clipped from back issues of children's magazines. You can also type student stories for this purpose with the student making an appropriate illustration.

POETRY Poems typed on the primary typewriter can be mounted on tagboard or construction paper. Use both original poems written by class members or favorites by well-known poets. Have students decorate the mounting for each poem.

PICTURE STORIES Type stories which substitute pictures for harder words to ease the difficulty of the reading. The pictures add to the interest of this type of story.

PICTURES AND QUESTIONS Mount pictures on stiff paper. Under each picture print several questions which can be answered YES or NO such as the following:

Do you see an apple tree?
Do you see four dogs?
Does the girl have a doll?

SETTING SAIL FOR READING

On a bulletin board arrange a lake cut from blue paper. Add trees and other appropriate scenery. Each child may add a small sailboat bearing his name when he has read a book.

Interest in words

Interest in words leads to greater interest in reading. The child is using reading skills as he completes these word activities:

SCRAMBLED SENTENCES Mix up word cards letting students rearrange them in order to make a sentence. Scrambled sentences can also be duplicated for individual work at each child's seat.

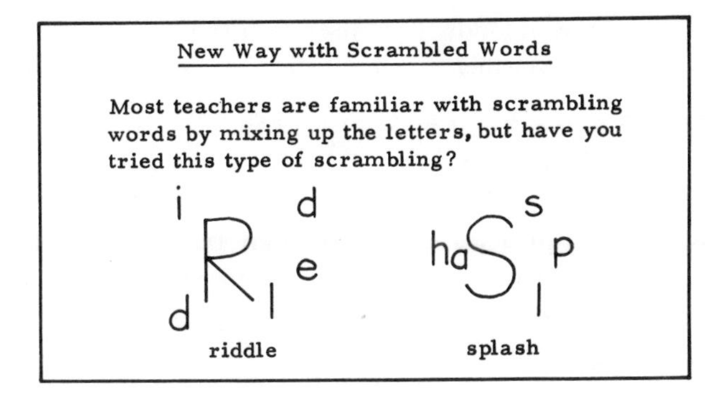

CATEGORIES Provide a list of objects (on the board or duplicated sheets). Each child is to read the words and arrange them in categories which you specify as in this example:

Given Words:

blue	horse	chair	cat
red	tiger	lion	yellow
stove	purple	table	stool

Categories:

ANIMALS	COLORS	FURNITURE
horse tiger	blue red	chair table

THE SILENT E To illustrate the effect of the E on many short words give each child a pair of these words (from a list compiled by the teacher)—*mad, made; bar, bare; fir, fire; pin, pine; gal, gale.* Each student can make a poster to show the difference between the two words. The class will become more conscious of this effect.

HOMONYMS Homonyms can also be featured on posters which illustrate the difference in meaning of the two or three words in the set—*four, for, fore; to, two, too; sane, seine; isle, aisle, I'll; fair, fare.* Have children conduct a Search for Homonyms which can be compiled in a class book, OUR HOMONYMS.

COMPLETION SENTENCES Prepare groups of sentences with words omitted as in the example. The child chooses the correct word from the words given. Students also learn much by constructing sentences like this using words taken from their reading lesson.

A ——— crowed loudly from the top of the ———.
fence farmer raindrops rooster horse

PREFIXES AND SUFFIXES On the board list the more common prefixes and suffixes—*ness, ful, est, un, re, dis, in,* and so forth. Write a root word on the board giving the class a few minutes to see which of the prefixes or suffixes can be added to the given root to make a new word. Given the root FAIR, for example, they might find: Fairness, Fairest, Unfair. Discuss the possibilities after each root has been used.

For more creative approaches to word study see *Exploring Words* by Sidney and Iris Tiedt. (Contemporary Press, Box 1524, San Jose, Calif.)

Reading stories aloud

Young readers enjoy reading a book which has first been introduced to the class by the teacher's reading it to the class. In this way some of the difficulty of new words is eliminated. Favorites will be read and reread. Recommended titles which we have especially enjoyed with young people in the classroom include:

Primary:

Dr. Seuss. *Horton Hatches the Egg* and *McElligott's Pool.*

Primary (*cont.*):

James Thurber. *Many Moons.*
E. B. White. *Charlotte's Web.*
H. A. Rey. *Curious George.*
R. and F. Atwater. *Mr. Popper's Penguins.*

Intermediate:

Robert McCloskey. *Homer Price.*
Ellen MacGregor. *Miss Pickerell Goes to Mars.*
Beverly Cleary. *Henry Huggins.*
Astrid Lindgren. *Pippi Longstocking.*
Lois Lenski. *Strawberry Girl* and others.

The reading circle

Select a number of favorite books (more than one apiece for the group) according to the abilities of your students. Arrange these titles on a READING CIRCLE (see the example) which is given to each student. As he reads each selection, he colors the box beside that title. Every student will read each book eventually although some will finish more quickly and will proceed to some other activity. The CIRCLES can be displayed on a bulletin board or kept in individual notebooks. No reports are given on these books, but encourage the sharing of reactions to books being read.

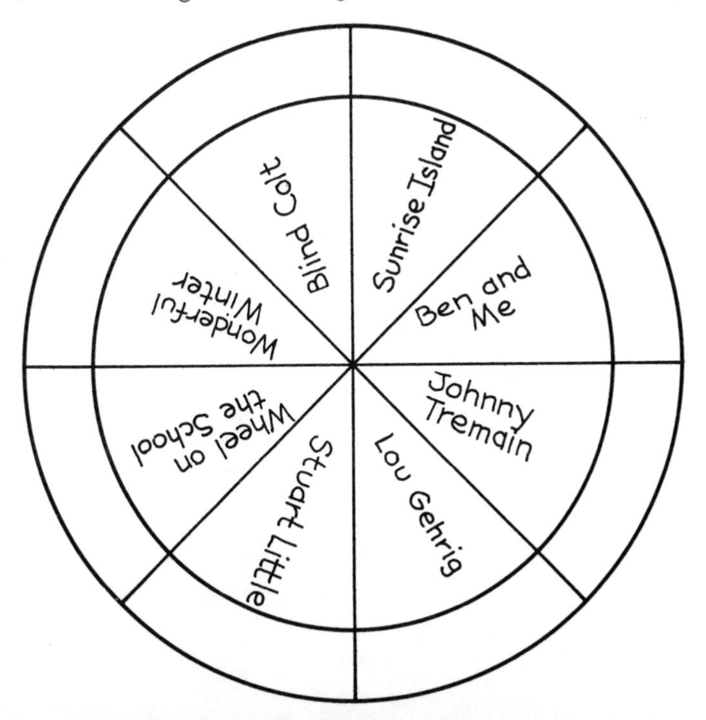

Booklists

Provide students with short reading lists (long ones may only discourage) for vacations or holidays. In December duplicate lists which can be mounted on green Christmas tree shapes or large red bells. Include about a dozen good titles TO LOOK FOR IN THE LIBRARY. In the spring a large Easter egg shape might hold another group of titles—EGGSACTLY WHAT YOU WANT!

Remember to feature books the children really like, not the ones someone says they should like. Follow up the distribution of a booklist by asking the children whether they found any of the titles in the library. Publicize the finding of any titles—"John found *Lentil* yesterday." or "Susan has brought *Charlotte's Web* to school, I see." Able students will also enjoy preparing special booklists for the class.

Inexpensive booklists—*Books for You* and others—are available from:

National Council of Teachers of English
508 South Sixth Street
Champaign, Illinois

Sharing magazines

Discuss some of the magazines that are published for young people. Show copies of these magazines if they are available. (Many companies will send you sample copies on request.) Encourage any students who subscribe to children's magazines to bring copies for the reading table.

If you have funds for this purpose, a magazine subscription is a good means for encouraging reading. Call attention to interesting items in various issues. Your interest will encourage the interest of the students. Remember, too, that many adult magazines will appeal to upper grade students—*Time, Life, Look,* and others.

Here are some recommended titles of juvenile magazines for the classroom. Other titles and addresses can be found in *Writer's Market,* a reference that will be in any public library.

Calling All Girls. (Bergenfield, New Jersey)
Children's Digest. (Bergenfield, New Jersey)

Children's Playmate Magazine. (Cleveland 5, Ohio)
Humpty Dumpty's Magazine. (Bergenfield, New Jersey)
Jack and Jill. (Independence Sq., Philadelphia 5, Penn.)
Wee Wisdom. (Lee's Summit, Missouri)

Bulletin board displays

Book jackets provide a colorful means for attracting the student's interest to reading. Here are several good ideas for focusing attention on books:

STOP! LOOK! READ!

Here is an *arresting* caption which can be used in combination with a cut paper traffic light or stop sign. Display a variety of book jackets with the books themselves on a table below the board.

CHECK THESE NEW BOOKS ✔

With this caption display book jackets with a large black check (cut from construction paper) touching each jacket.

LEADERS ARE READERS

This general caption can be used to feature a variety of books of interest to both boys and girls. It could be used with non-fiction.

INFORMATION—A TO Z

Here is a caption for use with interesting non-fiction. Feature books about numbers, electronics, automobiles, making things, travel, history, and so on. Include open books on a table below the display.

For more ideas about using the bulletin board refer to Chapter 1 which includes a section on Using the Bulletin Board as well as The Teacher's Calendar which would supply many dates related to reading.

The Book Fair

A good way to stimulate interest in reading for children of all levels and abilities is through the BOOK FAIR which may be sponsored by the PTA or students in the upper grades with the assistance of the school librarian. Local bookstores and publishers may be asked to cooperate with a display of books. Books from the school and classroom libraries can be shown as well as examples of children's magazines (with addresses for interested parents). Be sure to include some of the excellent paperback books for young people.

Let classes plan displays—a mural about a book theme, pictures drawn depicting favorite stories, original writing of students, skits or dioramas illustrating well-known works, taped discussions of books read, and so on. The BOOK FAIR can be held during Book Week (third week in November). Distribute paper bookmarks containing BOOKS TO READ and duplicated booklists including some for parents, for the reading parent will usually have a reading child. Prepare a list of books recommended for purchase as gifts for children.

Art and reading

Art correlates with reading to provide many stimulating ways of motivating interest in reading. Here are suggestions for activities which relate art and reading:

- BILLBOARDS Let students advertise their favorite books by constructing miniature billboards. They will need to review printing techniques and the spacing and wording required for a poster.
- MOBILES Mobiles can be used to depict any story with the student cutting from paper (or other light materials) the figures or symbols appropriate to his story. Hang the figures from two stiff wires (hanger wire) which are tied with black thread to form an X which is suspended from the ceiling.
- DIORAMAS Have each student construct a diorama picturing a dramatic scene from the book he is reviewing. Pipe cleaner figures can be made in proper proportion. Buildings, trees, landforms—all add to the telling of the scene being enacted. The making of the diorama serves as a Book Review.
- BOOK JACKETS Give renewed life to old books by having students make book jackets for books they have read. Use heavy paper on which the designer of the book jacket can draw an illustration which will catch the eye of the next reader. A "blurb" can be printed on the inside flap with a "Word about the Author" on the other flap or on the back of the jacket.
- PORTRAITS Have each student sketch the portrait of one of the characters in the book he has read. The artist uses his

imagination guided somewhat by the description written by the author. These portraits can be framed and displayed with names indicated.

Bookmarks

The making of bookmarks stimulates interest in reading as each student makes his bookmark and then uses it. Several simple varieties can be used.

Cut one corner from a discarded envelope to make a functional bookmark which slips over the upper corner of the book page. These markers can be decorated by pasting a cut paper shape over the point of the corner so the decoration projects beyond the edge of the book.

Another attractive bookmark which may be used as a Mother's Day gift is made from a strip of colored burlap which is decorated with yarn stitching that forms a design. The edges may be fringed to add interest.

A book party

Let the students of your class plan a BOOK PARTY with each one portraying a favorite character from a book. Each student can make simple costumes using paper, unbleached muslin, or discarded clothing items which can be decorated appropriately with crayon. Have each child enact an interesting part of the book; several children may represent characters from the same book with all sharing in the same short presentation.

Focus on word discoveries

Young people are intrigued by words—words with unusual meanings, strange-looking words, words that have peculiarities of pronunciation. Allocate a special bulletin board on which students can place interesting words which they have discovered. Words can be cut from newspapers or magazines, written on a 3 x 5 inch card, or printed on a strip of paper with a felt pen. Have the Discoverer supply a definition for the word. Several able students can prepare a book, WORD DISCOVERIES, of those words which are publicized on the bulletin board. Words can be arranged by letter so students can refer to the book when looking for one of these words.

> THE BOOK WORM
>
> As a child completes a book, let him add a segment to the body of a long Book Worm which can encircle the room on the wall above the boards and windows. Each child prints the title and author of the book he has read on a piece of bright construction paper which is trimmed to resemble part of the body which continues to grow behind the head which one student has designed.

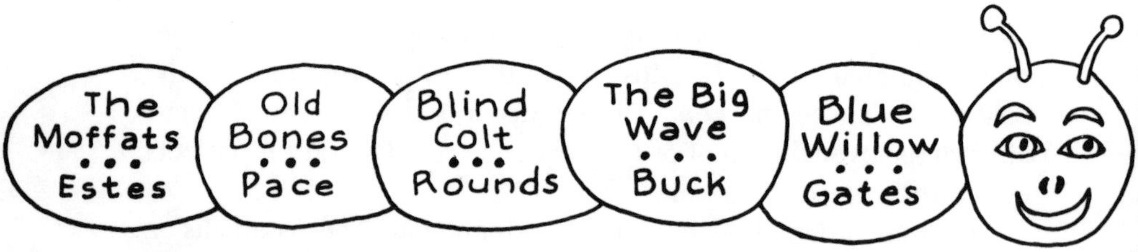

Mapping literature

Draw a large outline map of the United States or the North American continent (use an opaque projector to enlarge a small map). On this map let students locate the setting for stories they are reading. They can cut out figures to represent these books. Tom Sawyer, for example, would be placed in Missouri near the Mississippi River. List the titles of the books represented with the question: "How many do you know?"

Working with reading groups

Most teachers divide their students into three reading groups.

Working with groups requires real skill in planning so that all students have worthwhile work to do while the teacher is working, uninterrupted, with the individual reading groups. Here are suggestions for effective group work in reading:

• *Don't introduce a new story to all groups on the same day* as those who are working with new vocabulary will perhaps need more assistance. Those children who are reviewing a story will be able to work more independently while you introduce the new material to another group.

• *Vary your techniques for having students read stories orally* so the procedure doesn't become boring. Try these ideas for variety:

1. Have one person read until someone catches an error.
2. Choose one person to be the narrator while others read the dialogue parts.
3. Assign each student in the group a page of a story to prepare for reading aloud. When all have had time to practice, call the group to the front of the room where they read their pages (in order) so the whole class can enjoy the story. If the group is large, use two stories or more.
4. Let each student select one page from a story being reviewed. He is to practice that page until he can read it perfectly. When he is ready, he comes to your desk to read it aloud to you.
5. Have a child read until he comes to a specified word. Say, "Billy, will you please read until you hear the word, *help*?" or "Sue, you may read until you see the words, *Dan cried*."
6. Each child reads a line or a sentence with the turns moving rapidly. Each child can also read a paragraph.

• *Let students choose interesting names* for their reading groups—Rockets, Spacemen, Tigers. Don't think this naming fools children about ability levels, but then, why try to fool them?

Free reading time

Have some periods for reading or browsing through reading materials. Use the school library or the classroom library. Permit students to sit where they like with the understanding, of course, that reading and loud talking don't mix. Emphasize the pleasure of reading and permit them to read anything that interests them.

YOU READ, TOO! You may feel guilty as you read a novel or magazine during school time, but you are actually developing a sense of value for reading. Students often do not receive this feeling for reading at home when parents are not readers. They need to picture the adult as one who considers reading a pleasure, a necessary part of his existence.

Tell the students about the book you are currently reading, and encourage them to tell you about their books, too. Your pleasure and interest enhances their pleasure and interest. Reading becomes desirable, not something the teacher tells them they *must* do.

Building a background of stories

A student's background of stories adds to his interest in reading and is important for his general cultural background. Here are suggestions for adding to this background:

• *Play records* of stories which children should get to know. An example is the recording of Kipling's *Mowgli* and *Just So Stories* read by Basil Rathbone (Caedmon TC 1038).

You may wish to send for catalogs from the following companies which handle records of this sort:

Folkways Records, 121 West 47th St., New York 36, N.Y.
Educational Record Sales, 153 Chambers St., New York 7, N.Y.

• *Read stories to the class* (or tell them). Excellent collections for the teacher's desk are May Hill Arbuthnot's *Time for True Tales* and *Time for Fairy Tales* (Scott, Foresman). For variety try *taping stories* after school or at home. A group of students could tape a story perhaps incorporating interesting sound effects.

• *Activities focusing attention on the familiar stories* might include a puzzle like this example, THREE CLUES FOR THE DETECTIVE.

Can you guess the name of each storybook character with the help of the three clues given for each one?

1. ______ Hungry dog . . . bone . . . bare cupboard (Mother Hubbard)

2. ______ Seven little friends . . . wicked queen . . . princess (Snow White)
3. ______ Three bears . . . hot soup . . . broken chair (Goldilocks)
4. ______ Naughty bunny . . . garden . . . angry farmer (Peter Rabbit)
5. ______ Rabbit . . . deep hole . . . Queen of Hearts (Alice in Wonderland)
6. ______ Pie . . . thumb . . . plum (Jack Horner)
7. ______ Darling children . . . pixie dust . . . pirates (Peter Pan)
8. ______ Stepmother . . . fairy godmother . . . glass slipper (Cinderella)

• *An oral type of activity which features fairy tales and folk lore* presents hints about the story until someone guesses the right title. *Sleeping Beauty*, for example, might be described in this way:

> This fairy tale is about a beautiful princess. (Allow three guesses after which you can give the second hint.)
> Twelve fairies gave this princess wonderful gifts.
> One wicked fairy said the princess would die on her sixteenth birthday . . . and so on.

After the title has been guessed have someone briefly tell the plot of the story before going on to another.

Challenging the Gifted Student

In each room there will be at least several students who are reading much more advanced material than are the others in the same room. These students should be progressing in their development and should not, therefore, be confined to the basal reader which happens to be labeled with that grade number. These students may work as a small group or they may work individually on reading material which provides for their growth and stimulates their interest.

Individualized reading

Often it is possible to get sets of library books or paperback books which able students can read individually. Encourage students to bring to school books they have obtained from the public library; they can also share books which they own.

Records of reading can be kept in various ways (methods described in the foregoing section of this chapter are suitable for this use, too), but the record keeping should not become laborious work. Each student may develop his own Reading File (a small box) of three by five inch cards on which he records brief information about each book read thus:

Jesse Stuart.	January, 196__
The Thread That Runs So True.	Jim Hobbs
Charles Scribner's Sons, 1949.	

> Jesse Stuart was a teacher and superintendent of schools in Kentucky. He tells many interesting stories about his experiences.

Another method of recording individualized reading is the use of a duplicated sheet kept in a notebook or folder which is completed for each book read as in the example on page 61.

Getting to know authors

The able reader should begin noting the author of each book he is reading. He can learn to use *Current Biography* to find information as well as *Reader's Guide to Periodical Literature.* Each student may select one author to investigate developing a booklet of information about this person. The booklet might include a brief biographical sketch, illustrations, any appropriate magazine or newspaper clippings, resumes of books by this author, and so on. Library research should be used to locate as much information as possible.

Suggested authors for this type of study include: Robert Heinlein, Alice Dalgliesh, Walter D. Edmonds, Walter Farley, Marguerite Henry, Robert McCloskey, Jim Kjelgard, Sterling

Name: Pamela

Date: November 18

Author: Day, Clarence

Title: Life with Father

Publishing Information: Knopf, 1937

Pages: 258 Type of Book: Humor

List and identify the main characters:

Clarence Day, Jr. – author, son
Clarence Day, Sr. – father
Vinnie Day – mother

Write 3 new words found in this book. What does each one mean?

anthracite – kind of coal
affronted – offended
pottered – puttered, dawdled

What did you enjoy most about this book?

I enjoyed the many amusing personal experiences.

What did you like least about this book?

It wasn't long enough.

North, Armstrong Sperry, Robert Louis Stevenson, Mark Twain, James Thurber, and Edwin Tunis.

Literary debate

Two students could present a debate on a topic or about a book with each presenting opposite viewpoints. They should do wide reading to prepare their arguments, read reviews about the books in question, and locate other relevant information.

Poetry collection

A collection of favorite poems could be compiled by a student. The collection could include original poetry by this student also with each poem presented on a separate sheet. Appropriate illustrations and decorations can be added to make the book attractive.

Reporting unusual information

At times the gifted student can contribute much to the general knowledge of the class by researching a topic related to a unit of study currently under investigation. Reports of this nature encourage the reading of nonfiction and the use of library research either in your school or the public library.

Varied Approaches to Reviewing Reading

Book reporting can become so routinized as to be deadening rather than stimulating. What is the purpose of the book review? It is to check on the amount of reading done by a student and it may intend to stimulate the reading of this student and others. The average book report serves only the first purpose.

To encourage reading rather than discourage it use a variety of approaches to Book Reviewing. Described in this section are many different ways for the student to demonstrate that he has read a book while also "selling" his fellow students on trying that book, too.

Oral presentations

Have students prepare three minute oral reviews of their books. Group these reports so that only a few are given at any one time, for the audience gets tired even though the reports are well done. Included in each review would be: the title of the book, the author, and a brief statement of the general content of the book. Suggestions for variations might be:

Show the book to the class. An attractive cover may help interest your audience in reading this book.

Read particularly good sections to the class, being sure to explain what happened before, and perhaps after, the part you read.

Tell something about the life of the author who wrote this book. Name other good books he has written.

Read an exciting portion, stopping at a crucial point to ask your audience, "What do you think happened next?" After guesses have been made, you may tell them what the author wrote.

Show good illustrations to the class telling briefly what the illustration describes.

Checklists

Reading can be guided and checked through the use of a CHECKLIST which students can keep in their notebooks or in a classbook with a page for each child. Through the use of this type of list the teacher can emphasize various areas of interest which need to be developed. Include this type of item:

I have read a biography: ______________________________

I have read a book longer than 200 pages: ______________________________

____

I have read a book about science: ______________________________

____

I have read a book based on real history: ______________________________

____

Questions based on each book

Develop a file of cards (one for each book to be read) which contain the title and author and a group of questions about a number of specific books. As each child completes a book, he finds the card in the QUESTION BOX and answers the questions briefly, filing the answer sheet in his Reading Folder. Students can assist you in developing a file of question cards for books you have available.

The reading road

On a large sheet of mural paper assist a committee of students in developing a game to encourage reading called THE READING ROAD. The reading of a book entitles the student to move his car (cut from construction paper) one space or more according to the type of book—1 space for fiction, 2 for biography, 3 for other nonfiction. On some spaces add directions for a detour or other obstacle. On other spaces direct the Driver to draw a card which may direct him to move extra spaces or to move back several spaces.

Reading cards

On a large sheet of poster board mount a library book pocket for each child in the room with the names printed on each pocket. As a child reads a book he takes a 3 x 5 inch card (or slip of paper cut that size) on which he records the title, author, and a brief statement about the book. Each card is filed in his pocket. As time permits remove the cards from one child's pocket, calling the child to a small table for a conference about his reading. The individual discussion not only permits the teacher to determine whether the child is reading, but boosts his ego by giving him individual attention. It also permits the teacher to direct his progress, perhaps suggesting a book you know he would particularly enjoy.

Comic strip reviews

The student who enjoys drawing will be pleased to review a book by drawing illustrations comic strip style to tell about a particularly good incident. Displayed on the bulletin board this type of review will attract the attention of other readers.

Bulletin board display

One student might like to review a book by arranging a bulletin board display. He could cut illustrations from magazines or draw those he wishes to use. He might include a brief description of a thrilling part of the book or draw pictures of the main characters telling a little about each one. This type of activity encourages creativity on the part of the able student.

Models as review techniques

A student may present a book to the class by modeling a clay or papier-mâché bust of a famous person read about. This figure can be displayed in the classroom with the student telling the class something about the person represented.

Models of buildings, vehicles, or places can also be made to illustrate books read. Again the student could present the model while telling his reason for making that particular model and what significance it plays in the book he read. Models attract the attention of other students and interest them in reading the books represented.

Girls often enjoy dressing small dolls to represent the main characters of stories which they have read. A group of dolls might be dressed to represent the girls in *Little Women* or a doll might be dressed to resemble the subject of a biography.

Advertising books

A book can be advertised as in a magazine or the student can make a poster with a caption and illustrative drawings to "sell" the book. Book jackets are also excellent ways of reporting on the book read. Illustrations are made to decorate the front of the jacket while a "blurb" is written for the inside flap. These forms of advertising are effectively hung from a clothesline stretched along the wall.

Making slides

Students can make a lantern slide to illustrate part of a story. If several have read the same book, have each one illustrate a chapter or portion of the book. The slides can be shown while each student tells about that portion of the action. The verbal report can be taped for added effect and experience.

Professional reviews

Superior students in the upper grades will be able to read book reviews in adult magazines—*Saturday Review, Atlantic, Time, New York Times,* and so forth. Have them attempt to write book reviews in a similar style discussing a book's ideas and the quality of the writing. Their reviews will be surprisingly astute and mature in outlook.

Essays

As a form of book reviewing encourage the better student to discard the commonly used Book Report Form and simply analyze what the book has to offer him. He may write on the topic, for example, "What have I gained by reading this book?" The essay should cause the student to think about his reactions to the book and to say more than merely, "It was interesting."

Description of characters

A student can attempt to *write the biography (briefly) of one of the characters of a book* he has read (not biography). If pertinent information is not given, such as the date of birth, he may approximate these facts using any other dates given to guide him.

Another student might choose to *describe a character who would be a good model for anyone in the class to follow.* He should give his reasons for considering this character exemplary naming his good traits, and so on.

A report could feature THE CHARACTER I'D MOST LIKE TO BE in a book which the student has read. Again he must substantiate his statements giving evidence and reasons for his choice.

The reading log

THE READING LOG is another way of reporting on reading done by a student. He should note any books or articles read with brief reactions or statements about the content. Included in this notebook would be assigned readings as well as that done at home for pleasure. Clippings and other information relevant to his reading experiences should be part of the Reading Log.

If you wish to become a writer, write.

—*Epictetus*

3

WRITERS AT WORK

Through the use of widely varied techniques the student discovers that writing is fun; words are interesting. He learns how to express his thoughts on paper and finds that other people want to know what he has written. Emphasizing the positive aspects of his writing encourages the child to continue his writing efforts and helps develop his sense of individual worth.

Written language is used in many different ways in the classroom. Listed here are some of the forms which this writing takes:

Completing forms and test questions
Making signs and labels
Writing book reports
Creating titles and captions
Corresponding
Composing poetry
Writing stories
Preparing scripts
Writing news items
Compiling booklets
Reporting on research

Discovering Words

In order to write, to speak, to read we need to use the basic tool of language, the WORD. By the time the child enters school he already knows many words and he continues to add to this knowledge as he finds new ways of expressing himself.

Activities centered around words are good beginning activities for developing interest in creative writing. The child finds new ways of looking at words. He discovers that words are often composed of parts, that we have borrowed many of our words from other languages, and he begins meeting unfamiliar words, synonyms for the simple words he first knew. He discovers that working with words is fascinating.

Synonyms for common adjectives

Discuss the use of more exact and more colorful adjectives. Ask the class to suggest substitutes for commonly used words taken from their writing. Examples include:

small—tiny, wee, little, miniature
pretty—lovely, beautiful, gorgeous, attractive
big—large, tremendous, huge, immense, gigantic

Have each student keep a record of wordlists of this sort which will be useful when he is writing. Encourage him to add words as he finds them. Publicize any new synonyms which children may contribute.

Writing notebooks

Students can use small spiral notebooks to record new words which they learn or words which especially interest them. Pages can be marked for each letter of the alphabet to form an individualized dictionary. The notebook should also include space for things the student observes or imagery which he has heard or read. Titles which occur to him or topics about which he might like to write should be jotted down so these ideas can be remembered when wanted.

Dramatizing action words

When discussing synonyms for common verbs, have students take turns in dramatizing the action described. Have a child walk to the door. Write a sentence on the board describing the action in simple words: "John went to the door." Ask the children how they might make that action sound more interesting. They may suggest different words for *went* such as *sneaked, slipped, marched, ran, strolled, strutted, shuffled, charged.* Have the child who suggests the word go to the door in a manner appropriate to the word.

Other verbs which can be dramatized in this way include:

take: snatch, pull, steal, grab, pick, seize, remove
(Take a book from the desk.)
move: push, pull, lift, shove, carry
(Move the chair.)

Using a thesaurus

Children will be intrigued by books which list synonyms and antonyms. Any dictionary lists a number of synonyms, but the specialized dictionary of synonyms is a writer's tool with which children should become familiar. It is a good way to add to vocabularies and to the child's general interest in words. Two useful dictionaries for the school library are:

Mawson, C. O. Sylvester. *Roget's Thesaurus of the English Language in Dictionary Form.* Garden City, New York: Garden City Publishing Company, Inc., 1931. (Now in paperback edition: Pocket Books.)

Webster's Dictionary of Synonyms. Springfield, Massachusetts: G. and C. Merriam Co., 1942.

Writing similes

Introduce the idea of the simile by writing several familiar examples on the board: *as fast as a deer, as black as night, as cold as ice.* See if the students can discover the meaning of the word *simile* from the examples given.

Explain that the three comparisons made in these examples are so familiar that they have been overworked. Ask students to try to think of less common things with which to compare fastness, blackness, or coldness. Write suggestions on the board praising those which are unusual:

as fast as—
a shooting star
an angry bee
a snake's tongue
a jet streaking overhead

Changing accents

There is a large group of words which change their pronunciation and their meaning as you change their accents. Feature these words on a bulletin board with the caption CHANGING ACCENTS, and have students pronounce the words. Have them write two sentences for each word to illustrate the differences. Encourage them to add words to those displayed.

refuse	present	content
invalid	entrance	record
incense	permit	rebel

Describing sounds

Students can learn much just by listening quietly to sounds around them. Have them close their eyes and try to identify the sounds which they hear. Discuss words the writer uses to describe sounds: *scream, cry, shout, whisper, ring, scratch, scrape.*

You may wish to introduce the students to *onomatopoeia* (the forming of words which imitate natural sounds). Examples of words which sound like what they mean are: *buzz, chip, slice, tinkle, jingle, roar, crash, hum.*

Students can form lists of words which fall into this category. These words will be especially good for writing poetry.

Displaying words

In October prepare a Halloween bulletin board with the caption BEWITCHING WORDS. Mount a large black pot of construction paper with narrow strips of black paper signifying the steam rising from the brew. Small black bats can be cut out to fly above the witch's pot.

This display features words appropriate to Halloween stories: *ghost, spooky, witch, goblin, mysterious, broomstick, black cat.* Each word is printed on a small strip of white paper which is mounted on one of the bats scattered over the bulletin board. Use the display to motivate Halloween stories or poetry and to assist with the spelling of needed words.

The caption BEWITCHING WORDS can be used at another time

to feature words associated with magic: *enchanting, sorcery, wishes, fairy, wand, spell, elves, magician, conjure, charm.*

Collecting words

Encourage students to use a 3 x 5 card or strip of white paper as a bookmark while reading. As the reader encounters noteworthy words, he can jot them down on the bookmark for later entry in his notebook.

Changing words

CHANGE-ABOUTS represent a real challenge to better students. The object is to change one word into another in as few steps as possible. Each step consists of changing one letter to make another word until the desired word is reached. Duplicate one completed example with the others only partially completed so students can finish them. Include space on the sheet for the students to make CHANGE-ABOUTS of their own which they can share with others.

Heat to Cold	*More to Less*	*Green to Black*
HEAT	MORE	GREEN
HEAD	LORE	GREEK
HELD	LOSE	CREEK
HOLD	LOSS	CREAK
COLD	LESS	CROAK
		CROCK
		CLOCK
		BLOCK
		BLACK

Writing words

Give the class five minutes during which each is to write as many words as possible beginning with a given letter such as O. You may wish to use a beginning consonant blend such as BR or a prefix such as EX.

Emphasize the inclusion of more unusual words. If time permits, have someone begin reading their list of words. If anyone has listed the word which is read, they must cross out that word. This elimination continues until only less commonly used words remain. Count 1 point for each word a person has written which no one else listed.

> **TIP: Use an eggtimer for timing a short word game.**

Crossword puzzles

The crossword puzzle is a good device for stimulating interest in words. Here is an example which conceals four fruit names:

A'PEELING FRUITS

1 A	2 P	3 P	4 L	5 E
6 L	E	M	O	N
7 P	T		8 A	D
H		9 P	D	
10 A	11 L	L		12 O
13 B	E	A	14 S	T
15 E	G	Y	P	T
T		16 S	E	E
	17 R		18 E	R
19 B	A	20 N	D	
21 A	W	A	Y	
N				22 P
23 A	D	24 O	B	E
N		U		A
25 A	C	T	O	R

DOWN

1 ABC's
2 Pat
3 Afternoon
4 Burden
5 Finish
9 Dramas
11 Part of body
12 Water animal
14 Fast
17 Uncooked
19 Long yellow fruit
20 North America (abbr.)
22 Yellow fruit
24 Not in

ACROSS

1 Round, red fruit
6 Citrus fruit
7 Pint (abbr.)
8 Advertisement
9 Police Department (abbr.)
10 Every bit
13 Animal
15 Country in Africa
16 Use the eye
18 Common suffix
19 Musical group
21 Not here

Constructing crossword puzzles

Most students have worked Crossword Puzzles. They will learn more, however, through the actual construction of crossword puzzles of varying difficulty.

Duplicate a puzzle frame like the example shown. Students can use these frames to construct original puzzles. They should concentrate on arranging words which intersect, leaving definitions until they have filled the frame as completely as possible.

	V								
B	A	L	L	X					
	L								
	E								
	N								
	T								
	I								
	N								
	E								
	S								

Their puzzles may be smaller or irregular in shape. Compete puzzles (with answers) can be entered in a book of CROSSWORD PUZZLES compiled by the class. Especially good puzzles can be duplicated for distribution to the class.

Some puzzles may suggest shapes which can be drawn around the puzzle such as a heart, a flower, a fruit, or an animal.

Acrostics

Students will enjoy composing Acrostics which feature interesting words. In the Acrostic the first letter of each word used (read vertically) helps to spell a word.

Study	Backward
Children	Obnoxious
History	Youthful
Organization	Spoiled
Obedience	
Learning	

The Acrostic for BOYS above was obviously written by a girl; boys would enjoy composing an Acrostic for GIRLS. You may wish to supply a definition for each word indicating only the number of letters in the word. If the student correctly solves the Acrostic, he will FIND THE SECRET WORD.

Color words

Cut a large circe (18″ diameter) from colored construction paper or tagboard to form the COLOR WHEEL. Divide this circle into sixths with a felt pen. Print Color Words—Yellow, Green, Blue, Purple, Red, and Orange—on strips of colored paper which can be mounted at the end of each line on the wheel as in the sample below. Insert other Color Words around the Color Wheel to introduce students to less commonly used colors; add new ones as they are discovered by the class.

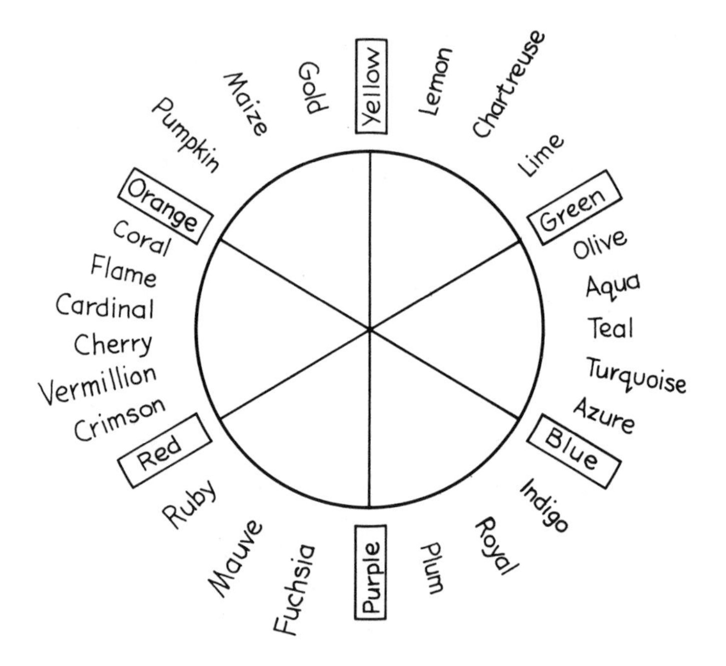

Adding letters to make new words

Give each student a sheet of paper containing ten sample words (without the answers) and these instructions: "Change each word to another word by adding the letter L. Do not change the order of the letters as they appear in the given word. Can you add an L to the word COT? By placing an L in two different places you can produce the words: CLOT, COLT. At the bottom of the page add any other words which can be changed by adding an L."

Here are samples which can be used on the prepared sheet:

sat–slat, salt	wed–weld
god–gold	jot–jolt
bad–bald	hat–halt
sip–slip	fatter–flatter
band–bland	can–clan

Anagrams

This word game increases the students' awareness of words. The object is to rearrange the letters of one word to form another word or words. Write several samples of anagrams on the board to illustrate the game:

SEAT, EATS, TEAS, EAST, (SATE)
SPIN, NIPS, PINS, SNIP
SALT, SLAT, LAST
RATE, TEAR, TARE
RIDE, DIRE
MATE, TAME, TEAM, MEAT

After solving several Anagrams together, let the students work independently to see what they can discover. Have them write their DISCOVERIES on the board or place them on a bulletin board. Several students could compile a class BOOK OF ANAGRAMS to which students can continue adding contributions.

Incomplete words

Tear or cut headlines or captions from magazines or newspapers so that only an irregular portion of each letter remains. Mount these partial words on a bulletin board around a large question mark. See if students can identify the words. Later produce the other part of each caption. This is an interesting demonstration of our method of gaining meaning from limited clues.

Antonyms

Have students make sentences in which a pair of antonyms (opposites) contrast as in these samples:

The *ugly* dog walked beside the *beautiful* girl.
The *huge* tree towered over the *tiny* boy.

To familiarize students with specific words you can provide a list of words to be used in this manner or they can discover their own pairs of words to be used. Encourage the use of the dictionary with this activity.

Word brackets

For this game print a word vertically on the chalkboard. Choose a holiday word, one connected with a subject being studied, or an interesting new word you wish to introduce. To the right print the same word with its letters reversed in order as shown. The object is to insert letters between those given to make new words, the longer the better, for every letter inserted gives the player a point.

G	n a	T	H	e a r s	E	F	r a m	E
H	i s	S	O	m e n	S	R	o	C
O	h i	O	R	o a	R	A	l l e	N
S	m a s	H	S	i l	O	N	o r	A
T	a	G	E	a c	H	C	o r n e	R
						E	l	F

If a student playing WORD BRACKETS with Horse, supplied the above letters, his score would be 13. If, however, he used Oysters for the second word, he would have gained another 2 points, and so on.

T__K__ ___T __ SH___T __F
P__P__R __ND __ P__NC__L.

Print this WORD FRAME on the chalkboard. See how many students can discover the message and follow directions without a hint!

Parts of speech

Choose a page from a book which all students have. After folding a sheet of notebook paper to form four long columns, head each column with the name of a part of speech—NOUN, VERB, ADJECTIVE, PREPOSITION, and so on.

Students then write each word taken from the selected page

in the appropriate column. After all have completed the page the lists can be examined with a discussion of the correct answers as each student corrects his work.

Verbs

To focus attention on the action verb ask students the following type of question which can be answered orally and listed on the board:

What can a dog do?—
bark
jump
wiggle
play

What can an airplane do?—
fly
taxi
circle
crash

You can change the questions to include,"What can you do *to* a dog?" "What can you do *to* a ball?" Answers might include:

I can pet a dog.
I can feed a dog.
I can bounce a ball.
I can throw a ball.

Spelling notebooks

Have students keep small notebooks with pages designated for each letter of the alphabet. Here each one can record words which he has spelled incorrectly during writing exercises as well as words which interest him, words that he would like to spell. At times children can test each other on words which are listed in their notebooks. You may wish to include words which appear frequently in individual notebooks as extra words to be added to the weekly spelling list.

Pre-testing for spelling

When introducing any spelling wordlist, give a pre-test before requiring all students to study these words. Have students study only those which were not spelled correctly. If there are students who are able to spell all the words without further study, let them use this time for further exploration of words such as activities listed in this section.

Initial blends

Teach or review the initial blends of consonants which begin so many words: *bl, br, ch, cl, cr, dr, fl, fr, gl, gr, pl, pr, sc, sh, sk, sl, sm, sn, sp, st, sw, spl, str, scr, tr.* Give students practice in hearing these beginning sounds by saying words and having them write the first 2 or 3 letters of the word. Select words which they won't necessarily know how to spell; they will delight in trying words they have never heard before—BIG WORDS! If they listen carefully to the sounds heard, they can often spell the whole word correctly; it's fun to try.

clamber	flamboyant
breeze	platitude
praise	drenched
striped	slovenly
scratch	sprightly

Display idea

Each month prepare a display captioned WORDS OF THE MONTH. This feature may be combined with a calendar. Mount appropriate words on a motif appropriate to the month. In February, for example, these words might be mounted on heart shapes: *George Washington, Abraham Lincoln, president, February, birthday, ground hog, twenty-eight, valentine,* and others which are associated with classroom activities at that time. The words can be hung from a branch, a mobile, or scattered on a bulletin board.

Similarities

When presenting a new list of spelling words, have the students notice similarities among the words. Remind them of words which were studied in previous weeks which had the same features.

p*er*fect	*pro*vide	r*ing*	*en*ter
bak*er*	*pro*test	tak*ing*	sp*en*d

Like endings

When teaching a word like *catch*, for example, point out the fact that many other words have the same ending. See who can change the beginning sound to make a new word: *batch, hatch, latch, match, patch, snatch, scratch.* By spelling one word the children really learned how to spell many others. You may also caution them about exceptions, in this case *watch* which is spelled the same but has a different sound.

Prefixes and suffixes

Children need to learn to spell the common suffixes and prefixes so that they will be able to spell words using them. The spelling of these syllables can be taught together with their meaning as the class lists words using various prefixes or suffixes. Here are some of the more common ones:

Prefixes	*Suffixes*
in, im, un, en	ing, ed, er
pre, per, pro	ness, less, ful
ex, con, dis	ly, y, le
de, re, be	tion, ment, ish

Spelling unfamiliar words

Point out the ease with which many seemingly difficult words can be spelled when the student knows consonant and vowel sounds as well as prefixes and suffixes. Say a word carefully, pronouncing each syllable clearly. Give the class time to try spelling the word before you have someone write it on the board. Try these words:

plantation	blatantly	clutching
discontinuing	entanglement	invocation
perfection	preferment	remarkable
understandingly	belaboring	vacationing

When presenting unfamiliar words, it is a good idea to provide a synonym or brief meaning for the word as many alert students will learn interesting words in this way.

Books about words

To stimulate further interest in words explore some of the following books which supply ideas and information:

Epstein, Sam and Beryl. *The First Book of Words.* Watts, 1954.
Funk, Wilfred. *Word Origins and Their Romantic Stories.* Funk, 1951.
Morris, William and Mary. *The Word Game Book.* Cornerstone Library, 1959. ($1.00)
Pei, Mario. *The Story of Language.* Lippincott, 1949. Monitor Books, 75¢.
Pei, Mario. *All about Language.* Lippincott, 1954.
Rand, Ann and Paul. *Sparkle and Spin: A Book about Words.* Harcourt, 1957.
Reid, Alastair. *Ounce, Dice, Trice.* Atlantic Monthly Press, 1958.
Tiedt, Sidney and Iris. *Exploring Words.* Box 1524, San Jose, California: Contemporary Press, 1963. ($1.00)

Writing Stories

The main object in teaching a child to write is to enable him to communicate his thoughts. Before he can communicate his thoughts, however, he must have thoughts. The purpose of the following group of ideas is to stimulate the thinking of the child, to awaken his imagination, which too often has been stifled or neglected, and to teach him the skills of effectively communicating his thoughts through writing.

Always preface any writing activity with at least a short period of discussion so that most children become interested and begin to have some ideas. If, for example, the class is going to write on the subject, "The Day I Was Invisible," encourage suggestions of the advantages and disadvantages of being invisible. Draw out a variety of responses from different children especially those who are more reticent. *When motors are warmed up,* then give the starting signal, "Write!"

Group dictation

Young children who are not yet skilled in writing words will gain much through group dictation as you print the sentences on the chalkboard or on a piece of tagboard (using a felt pen). The dictation may be based on the children's experiences of the day including sentences like these:

John saw a black dog.
Today is Susan's birthday.

Another time you may use a large picture to stimulate the construction of interesting sentences which describe the activities in the picture.

Mary is on the way to school.
She is wearing a blue dress.
Her dog is following her.

Using descriptive language

Write a simple sentence on the chalkboard such as: "A dog ran down the street." How can this sentence be made more interesting? Encourage the students to suggest answers to these questions:

What kind of dog was it?	*size, color, breed*
How did he run?	*scurried, loped, sneaked*
What kind of street was it?	*busy, quiet, crowded, narrow*

Have children share their rewordings of the sentence which may be something like this: "The little mongrel scurried along the crowded boulevard." Then present other sentences which can be made more interesting in the same way.

The man went into the store.
The woman carried a package.
We saw a child.

Inventing names

Students are intrigued by inventing names for people who might appear in a story. You might stimulate ideas for names by first discussing names of people the children have read about.

Dr. Doolittle	Yonie Wondernose
Pecos Bill	Henry Huggins
Mr. Popper	Flopsy, Mopsy, and Cotton Tail

What is it about these names that makes them different, that makes them more appealing? Let the class try to invent names that are unusual and might fit a character in a story—a young man who is always criticizing other people or a plump woman who is fond of baking cherry pies. Later a story can be written using some of the names invented.

Words suggest stories

Have each child write a Noun (or a verb or adjective) at the top of his paper. He then passes his paper to the person behind him who adds a second unrelated Noun as does a third person. The next passing provides each child with a paper containing three unrelated Nouns. He then writes a story about the three words which might, for example, be: NUT, DOG, BOOK or CARPET, PEACOCK, MAP. He must invent a situation which can encompass the three words given him.

Initial letters suggest stories

Write four unrelated letters on the board. Ask the students what these letters mean to them. Let them jot ideas on paper as they work out an idea. Write several suggestions on the board. No suggestions are rejected, for there is no idea of wrongness here. TCLA might, for instance, elicit these suggestions:

Ted coughs loudly, Alice.
Take crisp lettuce always.
Try Charlie's latest advice.

Letters should not be rearranged nor words inserted between letters. Dictionaries may be used for assistance in suggesting possible words. The ideas can be used as titles for stories or stories can be written to explain the meaning of the sentence.

Incomplete drawings provide ideas

Duplicate the following incomplete drawing. Let the stu-

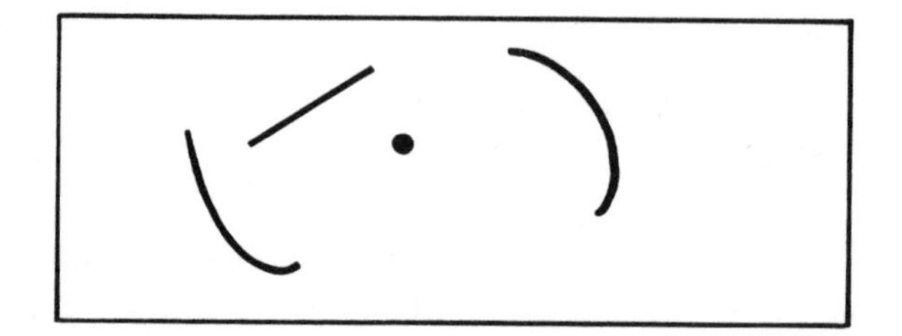

dents study the "picture" before they do anything. Then suggest that they write about what the incomplete drawing means to them. Permit students to add lines to the drawing if they wish.

The drawings may later be completed with color added. Some students may contribute other provocative drawings which can be used for this type of exercise.

Dictated sentences

One of the most effective ways of practicing punctuation, capitalization, and spelling all in one easy operation is through the use of sentences which are dictated to the class. You can construct sentences to emphasize any skills the class needs to practice, for example, quotation marks:

1. Dr. Baker cried angrily, "You know I wasn't there!"
2. "Yes, I saw you myself," replied Mr. Martin.

To present new sentences for study dictate the sentences to the students as a pre-test. Have the sentences written on the board correctly so each child can correct his own errors. Each will then know what he needs to study.

Practicing punctuation

Duplicate a page from a book to which all the children have access. As you copy the paragraphs, omit all punctuation. After each student supplies the needed punctuation, he can use his book to correct his errors. This exercise can later be used as a test if you make extra copies.

Punctuation changes meaning

How the meaning of a sentence can be changed by the change of punctuation! Have students read these sentences as the punctuation indicates:

Take that little baby.
Take that, little baby!

We'll be there on time.
Well, be there on time!

Mary Smith and I told you yesterday.
Mary Smith, and I told you yesterday!

Give it to her son.
Give it to her, son!

Constructing sentences

Give the students a FORMULA for a sentence to familiarize them with the Parts of Speech. Each student must substitute words according to the Formula, to produce a sensible sentence. Here is a sample Formula and two sentences which follow the given Formula:

Adj.	Noun	Verb	Adverb	Preposition	Noun
Lonely	Ruth	walked	slowly	to	school.
Clever	boy,	run	quickly	for	candy.

Quotation marks

Teach or review the use of quotation marks as you teach Synonyms for the verb, SAID. Have students compile a list of words which represent ways of *saying*—Scream, State, Cry, Whisper, Shout, Mutter. Direct them to use these interesting verbs as they compose sentences which will include quotation marks.

"Help!" cried the frightened child.
"I couldn't hear you," she explained.
"How could you do it?" the worried father asked.

Developing sentences

Supply a phrase which can be incorporated in a sentence. This technique should be used orally first. A student is called on to add a phrase to the given one; other students can suggest additional phrases until no more can be added. The original phrase may be in any position in the sentence. Here is an example:

Phrase: the fuzzy white cat

The fuzzy white cat leaped on the fence.

Meowing loudly, the fuzzy white cat leaped on the fence.

Meowing loudly, the fuzzy white cat leaped on the fence to get away.

Meowing loudly, the fuzzy white cat leaped on the fence to get away from the dog.

As the students gain facility in building sentences, you may let them work independently with given phrases. After all have written their sentences, the results can be compared to see various ways of handling the same original phrase.

Developing a theme

Write five words on the board around which the students are to write a story. Choose words which are directed toward one type of story as a fairy tale, a mystery, or a space adventure:

magic, wish, castle, journey, prince
ghost, hill, storm, tracks, shack
rocket, moon, craters, cold, gravity

When all children are writing on the same topic, it is interesting to compare the different types of ideas which develop from the same five words, a good demonstration of individual differences—interests, personalities, experiences—all of which influence their ideas.

Spelling and creative writing

As students write, encourage them to spell a word as it sounds or simply to write the beginning of the word leaving a blank space for the later completion of the word. *Concern with spelling should not be allowed to stifle creative thinking.* After the ideas are recorded, students can use the dictionary or other means to ascertain correct spellings.

Here are several suggestions for helping students spell the words they need as they write:

1. Each month prepare a list of seasonal or holiday words which will be helpful in written work. Students may have copies of this list in their notebooks or the list can be mounted on the bulletin board.
2. Individual spelling notebooks will record difficult words or words which a student has missed before. He can enter any word which he finds that he needs.
3. Designate one student in each row as the SPELLER OF THE DAY. Students in that row may then get help from this assistant. You may wish to limit the number of requests for help made by any one student. These positions will, of course, be rotated.

4. At times you may wish to spell words needed. Write any word requested on the board to eliminate second requests for the same word. If someone does ask the same word, simply point it out.

Completing sentences

This writing activity is so interesting that students enjoy using it as a party game. Even the poorest student is successful.

As you read the beginning for Sentence 1 (provided below), each student writes a possible ending for the sentence at the very top of his paper. His words are then covered up by making a narrow fold *toward himself*. (A consistent direction of folding will keep all answers on the front of the paper.) Each student then passes his paper to the person behind him. As you read the beginning for Sentence 2, each student writes an ending for that sentence on the paper he now has. Continue in this way until all sentences have been completed. For younger children you may use fewer sentences.

It was on a chilly evening that I met the boy named________.[1]
Walking with him was a________________________________.[2]
Quietly I asked him, "_____________________________.[3]
He answered almost angrily, "________________________.[4]
As he turned to go, he_______________________________.[5]
All I did was______________________________________.[6]
This was unfortunate because__________________________.[7]
The result of this adventure was_______________________.[8]

After the last sentence is finished, have the children pass the folded papers several more times. Each person then unfolds the paper he has received and reads the story with the use of your copy of the sentence beginnings. The results are often incongruous and very imaginative. With large classes you may wish to read each sentence asking students to volunteer to read particularly good endings. Students will enjoy constructing new "stories" to be used for this activity.

The beginning sentence

Discuss the importance of the beginning sentence of any story. Have students write five beginning sentences for different stories. As sentences are presented orally, class members can decide what sort of story would follow the sentences read.

Select ten provocative beginning sentences from these papers. Write them on the board the next day for use as the basis for student writing.

Writing fantasy

Here are a number of "What if . . ." ideas to give students ideas with which to work as they begin writing tales of fantasy. You may choose to use only one topic at a time letting students discuss the possibilities suggested by the idea. A warming-up period of this type leads to more enthusiastic and creative writing.

1. What if eating lemons made people sour?
2. What if you had a tiny dog the size of your pocket?
3. What if you had a pet monkey that was invisible?
4. What if you were the teacher of this class?
5. What if a rich man told you he would give you any two things you could name?
6. What if your uncle sent you ten dollars to spend any way you wished?
7. What if you were a stowaway on a ship?
8. What if cats could talk?

Provocative titles

An interesting title is often sufficient to motivate the writing of excellent stories. Listed here are several which you can use:

Boom!
All Night Long
What a Queer Animal!
It Happened at Noon
Two Plus Two
Snow in July
Keep Cool
Mother Told Me
My Day as King (Queen)
Just One Week Ago
Living in the Twenty-First Century

Correlating writing and social studies

Discuss the events that might occur if a person who lived one hundred years ago were to walk into our world today. What, for example, would Thomas Jefferson think of our government? What things would appear odd, amazing, wonderful, or distasteful to him?

Let each student choose a figure in history about whom to write a story. Have the student write his story pretending that he is the person who is suddenly transported to the twentieth century describing the events that happen.

Using a letter to motivate writing

Write the following letter on the chalkboard or duplicate it so each child can have a copy:

> Dear Mike,
>
> I hesitated a long time before writing you this letter, for I know you've suffered a great shock. I just want you to know that my offer still stands. Please call me soon to tell me your plans.
>
> Paul

The students can discuss the identities of Mike and Paul. Why was the letter written? What is the shock to which Paul refers? What is Paul's offer? What happens to Mike and Paul later? Each student can write a story about these two characters. Students can also construct similar letters on which stories can be based.

Publishing stories

Student writing can be published in the form of small literary mazagines. The magazine serves as an incentive for good writing and can include a variety of writing of varied lengths so that all students can contribute something. Short stories, poetry, interesting imagery, unusual words or phrases—these are some of the kinds of writing to be included.

Let students choose a name for the magazine. The magazine, which need not be published frequently, can be distributed to other classes and other schools to let them know what your school is doing. This publication is an excellent demonstration to parents of the work being done at school and can be given to them when they attend an Open House or can be prepared as a gift at Christmas time.

Recording stories

The tape recorder provides an effective means for presenting the writing efforts of your students. Each student can read a story or poem which he has written to produce a tape of materials to be presented to parents who visit the classroom. Tapes of this nature are also excellent items to exchange with schools in other lands to give them a picture of students in the United States.

Books to explore

Many books have been written about writing and writers. Here are a few which can be recommended for further exploration as you teach young writers:

Cowley, Malcolm, ed. *Writers at Work.* Viking, 1957.
Collection of interviews with famous authors who describe their writing efforts; includes biographies. (Now available in paperback.)

Mathieu, Aron M., ed. *The Creative Writer.* Cincinnati, Ohio: Writer's Digest, 1962. ($6.95)
Describes the writing process; an adult treatment.

Tiedt, Sidney and Iris. *Creative Writing Ideas.* Box 1524, San Jose, California: Contemporary Press, 1963. ($1.00)
Describes more ideas for motivating creative writing.

Yates, Elizabeth. *Someday You'll Write.* New York: E. P. Dutton & Co., 1962.
A book addressed to young people who want to write.

Composing Poetry

The writing of verse is very enjoyable. In order to stimulate the enthusiasm of students we recommend that children be introduced to poetry through the reading and writing of humorous verses. Other good varieties of poems for arousing interest are poems which tell a story and those which deal with topics that are especially current, for example, space, airplanes, and people. As children begin exploring verse writing, they will experiment with many forms and topics.

The limerick

Use the limerick to capture student enthusiasm for poetry. The humorous verse of Edward Lear will supply samples such as "There Was an Old Man with a Beard," and "There Was a Young Lady of Norway," which are included in the excellent anthology, *Time for Poetry* by May Hill Arbuthnot (Scott, Foresman, 1951).

Here is a limerick which can be written on the chalkboard to illustrate the form taken by these whimsical verses:

> There was an old man from Nome,
> Who never liked to stay home.
>   He missed winning a prize,
>   When out buying pies.
> Said he, "I'll never more roam."*

Notice that lines 1, 2, and 5 rhyme, while lines 3 and 4 have a different rhyme. Limericks often start with the words, "There was . . ." The class can write some limericks together before trying it individually. Stress the humor and enjoyment of the poetry rather than style.

Couplets

Lead your class in writing a poem together in couplets with one student supplying the first line and members of the class suggesting a second line. At Christmas time, for example, a first line might be:

> The bells are gaily ringing.

Different lines ending with a rhyme for *ringing* will be suggested with one being selected to be written on the board beneath the first, such as:

> Glad tidings to us bringing.

The poem can be continued with another couplet in the

* Unless otherwise stated poems, stories and songs are written by Iris M. Tiedt.

same manner until it is of sufficient length (8–16 lines). One child may then copy the completed poem for display on the bulletin board or in a collection of class writing.

There is no rhyme for Silver!

Reducing poetry to prose

Why write poetry? Why can't a person write prose with the same effect? To answer questions like these, have students examine a familiar poem and write the meaning of the poem in prose. The unknown poet's "I Have a Little Pussy," is a good example:

I have a little pussy,
Her coat is silver gray;
She lives down in the meadow
And she never runs away.
She'll always be a pussy,
She'll never be a cat
Because she's a pussy willow!
Now what do you think of that?

Reduced to prose, this poem says little more than that someone, who found a pussy willow bush growing in a field, compares it to a real cat.

Haiku poems

An interesting form of poetry which has lately become popular is the Japanese Haiku. The form consists of three unrhymed lines which fall into a syllabic pattern. The first and third lines each contain five syllables while the second line contains seven syllables.

These subtle little poems most often present a scene from nature, but with the ingenuity of the young writer can encompass any subject matter. The fact that there are no rhymes removes a certain artificiality which appears at times in children's efforts to follow rhyme schemes. Here are samples of Haiku which can be discussed with your students before they begin to write original Haiku.

Soft Lights
Candlelight flickers—
Soft shadows hide wrinkled age;
Sorrow is shaded.

Patterns
Look up to the blue!
Silken leaves pattern the sky
Fingering sheer air.

Welcome
When I return home,
Two brown eyes beg me to play.
A wet nose welcomes.

A Painting (by Pam, 10)
A painting is like
A flower nature fashioned
Delicately made.

Displaying Haiku

Have students use colored paper to fold small (4 x 6 in.) paper fans. Their Haiku can be printed on white paper (2 x 3 in.) which is attached to the fan. Scatter the oriental fans over a bulletin board with the simple caption HAIKU. For variety hang the fans mobile-fashion from the branch of a tree or distribute fans to classroom visitors at an Open House.

Triplets

The triplet is a rhymed form of poetry that is relatively easy for the young poet. Since each triplet consists of three lines which end with the same rhyme, the best way to start is by making Rhyme Lists. Suggest that each child choose the name of something which interests him—*plane, play, lake, school, game, pet, cat, dog, jet, boat, train, map, sea, town, toy.* (Encourage the selection of words which rhyme easily like those in this list.)

Each child then makes a list of words which rhyme with the selected word. If, for example, he selects the word *play*, his list will include many of these words: *bay, day, gay, hay, lay, may, pay, ray, say, way, clay, gray, pray, play, stay, sway, stray, tray.* From this list he can choose three words to use in his Triplet. The result might be something like this:

Our cat likes to play.
His antics are gay.
"See me?" his eyes say.

The Triplet, as described here, is really a brief story told in rhyme. Here is another example of a Tri based on the word SEA:

Standing silent before the sea,
I thought the water talked to me
Then laughed aloud with sudden glee.

Displaying triplets

Have each child cut out large (9 x 12 in. paper) flower shapes in bright colors for a spring bulletin board. The centers for the flowers can be cut from yellow or orange construction paper (4 x 6 in.) on which a Triplet is carefully printed. Add stems and leaves to the flowers which can be grouped on a bulletin board beneath the caption GARDEN OF VERSES. Smaller flowers can be used if space is limited.

Sharing poetry

Each student may contribute his best Haiku or Triplet to be included in a class booklet. Use a long, slim format for these short verses with a cover designed by a class member. Type (or print) the verses in two columns on a duplicating master; each column will then constitute a page in the booklet. Prepare class quantities of the booklets to be used as Christmas gifts for the students' parents.

Guiding Student Development in Writing

In order to help the individual child develop to his fullest ability in writing creatively the teacher must do a certain amount of reading what the child has written, noting errors, and guiding his correction of these errors.

One of the chief reasons that teachers avoid use of creative writing is the knowledge that anything of this nature represents a time-consuming task of grading. Let us consider, therefore, effective methods of helping the student while at the same time minimizing the amount of teacher-time required. Remember to vary the techniques used, for any method loses its effectiveness if overworked.

Oral evaluation

Short compositions can be shared with the class by reading them orally. Class members should learn to listen carefully in order to comment on the work. While the oral presentation takes place, you can use a small tablet or slips of paper to jot down notes for each author in this manner:

> John—
> What a good story! I like the first sentence which certainly caught our attention.
> Check pronunciation of magnanimous.

You can pass these notes to the individual students while they are filing their writing in Writing Folders.

Proofreading marks

Develop a set of simple proofreading marks so that you or Student Editors can use these marks to simplify making corrections. A key for the marks can be kept on a card to which a student may refer if he forgets the meaning of a mark. Here are some you may wish to use:

- P Start a new paragraph here.
- S This group of words is not a sentence.
- <u>Underlining</u> This word is not spelled correctly.
- √ See me about this part.
- ★ What a wonderful way to say that!

Projected writing

Use the overhead projector to project written work on a screen so that the whole class can view a paper at once. New methods of preparing transparencies for this projector permit the teacher to reproduce pencil-written compositions quickly and easily for this purpose. You may wish to remove the name of the writer so that no embarrassment will be felt.

The values of this type examination of written work are that all students are viewing the same work as you suggest corrections and mark directly on the transparency. Discuss the paper, pointing out errors, but emphasizing those aspects of the paper which are praiseworthy—interesting imagery, use of a new word, a well-phrased sentence, some good dialogue, or a catchy title. Working with the group in this way demonstrates to the whole class the sorts of things you value in their papers. Their own thinking will be directed along these lines as they write and as they evaluate the work of others.

Recognition of good work

Read aloud stories or parts of stories which you consider particularly effective. Indicate your reason for being impressed with the writing you present in this way. At times let the author come forward to read his own work, but students are also honored to have you do a more expert job of reading their stories.

Always make it class policy that any time a student is writing about something which he does not care to have read aloud, he may simply mark it—NOT TO BE READ ALOUD. You may otherwise miss some very revealing writing from students who might confide in you through their writing.

Student editing

Occasionally select one child from each row to act as Student Editor. It is the Editor's duty to read the papers of each child in his row carefully marking any errors in spelling or grammar. He can employ the Proofreading Marks regularly used by the class. These papers can then be corrected before they are handed to the teacher. Rotate this job so no single person is overburdened.

Self-selection of work

It is not necessary that all written work be turned in to the teacher. The successful creative writing program requires that the student write almost every day; some students are especially enthusiastic and continue their writing efforts at home. Each student should have an individual folder where all of his writing is filed.

Designate one day each week, perhaps Friday, as the time for examining the writing done that week. Each student reviews the material he has filed that week and selects the piece of writing which he considers his best selection. He then rereads it, makes corrections, and copies this one selection to be presented to the teacher for evaluation.

This aproach to the encouragement of creative writing works well for both the very able student and the low-achiever. Emphasis is placed on development rather than grades. Each student progresses according to his ability. The able student can use extra time for working in this area, so that he always has a project on which he can work.

Publicizing writing

Help the students publish a brief bulletin or magazine which is an outlet for good writing. Columns can feature Picturesque Phrases, Willing Words, and so forth. Short stories and poetry can also be included. Publications of this nature add an incentive for writing and they point up the qualities of good writing. Do make certain that all students contribute something even if only a word or phrase.

A publication can be as simple or as elaborate as time and desire permit. It can include only work from your class members or it can become a school project with representative writing from children of all grades.

Reporting Facts

Much of the writing which is done by the student is in the nature of a report. Besides knowledge of the mechanics of writing, there are a number of other skills involved in the writing of reports. A student must develop research skills, ability to take good notes, accuracy of reporting facts, and ability to state information clearly.

Developing observation skills

Prepare a quiz to illustrate the fact that few of us really observe what goes on around us. Questions might be of this variety:

What color is the wall in the hallway?
What is the number of the room directly across the hall?
Does our principal wear glasses?
What object have I removed from this table?
What color is your mathematics textbook?
How many exits are there from the school building?
How many swings are on the playground?

The children will be amused and amazed to learn how many inaccuracies are revealed by the answers to this test of their powers of observation. Let certain students verify the answers by going to determine the correct answer. This activity can be conducted orally for primary children.

Taking notes while listening

Use the tape recorder to present material on which students are to make notes. This technique provides an opportunity to repeat the same material at a later time after you have discussed the notes which were taken and have suggested improvements.

Students will gain much skill in listening attentively as they take notes from oral material. Use this technique before having a speaker address your class in connection with a social studies unit. Some records present material appropriate for this method of note-taking also.

Taking notes while reading

Select a page or two from a textbook which all students have. Take notes together as a way of introducing the idea of note-taking. Let students suggest the notes to be recorded by one student writing on the chalkboard. This method clearly demonstrates the avoidance of copying whole sentences, paragraphs, or pages.

After the notes have been recorded for the selected material, have these notes erased from the board. Each student can then reread the same material taking notes individually, trying to produce notes similar to those recorded by the group.

On another day assign different pages from the same text for note-taking. Again the entire class is working on the same material so that the results can be compared. When the assignment is completed, permit each student to refer to his notes and to the textbook while notes are again recorded on the board. Point out the reasons for including some items and not including others. This process may be repeated according to the needs of the class. Some individuals may require more work as a small group after the majority of the group is ready to work on individual research.

Using reference books

Prepare a Treasure Hunt to be done in the library or in the classroom using those reference books available. All students should become familiar with these basic reference tools:

Encyclopedias
Unabridged Dictionary
World Almanac
Atlas

Include questions such as the following based on the reference tools you have available:

1. What is the population of France?
2. During what years was Lincoln president?
3. Name two synonyms for *Transparent*.
4. What does the abbreviation S. R. O. mean?

Each student is to write the name of the book in which he finds the answer and the page number. The answer to the question is not as important in this case as is knowing *where* to look for the answer.

Using the card catalog

Each student should become familiar with the use of the library's Card Catalog. Even if your school does not have a central library, this information is important if the student is to use a public library. Duplicate or copy on the board the common forms of library cards—Author, Title, and Subject. Included here are samples of these cards:

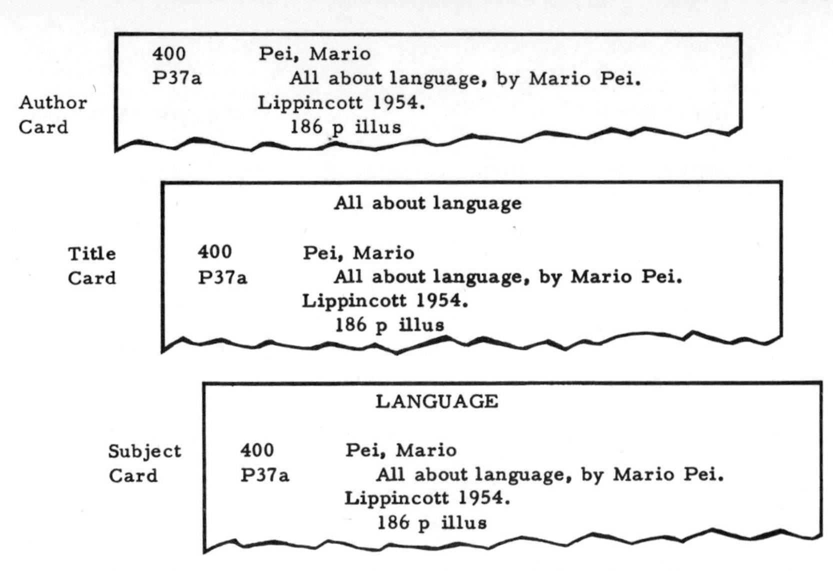
Author Card

400 Pei, Mario
P37a All about language, by Mario Pei.
Lippincott 1954.
186 p illus

Title Card

All about language

400 Pei, Mario
P37a All about language, by Mario Pei.
Lippincott 1954.
186 p illus

Subject Card

LANGUAGE

400 Pei, Mario
P37a All about language, by Mario Pei.
Lippincott 1954.
186 p illus

Ask students questions about the book listed on these catalog cards. Let them find the information from these cards before you have the questions answered and discussed. You may also find it helpful to have each student make printed catalog cards (use 3 x 5 inch slips of paper) for library books which they have on hand so that they thoroughly understand the information included on these cards. Here are questions which might be asked:

1. Who is the author of this book?
2. What is the title of the book? Is the title capitalized the way we would capitalize it in a report? Why not?
3. What does the number 400 tell you? Why are numbers like this one used? (Opportunity to introduce the Dewey Decimal System in brief.)
4. Why does this book have three cards? Might a book have more than three cards?
5. What does the number P37a mean? (This is a Cutter number, used in public libraries to aid shelving of books. P stands for the author's name; *a* indicates the first letter of the title. Students should know what this number is simply to avoid confusion.)
6. How many pages are in this book? Are there any illustrations?
7. Who published the book? In what year was it published?

Preparing the bibliography

Students should learn to keep a bibliography whenever they are doing any sort of research. Have them learn a simple, but consistent form for listing a book, a magazine article, and information from encyclopedias. Each entry should be listed on a separate card or a card-size slip of paper which can be used to prepare the bibliography at the end of the report or paper. If notes are to be recorded on the same cards, use a large card size (5 x 8 inches).

Here are sample acceptable forms for recording bibliographic information:

BOOK: Pei, Mario. *All About Language.* New York: Lippincott, 1954 (note pages read).

ARTICLE: Witty, Paul. "A Summary of Yearly Studies of Televiewing—1949–1963." *Elementary English.* October, 1963. pp. 590–597.

ENCYCLOPEDIA: *Britannica Junior.* "Alaska." Volume I, p. _____.

Accurate reporting

An interesting technique to demonstrate the need for accurate reporting of facts is the presentation of an unexpected event about which students are later questioned. Arrange to borrow three reliable students who can enact a brief skit unexpectedly before the eyes of your class to test their skill at reporting an event which they witness. Talk to these actors ahead of time to explain their role in this skit letting them practice the act briefly so that it goes smoothly. At a pre-arranged time have the actors enter your room to enact a skit something like this:

1st Boy—Wears coat, carries umbrella, rushes into the room, hides umbrella in wastebasket, leaves.

Girl—Wears scarf over head, enters crying, "I must find my purse or Mother will be angry!" She finds umbrella, says, "Oh, there it is."

2nd Boy—Wears jacket, hands the girl something small, unseen, says, "You were foolish to give this to Tom Warren."

The actors return to their classroom as arranged, and you ask your class to take paper and pencil so that they can record what happened before their very eyes. Ask questions about the event:

What object was hidden in the wastebasket?
What did the girl say when she came in the room?
What was the first boy wearing?
What color was the scarf the girl wore?

What did the second boy give to the girl?
What were the exact words of the second boy?
What was the first boy's name? (Do they know this?)
What was the girl searching for?

It is interesting to tally the different answers given to see how inaccurate we really are when we report what we think we see.

> Speech was made to open man to man and not to hide him . . .
>
> –*David Lloyd*

4

FOCUS ON SPEAKING AND LISTENING

Both speaking and listening have become increasingly important in our verbal society. Described in this chapter are techniques for focusing attention on the abilities of effective speaking and listening in the classroom. Included are both individual and group activities which will assist the teacher by varying the techniques used in developing the skills of speaking and listening.

Developing Speaking Skills

In this section we shall focus attention on creative approaches to effective speech. Every child knows how to talk upon entrance to school, but ability to communicate requires more than mere talking. He must be able to speak with confidence and to speak so that others understand. In order to develop these abilities the student must have the opportunity to speak frequently through the use of oral activities such as those which follow.

Teaching language usage

Give students an opportunity to speak while at the same time emphasizing correct usage. The PROGRESSIVE CONVERSATION is a method which we find highly successful. Students respond more positively to this method of studying correct usage than they do to the traditional lengthy written exercise.

To provide practice in the use of *was* and *were,* for example, begin a conversation like this:

Teacher: "Was John late today, Mary?"

Mary: "No, John was not late today."
"Was the sun shining yesterday, Susan?"

Susan: "Yes, the sun was shining yesterday."
"Were you at home last night, Jim?"

The Progressive Conversation continues around the room in this fashion with each child constructing a sentence using either *was* or *were.* With large classes divide the class into 2 or 3 conversation groups with a student leader assigned to each group while you walk from group to group guiding progress. If a sentence causes difficulty, write it on the board to discuss the correct usage, and then continue. After all have participated lead the class to make generalizations about the use of *was* and *were* such as the following:

Both WAS and WERE tell about something in the PAST.
WAS is used when you are talking about only ONE thing.
WERE is used when you are talking about more than ONE thing.
WERE is always used with YOU.

A class book, USING WORDS, may be compiled for each discussion about usage. A student may be assigned, for example, to print the above generalizations on a page for the book headed simply: WAS and WERE. Examples may also be included to illustrate each generalization.

ADVANTAGES of oral study activities like the Progressive Conversation:

All students participate with interest.
Errors are corrected immediately.
All students complete work together.
No worksheets are prepared.
There are no exercises to correct later.

Oral word games

Here is a type of oral review which features Prefixes and Suffixes. The Leader says a Prefix or a Suffix as he points to a specific student. Then he begins counting from one to ten or any other specified number. As the Leader counts, the other student names as many words containing the stated Prefix or Suffix as possible. The Leader might say, thus: "CON–1,2,3,4,5,6,7,8,9,10." The student he points to meanwhile says, "Conference, conclusion, convict, conduct, contest."

The class can be divided into teams with score kept (one point for each word named by a team member). Students can prepare a list of common prefixes and suffixes to be used by the Student Leader. Activities of this nature produce much interest in learning new words as well as providing an opportunity for students to think and speak. You can use this same method to study parts of speech with the Leader saying, "Verb, Adjective, etc."

Voice qualities

Of interest as students try to speak well is the student's voice itself. Listen to records of different voices (tape portions from records of people like Robert Frost or Dylan Thomas). Have students tape their own voices. After listening to a variety of voices have the students discuss the qualities which are involved in the use of the voice as a means of communication. They may list some of these qualities: *Loudness, Softness, Contrast, Clearness, Pronunciation, Naturalness, Accent, Warmth.*

After discussing the qualities which make for a pleasant voice let each student write a critical analysis of his own voice. Encourage each one to think of ways to better his voice as an instrument for communication. Repeated use of the tape recorder will make the students more conscious of their own voices as others hear them.

Tape recording

The tape recorder lends interest to a study of speaking skills. Here are several ideas for encouraging effective speech habits through the use of the tape recorder.

Perhaps you can prepare *a tape to accompany a series of photographs or pictures clipped from a magazine.* Students can also draw or paint illustrations for this purpose. A script can be written to accompany the pictures used or each student can speak about his own picture. Focus the set of pictures on one theme, for example, WINTER SPORTS, with each child telling about one sport or describing the activity pictured. His contribution might also be a short story based on the picture. The pictures can be held by each child as his taped message is heard or the pictures can be mounted (in the order taped) on a continuous strip of paper to be used in a Scroll Theater.

Tape messages to children in other schools. The class with whom you exchange tapes can be across the hall, in another city, or across the ocean. Students can prepare stories, poems, or plays which they have written. At times they can tape material individually or they can tape some things as a group. Illustrations and written materials can also be sent in conjunction with the tape. Here are two addresses you might wish to write to for information about sending tapes abroad:

Scholastic Magazines—Living Letters
33 W. 42nd Street
New York 36, New York

World Tape Pals
Box 9211
Dallas 15, Texas

Developing confidence in the young speaker

Many students are extremely shy about speaking before the group. Suggested here are several techniques for encouraging these children:

Using props when speaking assists the speaker in having more assurance. Assign "How-to" topics for speaking which require the student to show the class, for example, "How to fold a paper airplane" or "How to open a new book." The student who holds something in his hand, and has something to manipulate, will not feel that all eyes are on him; they are on the object he is handling. He will lose somewhat his feeling of self-consciousness as he explains about the paper airplane or the opening of the book.

A *speaker's stand* also gives the student a sense of security.

He may stand behind a table or desk or you can construct a simple stand which will hold notes and add to the reality of the atmosphere.

Make speeches brief for those who have more difficulty. One type of speech which remains short for all is the telling of a joke. The material readily gains the interest of the audience, so the speaker feels a sense of support from their obvious eagerness to hear the "punch" line.

Taping a speech is not as awesome for many students as speaking before the group. There is a certain feeling of anonymity with the tape recorder, for no one's eyes are on you.

Puppetry also permits the student to lose his identity in that of the character he is portraying. Even the shyest child may be able to shout triumphantly, "I've caught you at last, you wicked old rascal!" as he kills the wolf in *Red Riding Hood.*

Group speaking is another method for encouraging the shy child. He can speak with confidence as part of the group. Have him work in smaller and smaller groups.

TALKING TIME (TT)

Write the letters TT on the board to signal students that it is Talking Time. This signal soon becomes familiar as students put away work, perhaps arrange seating less formally, and prepare to talk. Anyone may initiate a subject; others comment. Be sure to have a store of topics to introduce if this technique "bogs down" at first.

Storytelling

Discuss with the class the art of storytelling. Compile a list of statements about what they like about some storytellers. Have them listen to records of people telling stories. Then they can compare their reactions to the way the story was told.

Let each child choose a story to tell to the class. They may wish to begin with very simple familiar fairy tales or nursery stories. Each child should be encouraged to tell his story freely, even briefly, in order to achieve a feeling of success with storytelling. Mentioning something complimentary about each presentation not only boosts the morale of the speaker, but also points out aspects of storytelling which are considered desirable.

Storytelling can also be taped and used to send to other students. Encourage the selection of longer stories by those who are more able. Never try to have the whole class tell their stories on one day. Rather arrange to have a few each day at a specified time until all have a chance to participate.

The teacher, too, can enjoy storytelling with the class. Her telling of stories will lead the way to student enthusiasm. Students can form a STORYTELLERS' CLUB which presents stories to children in lower grades.

Conversations

Because most people usually engage in speaking in the form of various types of conversation, it is important to discuss the skills involved in conversing. Set up conversation situations in which several children play a role and engage in conversation together. The following situation would include two boys and two girls:

> Barbara and June are walking toward the grocery store where June is to buy bread for her mother. They meet Jim and Chuck, who are in their room at school.

Let several groups play these roles. What do the girls talk about as they approach and enter the grocery store? What do the girls say to the two boys? What do the boys say in reply? What do both groups say after they have walked on? Have the class invent other situations which would involve conversation.

Group stories

To provide an opportunity for each student to talk for at least a brief time begin a TRAVELING TALE like this:

> As I was climbing into the boat to continue our journey up the Amazon, I suddenly heard a peculiar cry. Was it human? It was difficult to tell, so I . . .

At this point call on a student to continue the story. Use an eggtimer or the second hand of the clock to time each student. At the end of perhaps one minute ring a small bell as you call the name of another student who continues the story where the previous storyteller broke off.

Traveling Tales can be fitted into odd moments of time while you wait for recess or afternoon dismissal or while some students are still clearing away their work. This technique gives the teacher an opportunity also to call on students who are shy or less skilled in speaking without its being so formal a situation. Frequent chances to speak informally increase student confidence.

Completing stories individually

Prepare (or have a team of students prepare) several beginnings for stories which can be completed orally. If enough UNFINISHED STORIES are collected, each student can draw one from a box. He reads the story aloud to the class and adds his own ending trying to continue so smoothly that his audience does not notice the break. Here are examples of UNFINISHED STORIES to be completed aloud:

> Jim sauntered slowly along Phillips Avenue. All was quiet in the little town of Greenville. It was Sunday afternoon, and as usual, the August afternoon was hot and smothering. Suddenly the summer haze was pierced by the sound of . . .
>
> Larry and Lucy scrambled out of bed before six on Saturday, April 15th. It was the twins' birthday, and Uncle Bill was arriving by plane from Chicago. They wanted to be at the airport on time because his letter had said clearly that he was bringing the twins a surprise—something that they would both like. As Uncle Bill came down the ramp neither Larry nor Lucy could see anything, but then Larry cried, ". . .

Combine this oral activity with creative writing as each student prepares an Unfinished Story. Have everyone pass his story to the person on his right (several times). That person can read the story he is to finish and after a few minutes for thinking out a good ending, present the story orally.

Word fun

Interest in words and their use can be stimulated by oral activities. Students are very much intrigued by the sounds of words as well as the feel of them. Some words are fun to say because they roll on your tongue. Let students try these words aloud together: TINTINNABULATE, SARTORIAL SPLENDOR, EFFERVESCENT, SPONTANEITY, PHILANTHROPIC PHILATELIST.

Rhymes also lend enjoyment to the use of language. Young students like to list orally as many words in one rhyme family as they can—*cat, mat, fat, tat, rat, pat, flat, chat, scat.* Older students can construct humorous sentences composed of groups of rhyming words such as the following:

"Slide, Clyde!" called bald Larry McNary.
"Whoo, Whoo," tooted and hooted the plain grain train.
"OOOooo, BOOooo," groaned and moaned hosts of ghosts.

Conducting meetings

Many classroom activities can provide students with the opportunity to conduct meetings. Organize your classroom with student officers who are responsible for regular meetings to discuss student affairs. These officers are selected by the class, but positions should be rotated so that all students participate actively.

You can assist the students in conducting the first election of officers. Subsequent elections can be organized by the students who have been introduced to the rudiments of nominating, voting, and counting the votes. The election of new officers can be the last function of the outgoing officers.

Officers as well as other members of the class will need to learn the skills of discussion, stating motions, and voting. Students will also participate as they present reports to the group. Minutes can be kept in a notebook for that purpose. An agenda can also be written on the board before the meeting begins to assist the group in concentrating on the business at hand.

Officers for a classroom might include the following:

President, Vice-President, Recording Secretary, Corresponding Secretary, Treasurer

Chairmen: Displays, Decorations, Hospitality, Attendance

Introduce older students to *Robert's Rules of Order*. Committees can make charts presenting the correct procedures to be followed.

Study of communication

Let students investigate the various methods of communicating—SIGN LANGUAGE, PICTURES, WRITING, SPEAKING, MUSIC, and others. Have them explore some of the following questions:

> How do you communicate with a person in a foreign country if you don't know his language?
>
> What helps you to understand a person's meaning besides the words he says?

Conducting interviews

Conducting interviews lends interest to a study being made in social studies or other areas. It also provides students with excellent practice in speaking with another person, often an adult. A good method to use as an introduction to the art of interviewing is the Student Interview. Let each student interview someone else in the room so that each student serves as both Interviewer and Interviewee. Some interviews should be conducted in front of the class as a teaching technique; others can then be conducted independently by students as time permits.

Invite a speaker to address the class on a topic of interest. After he has spoken, several students (or the entire class) can serve as reporters to interview him. Interviews should be well planned with a questionnaire developed before the interview so that all pertinent questions are covered.

Encouraging student participation in discussions

How do you get all students to participate in a discussion? How do you restrain the talkative student who monopolizes the discussion? These are the problems of conducting a good discussion.

To encourage the quiet child to participate try these methods:

> Address a question to him (not to embarrass him) thus: "John, did you ever know anyone who had an experience like that?"
>
> Ask a general question, then call on someone who has not been active thus: "How many of you have ever been on a boat or a

ship?" (Pause for response; select a quiet student first.) "What kind of boat were you on, Joan?"

Watch for signs of interest and desire to respond; take advantage of these responses by calling on that child: "Did you have something to add, Sue?"

Make it clear that each response is valued. Make a point of praising contributions of the child who needs encouragement.

The extremely verbal child, on the other hand, can at times monopolize discussions in such a way that less aggressive children are discouraged. Try to *control his participation while at the same time not discouraging* it.

Ignore his waving hand *part of the time* to call on others.

Give him something else to do as part of the discussion such as recording ideas expressed.

Let him act as Discussion Leader (after discussing the qualities of a good Leader).

Ask him or her to call on someone else.

Limit his answers thus: "Bill, will you tell us *one* more thing we can add to our list?"

Explore with the class the art of discussing so that they become conscious of their roles in a discussion. Examine the types of questions to be asked. Have them observe discussions on television.

Speaking to the group

Students should be given many opportunities to speak in various ways. At times you will *assign (or permit a choice) a topic or type of speech* to be prepared by the student. If all students are to speak, it is best to keep each speech short (2–3 minutes). Assign groups of students to give their speeches on different days so the period never exceeds half an hour. Here are several topics which are suitable for the young speaker:

My Ambition	A Trip I'd Like to Make
Who's Who in My Family	What I Like to Do on Saturday
What Will Tomorrow Bring?	My Favorite Television Program

Occasionally *have the students speak extemporaneously*. Collect a box of small pictures clipped from magazines. Mount these pictures on 4 x 6 inch unlined filing cards for easy storage and reuse with this activity (or creative writing). You may permit each student to select a picture from six laid on your desk or you may simply have each speaker take the one on top of the pile. Give the speaker thirty seconds to think about what he will say and then have him begin telling the class about the picture. The picture helps the less verbal child to think of something to say.

Later you may wish to use the same technique with titles printed on cards. Try some of the following:

What a Horrible Day!	He Just Followed Me Home
I Knew I Could Do It	Help! Help!
My Big Moment	Looking Ahead
Stop! Look! Listen!	Only Four Minutes

Skills of speaking

Before students make their first speeches to the class have them discuss the techniques of giving a speech. Elicit some of the following general suggestions for making effective speeches:

Don't speak until you face your audience.
Look at the audience.
Speak so you can be heard.
Don't read your speech (with notes).
Speak slowly rather than too fast.

Have a student make a chart of these REMINDERS FOR SPEAKERS. After the students have completed their first speeches they will be able to add other suggestions. You may also teach several techniques to assist them in speaking such as the following:

At the end of a speech summarize the points you have made.
Occasionally repeat statements which should be emphasized.
Sometimes use a question as an opening sentence.

Evaluating oral presentations

Encourage students to give constructive criticism. Your own attitude toward the students' speaking will guide that of the students. Rather than pointing up errors in pronunciation, the way the speaker stood, the content of his speech, *ad infinitum, praise one aspect of the student's presentation.* You may also *suggest one specific area for improvement,* remembering that too many suggestions or criticisms tend to confuse rather than to assist the student.

Students will develop greater enjoyment of speaking and will be interested in developing skills of speaking if they have a positive feeling toward oral activities. Any speech impediments and errors in articulation should not be emphasized during these speaking activities; refer these children to a speech specialist, if possible.

When children are speaking to the class, try sitting in the back of the room so the speaker speaks to the group rather than half turned to the teacher who is sitting near him.

Oral interpretation

A type of oral presentation which is easier for the shy child is reading orally. Discuss with the class the *art of reading well* and interpreting without exaggeration. Help them list suggestions to follow, such as these:

Know the material well, so your eyes can look at the audience.

Read in sentences rather than words.

Use expression according to the material—excitement, softness, speed, pauses.

Various types of material can be read. Poetry, excerpts from books read, short stories—all lend interesting variety to oral presentations. Let each child plan to read aloud to the class after recess assigning one or two children to each day. At times have each student select his best piece of writing to read to the class. Tape these presentations for use during an OPEN HOUSE.

Memorizing

Encourage students to memorize favorite passages of poetry or prose which they like. Memorization should never be used as a punishment or time filler, however, for it can quickly kill the child's liking for poetry.

Memorization occurs naturally as children pick up words, phrases, lines when working with choral reading or speaking. Have a Poetry Hour when students can present a poem or just a phrase which they memorized because they liked it. You share your favorites, too, for your participation will enhance the children's appreciation of both poetry and prose.

Broadcasting

Another type of oral activity is Radio or Television Broadcasting. This activity can be combined with the study of Current Events or the writing of stories and plays in Language Arts. Rotate the positions of reporter, announcer, or radio actor, so that all students eventually have speaking roles. The Television broadcast makes an effective presentation as a student assembly.

A weekly or even daily program can be planned which might include: commercials, news reports, a continued story, a quiz program, and so on. Students can make simple props as needed for the broadcast. In television productions cameras can be constructed from cardboard cartons. For both radio and television you can make standing microphones from small painted boxes attached at the end of dowel rods or old broomsticks. Small individual mikes can be made from short pieces of doweling or broomstick to which are attached heavy cords for hanging around the speaker's neck.

You can construct a large TV screen from a big packing box if you wish actors to "appear on the screen" for the viewers. This method is especially effective for primary children.

Different ways of saying things

Students will enjoy experimenting with different ways of saying the same words or sentences. Let them try saying the following sentences first *laughingly*, then *sadly*, and last *angrily:*

Am I going with you?
It just doesn't seem to fit.

What in the world have you been doing?
He told me he was going to fly across.

As students try these sentences, have them suggest situations in which the sentence might be used as they said it. Brief impromptu skits can be developed as the students think about the situation.

Another technique along the same line is the *emphasizing of different words in the same sentence.* Let students say this same sentence each accenting the word indicated. Try other sentences, too, to point up the fact that THE WAY YOU SAY SOMETHING IS SOMETIMES MORE IMPORTANT THAN WHAT YOU SAY. Discuss the differences in meaning conveyed by the different interpretations of this sentence:

I don't care what you say!
I *don't* care what you say!
I don't *care* what you say!
I don't care *what* you say!
I don't care what *you* say!
I don't care what you *say!*

Other sentences you might try in this same way are:

She was right here.
Did you hear that awful noise?
Mary wore that big red hat.

> How many ways can you say, "Yes"?
> Can you say, "Yes" so that it sounds like "No"?

Projected materials to stimulate talking

The opaque projector can be used to project a variety of pictures which students can discuss briefly. As you show a picture, call out three or four student names. Each student called is to say a sentence or two about the picture.

Another time simply ask questions about the picture shown—Why is the dog running? What kind of dress is the girl wearing? Where is she going? Who lives in this house? This type of oral activity is excellent preliminary preparation for writing about a picture.

Use slides and film strips also to stimulate speaking in the same fashion. As you show a slide, have students take turns in making some comments about the picture. The film strip can be stopped to allow for more comments by the students. Develop a collection of provocative slides for use in this way—an old house, a child at play, a dog running down the street, a mysterious object.

Sharing time

A frequently used technique for oral presentations is the informal *Sharing* or *Show and Tell Time.* Basically a good method for providing oral language experiences, this technique often becomes so routine as to be ineffective. Like most activities Sharing of Experiences should be a varied method, for any technique becomes dull and uninteresting if overworked. Here are some suggestions for varying the routine to maintain a high level of interest and participation:

Don't have Sharing Time every day or always at the same time.

Select a theme for the Sharing period—My Best Friend, Was I Scared!, Work Can Be Fun, An Exciting Moment. Announce the Theme the day before.

Use an unusual seating arrangement—circle, semi-circle, sitting on the floor.

Tape the speaking occasionally for evaluation by students.

You listen, too, and comment with interest. (Don't be obviously busy with paperwork.)

If a child has something exciting to share, let him, even if Sharing is not on your schedule. Take advantage of this show of interest.

The poetry choir

Here is an excellent way for students to develop an appreciation for poetry. Work with choric speaking should be informal with emphasis on pure enjoyment rather than long memorizing assignments. Students will soon learn the lines through repetition. Several poems we have found especially suited to this type of activity are the following which are found in May Hill Arbuthnot's *Time for Poetry:*

Beatrice Brown: "Jonathan Bing"
T. S. Eliot: "Macavity: The Mystery Cat"
Edward Lear: "The Owl and the Pussy-Cat"
A. A. Milne: "Puppy and I"

One of the poems we like to begin choric speaking with is "Poor Old Woman," an anonymous nonsense poem, which contains all the necessary elements to introduce students of any age to the pleasures of speaking in a chorus. Here is the version we have used with suggestions for grouping and interpretation:

Poor Old Woman

LEADER	There was an old woman who swallowed a fly.
CHORUS	What, swallowed a fly? (Great amazement)
	Poor old woman, she surely will die! (Sadly, slowly)
LEADER	There was an old woman who swallowed a spider
	Right down inside her she swallowed a spider. (Pointing)
SMALL GROUP	She swallowed the spider to kill the fly. (Aside)
CHORUS	What, swallowed a fly?
	Poor old woman, she surely will die!
LEADER	There was an old woman who swallowed a snake
	Oh, my, her stomach did ache!
SMALL GROUP	She swallowed the snake to kill the spider
	She swallowed the spider to kill the fly.
CHORUS	What, swallowed a fly?
	Poor old woman, she surely will die!
LEADER	There was an old woman who swallowed a bird
	How absurd to swallow a bird.
SMALL GROUP	She swallowed the bird to kill the snake;
	She swallowed the snake to kill the spider;
	She swallowed the spider to kill the fly.
CHORUS	(Repeats same two lines as above)
LEADER	There was an old woman who swallowed a duck
	Wasn't that just terrible luck?

Poor Old Woman (cont.)

SMALL GROUP	She swallowed the duck to kill the bird; She swallowed the bird to kill the snake (and so on)
CHORUS	Two lines as above
LEADER	There was an old woman who swallowed a dog She went the whole hog; she swallowed a dog!
SMALL GROUP	She swallowed the dog to kill the duck (and so on)
CHORUS	Two lines
LEADER	There was an old woman who swallowed a pig She swallowed the pig while dancing a jig.
SMALL GROUP	She swallowed the pig, etc.
CHORUS	Two lines
LEADER	There was an old woman who swallowed a cow I don't know how, but she swallowed a cow!
SMALL GROUP	She swallowed a cow, etc.
CHORUS	Two lines
LEADER	There was an old woman who swallowed a horse (Long pause) SHE DIED, OF COURSE!

This fun poem can be varied as your class composes new verses. When students are familiar with the poem, have a small group of students speak the part of the Leader.

Finger plays

Primary children have fun with finger stories which provide an opportunity for speaking together. Each child tells the story as he uses his fingers to portray the action. These stories can also be invented by the class or individuals. Encourage the class to suggest innovations as they repeat familiar finger plays. Small groups may tell a story to the rest of the class to add experience in speaking before a group. Here is a story which you can use as a starter toward the enjoyment of Finger Plays:

How Mrs. White Rabbit and Mrs. Black Rabbit Missed Each Other

Mrs. White Rabbit lived in PRETTY PRAIRIE on the LEFT side of HIGH HILL. (Peak hands to form the hill; lean head toward the Left side.) Mrs. Black Rabbit lived in MERRY MEADOW on the

RIGHT side of HIGH HILL. (Lean head toward the Right side of High Hill—the hands.)

One day Mrs. White Rabbit crept out of her house under the bushes in PRETTY PRAIRIE on the LEFT side of HIGH HILL. (Fingers of Left hand are cupped to represent bushes over the thumb which is the Rabbit; thumb is moved slowly from beneath the bushes.) Mrs. White Rabbit looked up at the blue sky, "It is a lovely day. I think I shall go visit my friend Mrs. Black Rabbit who lives in MERRY MEADOW on the RIGHT side of HIGH HILL." And she began hopping slowly around HIGH HILL (imagined now). Hop, hop. (Make the rabbit hop two times close to the chest.)

On the same morning Mrs. Black Rabbit crept out of her house under the bushes in MERRY MEADOW on the RIGHT side of HIGH HILL. (Cup fingers of Right Hand to form bushes over the thumb which is the Rabbit; move thumb slowly from beneath the bushes.) Mrs. Black Rabbit looked up at the blue sky, "It is a lovely day. I think I shall go visit my friend Mrs. White Rabbit who lives in PRETTY PRAIRIE on the LEFT side of HIGH HILL." And she began hopping slowly around HIGH HILL. Hop, hop. (Make the rabbit hop twice *this time at arm's length.*)

Each rabbit lady continued on her way. Mrs. White Rabbit hopped to Mrs. Black Rabbit's house while Mrs. Black Rabbit hopped toward Mrs. White Rabbit's house—Hop, hop, hop. (Make the two rabbits hop; the arms will be crossed.)

Knock, Knock, Knock. (Make each rabbit knock simultaneously.) "Oh, dear, nobody is home," said Mrs. White Rabbit. "Oh, dear, nobody is home," said Mrs. Black Rabbit. So they both hopped slowly back home—Hop, hop, hop, hop, hop.

"I am so tired. I think I shall take a nap," said poor Mrs. White Rabbit as she crept into her house under the bushes. (Make rabbit disappear beneath the finger-bushes.)

"I am so tired. I think I shall take a nap," said poor Mrs. Black Rabbit as she crept into her house under the bushes. (Make rabbit disappear beneath bushes.)

And that is how Mrs. White Rabbit and Mrs. Black Rabbit missed seeing each other. (Ask the class why the rabbits missed each other.)

When presenting Finger Plays, first tell the story to the class with the finger actions. Then ask them if they would like to help you tell the story. Tell the story again in the same way letting them join in as much as possible. Another day tell this same story once or twice again so children gradually become acquainted with it. Add other stories as the class is ready and soon they will have a pleasant repertoire of these oral activities which can assist the study of numbers, or in this story the concepts of Right and Left, as well as provide for opportunity to speak, to follow the sequence of a story, and to listen carefully.

Creative drama

• A good way to introduce students to the possibilities of acting freely is the PANTOMIME which, of course, requires no spoken language on the part of the actor. Let students take turns in portraying (through actions only) some type of activity while the class tries to guess what they are doing. Several activities which lend themselves to pantomime are:

Eating a banana	Cutting flowers
Eating spaghetti	Typing a letter
Hanging clothes on a line	Wrapping a package
Sweeping the floor	Jumping rope
Painting a picture	Petting a dog

• Another type of creative drama is ROLE PLAYING in which several children play assigned roles in a given situation. The situation is merely described, the roles assigned, and the action and script develop according to the desires of the actors who may speak freely as they think the person would speak in the given situation. Described here is one situation which can be used as a starter:

> Mr. and Mrs. White have just returned from shopping to find their three children—Mary, Jim, and Ralph—fighting over a toy while the babysitter, Joan, stands helplessly at one side of the room.

• Familiar stories such as *Red Riding Hood, The Three Bears,* and *The Little Red Hen* can be dramatized by primary students. Older students will know and enjoy dramatizing *Jack and the Beanstalk, Ali Baba and the Forty Thieves,* or *Aladdin and the Wonderful Lamp.* Be sure that all students know the story to be used. If there is any doubt, especially with less common stories, have the students tell the action of the story. Remind them that there are many variations of these tales which have been handed down by word of mouth; this concept will encourage them to add variety to their presentations of the stories.

Rotate the roles and add roles to the story to permit all to participate. No scripts are prepared in written form, however; the dialogue develops as the students explore the story and begin working with it orally. It does not matter if a speech varies slightly every time it is said as long as it serves to move the story action along as needed.

• As children become accustomed to working with creative drama, you may wish to *develop a new story which you have just read to the class.* Select a story which is not too long or involved and one that the students enjoyed thoroughly. Discuss together the characters required and others which might be added (crowds, groups of people, animals, friends, relatives, servants).

Then review the action of the story to decide what scenes are necessary to the action and what actually happens in each scene. Let the students begin acting the story. Other changes will be suggested as the story is worked out. You may wish to have half the class present the play one day while the other half assumes the same roles another day. Or each half may be working on two different stories. Grouping arrangements will depend on the size of your class and the complexity of the story chosen.

Try a THEATER IN THE ROUND for creative drama with the "stage" in the center of the classroom. This arrangement provides an effective setting and makes certain that *all can see and hear.*

Puppetry

Puppets provide an excellent means for encouraging students to speak effectively. Many shy students find it relatively easy to speak behind the puppet stage, for it is not they who speak, but the characters represented by the puppets.

Try a variety of puppets, none of which need to be time-consuming projects. Easily constructed puppets for instant use are the stick puppets which consist of paper figures pasted on one end of a tongue depressor or other flat wood or cardboard. See Chapter 8 for directions for making other varieties of puppets suitable for classroom use.

With puppets use some of the techniques described earlier in this section for encouraging children to talk. Role playing is very successful with children manipulating puppets who speak freely about the situation portrayed. Again emphasize free speech rather than lengthy memorization of written scripts.

Costumes

Spending money and time on elaborate costumes can seldom be justified for the dramatic activities of the classroom. Children should be encouraged to use their imaginations to provide settings and costuming. At times, however, a few simple items will assist the development of atmosphere. Here are several suggestions:

MASKS, like puppets, assist the shy child in playing a role before the class. One of the simplest masks is that fashioned from a large paper bag. Fit the bag over the child's head to mark the eyes and nose. Then add appropriate features. For a mouse, for example, add pointed ears and nose as well as pipe cleaner or paper whiskers. Masks of people can have hair of yarn or cut paper. A paper plate also forms a good base for this type of mask. Attach elastic to the plate to hold it on the student's head.

CLOTHING can be made from tissue or crepe paper as well as old cloth. Pinchpleat crepe paper to a cloth band with staples or needle and thread to make simple aprons. Crepe paper sashes or belts are quickly cut and decorated as desired. Serapes and shawls are straight pieces of crepe paper or cloth draped across the shoulders. Crepe paper ribbons, bows, scarves, and ties can be effectively used. Vests or boleros can be cut from paper or cloth which children can stitch together.

Listening to Learn

Since speaking and listening are handmaidens in communication most of the oral activities already described in this chapter involve listening. The techniques reserved for this section of the chapter are those which stress the development of efficient and effective listening skills.

It has been said, "Nature has given to men one tongue, but two ears that we may hear from others twice as much as we speak." Listening, however, means more than just *hearing*, for what is heard must be assimilated and used. We use the term AUDING to mean listening with comprehension and appreciation, for *Listening is to Speaking what Reading is to Writing.*

Estimates tell us that half of the child's time in school is spent in listening. He listens to stories, reports, directions, announcements, recordings, radio and television programs, lectures, and sound films. Unless he does more than *hear* the material presented, half of his school time is wasted. Teaching listening skills, therefore, becomes a vital necessity in this verbal world, for these skills will be used throughout adult life.

Many of the listening activities described here require only five or ten minutes so they can be tucked into the schedule at odd moments. You can motivate the students' interest in listening by using a variety of techniques and by remembering these guidelines to effective teaching:

Consider the attention span of the children being taught.
Insert humor to arouse interest and response.
Use audio-visual devices for a change of pace.
Ask questions about the material being heard.

Listening to sounds

Many sounds are never heard. We are so accustomed to some of them that we ignore them. To help students become more aware of sounds which occur around them have them sit quietly for three minutes as they listen closely to any sounds that may be heard. (This activity can be done in the classroom or out-of-doors.)

After the time has passed have the students write (or name) those sounds which were heard during the listening period—breathing, squeaking, honking of a horn, shuffling of paper, a plane, coughing, wind or rain, people in the hall. Discuss the need for both *visual and auditory observation* for exact writing.

List words which describe sounds, such as *harsh, melodious, tinkling, whispering.*

The importance of listening

• To emphasize the importance of listening in our lives have students make a list of vocations which interest them. Discuss what part listening would play in the work of a doctor, an airplane pilot, a teacher, a secretary, a mother.

• Have each student compile a diary of what he listens to over a period of one day from the time he awakens until bedtime. The next day compare these LISTENING DIARIES to notice the kinds of things students listen to, the sheer number of different things they listen to. *Have them estimate the total amount of time they spent listening* during the one day. How many hours will they spend in one week, in one year? What percentage of their day is spent in listening?

• Let each student *write a story illustrating the importance of listening*. Read some of the stories and discuss the need for effective listening. List events which might occur as a result of a person's not listening carefully. Here are some titles which may be used to motivate the writing of these stories:

I Heard You the First Time
That Isn't the Way I Heard It
What Did He Mean by That?

Following spoken directions

Perhaps the most important thing we listen to is the spoken direction. Students should be given much practice in following verbal directions exactly. Here are several ideas for providing this type of practice:

MENTAL MATH is an excellent method for providing this practice in listening as well as using arithmetical skills. According to the ability level of your group, give students oral problems to which they can write the answer (or give it orally):

Take 3; add 2; subtract 4; double your answer; add 5. What's your answer? (7)

Take 10; add 5; divide by 3; add 7; multiply by 2; divide by 6. What's your answer? (4)

Do as I say is a game in which the class listens carefully to a set of directions and then tries to follow them exactly. Try these types of directions:

> (Say the whole paragraph while everyone listens—*no writing or questions.*)
>
> Write your name on the last line of your paper.
> Write the numbers from 1 to 10 all on line 4.
> Write the colors of our flag on line 10.
>
> (Repeat the directions twice; then students act.)
>
> All boys with blue eyes are to line up against the back wall.
> All girls with brown eyes stand near the windows.
> Boys with brown eyes line up near the door.
> Girls with blue eyes stand in front of the chalkboard.

The tape recorder can assist you in preparing material to provide practice in listening. Make a tape of a story that people know very well, but make some slight changes. See if the class can spot them. You can also tape a story which you play once and then play halfway through again. See if students can finish the story after having heard it only once.

Folded paper projects offer another opportunity for following oral directions. Begin with simple folding of paper into fourths and eighths. Combine this folding with cutting to make boxes and baskets. More advanced students can try Origami (oriental paper folding) or figures such as Polyhedrons.

Graph paper can be the basis for an interesting method of practicing directions. Use a paper with lines about 4 squares to an inch. Give oral directions so that, if correctly followed, a figure will result. Here are two sets of directions you may try; others can be developed by students who will benefit from trying to write exact directions.

Color a block which is five spaces from the left side of the paper. Now blacken 10 more blocks in line below the first block. Color 6 blocks directly to the right of the first block. Color 3 blocks to the right of the 6th block from the top. Color 6 blocks to the right of the 11th block. What have you made? (The letter E.)

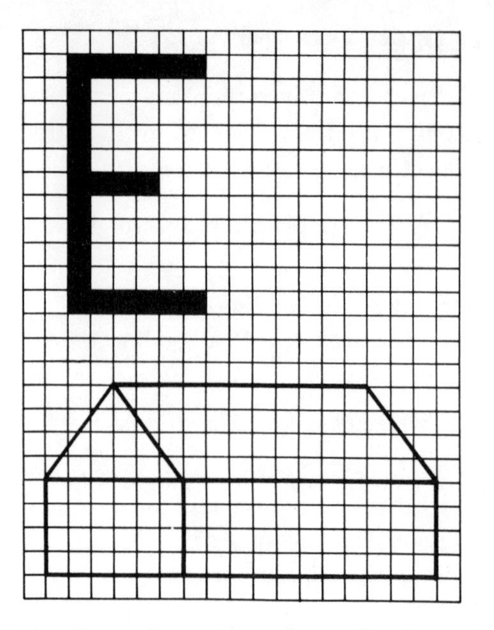

Put your pencil on the point where the lines intersect four blocks up from the bottom of the paper and four blocks from the left side. At this point begin drawing a line to the right 17 blocks. Four spaces above this line draw another identical line. Connect these two lines at each end and six spaces from the left side. Four spaces above this box draw another line which is centered above the box but is only 11 spaces wide. Now connect the left end of this line with the top left corner of the box. Connect the same end of the top line with the top of the box six spaces from the left of the box. Last, connect the end of the top line with the top right corner of the box. What do you have? (A house or barn.)

LISTEN, THINK, ACT is another game for following directions. Say, "LISTEN," and then give directions (before calling an individual student's name) while all listen. Then say, "THINK," while all try to remember the directions. Last, call one student's name, "Joe, ACT." The class watches carefully to see if the person is able to follow the oral directions exactly. This activity can be played with teams. The child who carries out the directions then gives a set of directions in the same way (the number of items included each time should be set according to the ability level of the group). Here is an example of directions to be given at one time:

> Walk to the door. Turn around three times. Touch the teacher's desk. Write your name on the left side of the chalkboard.

Giving oral directions

Almost as important as being able to follow oral directions is the ability to give oral directions. As teachers, we must also develop skill in giving directions that can be followed. Here are several suggestions to assist you in giving good oral directions:

Be certain that students are giving you their attention.
  Have them put away distracting objects before you talk.
  Have them turn their eyes toward you.
  Never begin speaking until they are ready to listen.
Speak clearly, distinctly, so all can hear.
Ask if there are questions.
Have one or two students repeat the directions.
Ask a question or two about the directions to be followed.
Do not answer questions about directions after work has begun. (You will have to develop this practice gradually, but it is effective in teaching students to listen carefully.)

Students, too, can learn to give oral directions. Let them practice giving directions to each other by playing LISTEN, THINK, ACT (described in detail on page 126) or by telling the class how to do or make something—How to make a paper fan, How to cross an intersection safely, How to use an index. Students can also practice giving directions on a map. If each student has a road map, the leader can give directions for getting to a specific town or locality in conjunction with social studies.

ARE YOU LISTENING?

Tell students you are going to make several mistakes sometime during the day. At the end of the day you will ask them to tell you the mistakes that were made—misspell a word, mispronounce a word, call a student by the wrong name.

Listening for a specific purpose

GUIDED LISTENING is usually more effective than listening without any specific purpose. Play a recorded story first to hear the story; then play it again so students can listen for interesting ways of using words. You may have each student list on a paper all the different adjectives he hears as you play a short story to develop vocabulary and interest in words. After the story is completed compare the words listed, discussing the meanings of some of the more unusual ones.

TAKING NOTES from taped or recorded material is good practice in listening for a purpose. You can quickly tape a page or two from a textbook which lends itself to outlining. Play the tape first to let the students listen to the content without writing. Then play it again while they take notes without further preparation. Discuss the notes taken; compare by having students write portions of their notes on the chalkboard. Point out good qualities and suggest improvements to be made. The next day review the notetaking experience and play the same tape to see whether students are able to take better notes. Provide this type of practice often for upper grade students as it will benefit their notetaking from printed material also. After notes are taken *give a test letting each student use his notes to help him answer the questions.* This activity demonstrates the value of good notes.

REPEATING what was said is another way of developing listening skills. You may say any series of words, numbers, or names to see if students can repeat them aloud or write them. Say a series of numbers asking the students then to write the series in reverse order. The number of items will vary with the ability of the students.

Auditory discrimination

One of the skills of listening is that of distinguishing differences. Give students practice in noting differences in words and sounds. Here are several activities which assist auditory discrimination:

• Read groups of words to students who are to designate one word which is different from the rest.

Time, climb, same, lime	(Which word does not rhyme?)
Room, rabbit, bounce, round	(Which word does not begin the same)
Bending, walking, helped, coming	(Which word does not end the same?)

• Play notes on any musical instrument to provide practice in distinguishing between high and low tones. As you play groups of two or three notes, students can decide whether 1, 2, or 3 was the Highest Note and which one was the Lowest Tone.

• Tell the students to listen for a word which sounds like, for example, BIRD, as you say the following sentence: "I *heard* the wind blow hard." You can designate different types of words for which they are to listen according to the level of your group as in these examples:

Listen for a 3 syllable word:	"That was an *excellent* book," said Robert.
Listen for the adjectives:	*Poor, tired* Rover drank the *cool* water gratefully.

• HELLO, PETER O'FLAHERTY is a game which students of all ages enjoy. Used for indoor play it also serves to exercise the child's auditory discrimination. One child sits on a chair with his back to the class while another serves as the Leader. The Leader indicates one person who speaks thus: "Hello, Peter O'Flaherty. How are you today?" The child with his back turned gets three guesses to try to identify the speaker. If he successfully identifies the speaker, he gets another turn; otherwise the speaker comes to the chair to be Peter O'Flaherty.

Mathematics possesses not only truth, but supreme beauty.

—*Bertrand Russell*

5

MODERN APPROACHES TO MATHEMATICS

Presented in this chapter are a variety of ideas for stimulating student interest in mathematics. Attention is focused on ways to assist students in recognizing and writing numerals, understanding number concepts, and using arithmetical facts.

Introducing Number Concepts

The pre-school child, the kindergartener, and the child in the primary grades are being introduced to numbers according to their ability. It is becoming increasingly evident that most children are ready for this introduction at an early age. Few children, for example, enter school without knowing any number concepts. Suggested here are methods for clarifying these concepts and adding to the child's understanding of numbers.

Using numbers every day

Discuss with students the many ways we use numbers in our daily lives. List these ways on the chalkboard, for example:

Taking attendance
Telling time

Telling your age
Measuring your height, weight
Taking a temperature
Reading maps, telling how many miles traveled
Buying food in the grocery store
Telling how many times we jumped rope
Buying tickets for an airplane
Telling the date

Have each student draw pictures to illustrate THE NUMBERS IN MY LIFE. Let them discuss the numbers which directly affect them—phone number, address, age, birthday, classroom number, number of students in the room, and so on.

Making comparisons

Children need to develop concepts of comparison. To do this you can compare numerous items in the classroom including the students themselves who can compare their heights. Who, for instance, is taller than John? Who is the tallest in the room? These concepts can be combined with the teaching of words of comparison and the forms they take:

tall, taller, tallest
big, bigger, biggest
small, smaller, smallest
many, more, most
few, less, least

Recognition of numerals

- Have each student make a NUMBER BOOK which contains a page for each numeral from one to ten. On each page he can mount clippings from newspapers and magazines illustrating that number concept. Included can be the figure itself as well as pictures which illustrate this number as: two dogs, three ducks, or four horses. Older students can collect numerical figures used in various ways—prices, sizes, quantities; problems can be constructed using the information collected.
- For MATCHING NUMBERS use a shoe bag with a numeral on each compartment. Cut figures from old calendars which children match with those on each pocket.

• Play WHAT'S MY NAME? with young students who are learning to recognize numerals. Write on the chalkboard (or use cards) a figure like 7, asking, "What's my name?" The students can answer in unison or you can call on individuals.

• Give each child a paper with numerals in squares to play CAN YOU FIND ME? As you call out, "My name is 7; can you find me?" each child must cover the seven with a square of construction paper. To introduce the numerals you can show a card or write the figure on the board as you speak the words so children begin to associate the name with the shape of the figure. This activity can be used with progressively advanced numbers.

• Knock on your desk (or a drum) while the children count the number of beats. Have one child select the card which tells how many beats there were. (Use this technique having the children write the figure also.)

TIP: Call on the children to answer by showing their name cards.

• Display numerals around the room. They can be used in conjunction with words for both number and word orientation, for example: 1 desk (taped on your desk), 5 windows (taped on the window area), or 2 doors (taped on a cupboard). Talk about the meanings of the figures and words on these cards, so that students become familiar with them. Refer to the cards during school and point out other number concepts illustrated around the room such as on the calendar.

• Play I SPY A SET. Call, "I spy a set of TWO." The class tries to guess what pair of things you see—2 shoes, 2 girls, 2 wastebaskets.

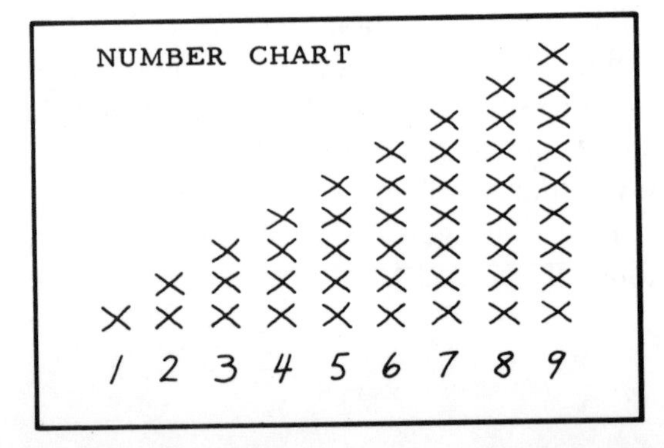

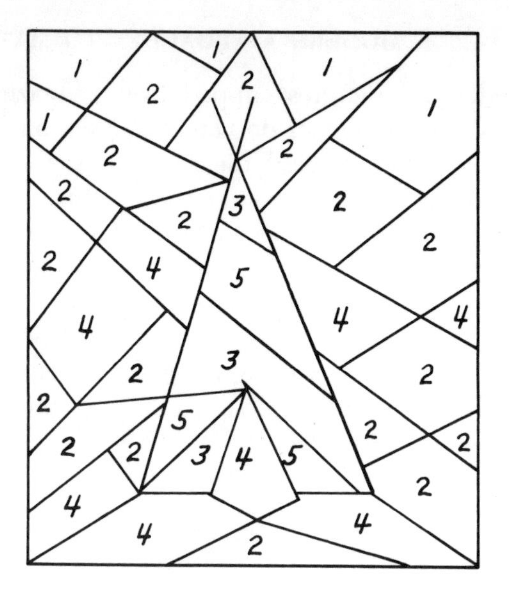

1 = blue
2 = green
3 = yellow
4 = brown
5 = orange

• Prepare COLOR BY NUMBER pictures to help students learn to recognize numerals (not a substitute for Art).

Writing numbers

• To provide beginners with practice in writing numerals have each one draw his house with his house number written on it. Students can practice reading the house numbers of their classmates.

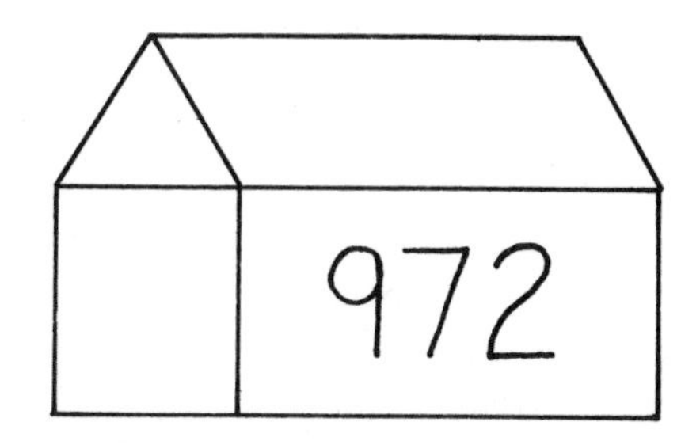

how students pictures clipped from magazines to play ANY? How many horses do you see? Each one must write gure as you walk around the room to see that they are ng it correctly. Then show another picture again asking, many?" Children can also write the answers as you hold up fingers or ask questions such as—How many ears do you have? How many toes do you have on one foot?

• Have each child make his own calendar in September and October to give practice in writing numerals in sequence. Duplicate the calendar form with space at the top for the name of the month thus:

S	M	T	W	T	F	S

Use old calendar pages to play CALINGO as children cover the numbers called.

In connection with this activity teach related facts such as the days of the week, the number of days in the month, the number of months in a year, and so on. Later use the calendar for introducing simple story problems such as:

Today is the eighth of November. Four days from now will be ______ .

Yesterday was the seventh of April. One week from yesterday will be ______ .

• Place several number cards on the chalk tray. Have children hide their eyes while you remove one of the cards. Then ask, "Which one did I take away?" Emphasize the figures which are more difficult to identify, but include some of the more familiar ones.

Number sequence

• Place number cards from one to ten in sequence on the chalkboard tray. Remove one card while children hide their eyes. What figure is missing? Remove more than one. What numbers are missing? Arrange the cards to count by two's or fives. Then let the students supply those which are missing.

• Sing NUMBER SONGS which help children learn the numbers in order. "Ten Little Indians" and "This Old Man" are familiar tunes which can be sung for fun. Have each child hold up his number card at the appropriate time in the song.

• Give each student a number tag. Then have the class line up for lunch or recess by number turning their tags toward you so you can quickly check the correctness of their order.

• Use a box full of small objects (nuts, pebbles, beans) to encourage counting. Have one child count to twenty-five while another gathers as many of the objects as possible moving them one-by-one from the box to the table. See which child can gather the most nuts.

• Mount numerals on flower shapes (airplanes, animals) which students can use on the flannel board as they practice putting them in the correct sequence.

• Distribute number cards from 1 to 100. Have the class count together slowly as the cards are brought to you in order. Hold the last card up each time so that students see it.

• Have the class or a group of children act as counters while children jump the rope, hop, or bounce a ball. Record the scores on the board to introduce a variety of written numbers.

• Card games using the numbers from one to ten are excellent ways of developing skill in numerical sequence. Students can make cards in sets of four or you can use the numbered cards from any deck of playing cards. Play these two simple games with small groups who will soon learn to follow the rules and the correct sequence:

C'EST TOUT (*That's All;* French pronunciation—*sĕ too*); Deal 4 cards to each player (4–5 players with deck of 40 cards). Place four cards face up as in the diagram with the pile in the center. The player to the left of the dealer begins by taking one card from the pile and then playing any card in descending sequence matching suits or colors. A TEN (or the highest card in your deck) can be played in the empty diagonal spaces. As each player finishes playing, he says, "C'est tout." The object of the game is to get rid of all cards.

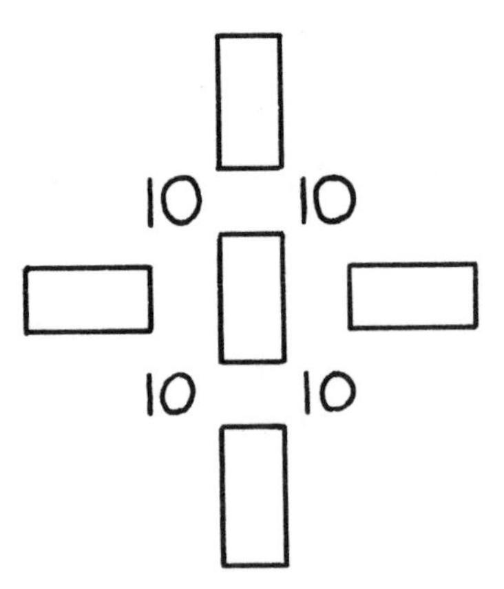

CHINESE RUM: Deal 4 or 5 cards to each player. Place the pile in the center with one card face up. In turn each player plays a card, if he can, matching either the color or the numeral. On a green eight, for example, he may play any green card (the same suit) or he may play an eight which will change the suit or color.

When a player cannot play a card, he must draw one from the pile. The first player to be rid of his cards wins.

• Have students estimate (write estimates on the board) the number of items in a group and then count them to discover the exact amount. Use beans, macaroni, nuts or bottle caps in a jar. For a real treat use paper-wrapped candy (enough for the class) and have the counter pass each piece to a student who gets to eat it!

• Play a circle game with each child holding a number card. One person walks around the circle and tags a person on the back. The tagged person must count out his number, perhaps 5, then may chase the tagger. The object is to catch the tagger before he gets all around the circle.

• Primary children can keep a COUNTING DIARY in a notebook with one page per student. Each child should record any items he has counted. Each morning pass out the individual pages as the children record items counted the day before. A class mural can be made with illustrations of THINGS WORTH COUNTING.

• Prepare FOLLOW THE DOTS sheets, using appropriate shapes according to the season to teach number sequence (not a substitute for art). Here is an example which you can prepare on a ditto master showing the numerals only:

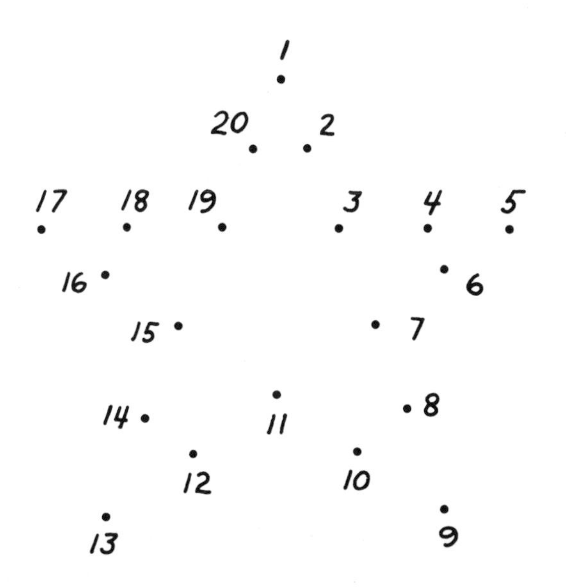

Learning Arithmetical Facts

Usually a certain amount of repetition is necessary before students know addition, subtraction, multiplication, and division facts so that they are able to use them easily. The creative teacher is the one who can provide the necessary practice for learning these facts without this practice's degenerating to dull, uninteresting drill which may kill the student's interest in mathematics.

The techniques suggested in this section are those which will assist the teacher in maintaining a high level of interest in mathematics while providing this drill. The key to success in this venture is VARIETY, for any effective technique will become dull and routine if overworked.

Remember: All students do not require the same amount of drill or practice.

Using number cards

Give each student a number card (suitable to the facts being learned). The teacher then asks the class questions like these:

Addition: "I have five (holding up the 5 card). Who can make it eight?"
The child with the 3 card comes up to join her.
Subtraction: "I have ten. Who can make it three?"
Multiplication: "I have seven. Who can make it 56?"
Division: "I have 81. Who can make it 9?"

Also use number cards for showing answers as you rapidly give multiplication facts. You can quickly see who knows the correct answers.

Fact tests

After students have studied the facts of one process, duplicate all the facts of that process on a sheet of paper. (Duplicate many extras for retesting and practice.) Give students a timed test to see how many facts each can correctly answer in five minutes. At the end of five minutes have each person draw a line to indicate those problems completed before the time was up. Let them then complete the unfinished problems. Each student corrects his own paper so that he knows which facts he needs to study.

Repeat the timed test in the same way every other day with periods of practice in between testings. Each student records his scores on a graph showing the number of problems correctly answered in five minutes. When any student is able to answer all facts correctly within five minutes, he is permitted to use this study time for other projects requiring independent study (see the last section of this chapter).

Omitting figures from the problem

Usually students are required to find the missing answer. For variety and increased understanding of number facts omit different figures from the problems on a page as in the examples below:

4	?	7	9	?	7	9
+?	+9	−?	−2	?	?	4
7	12	5	?	7	3	?
				14	4	7
					20	27

Magic squares

• MAGIC SQUARES provide practice in using facts, but the form of the problem is so different that students scarcely realize that they are really drilling on number facts. Here are samples of varieties which students can construct:

6	1	8
7	5	3
2	9	4

8	?	6
?	5	?
4	?	2

1	?	2
3½	2½	?
3	?	?

Progressive addition

Each student writes an addition (or multiplication) combination such as 9 + 6. This paper is then passed to the person behind him who writes the answer to the first combination (15) and adds another figure to be added, perhaps, 7. The papers are passed again with each student adding the combination and writing another numeral for the next student to add. Continue passing the papers until they come back to the person whose name appears on the page (or stop when time runs out). The owner of the paper must check the addition to see whether errors were made. Here is a portion of a progressive problem:

$$\begin{array}{r} 9 \\ +6 \\ \hline 15 \\ +\ 7 \\ \hline 22 \\ +\ 9 \\ \hline 31 \\ +\ 6 \\ \hline 37 \end{array}$$

Chalkboard activities

• THE WHEEL OF NINE is constructed like the example shown here. It can be used by several people who are studying the multiplication or division facts involving *nine* (other numbers may also be used). A leader uses a long rubber-tipped pointer to indicate a figure like 7 which the players must multiply by nine and compete to indicate the correct answer (63). For division the leader would point to the outside figures like 72 which the players must divide by nine and try to indicate the correct answer (8). Other circles can be constructed for facts which present difficulty such as 6, 7, and 8. Circles can also be made for addition and subtraction.

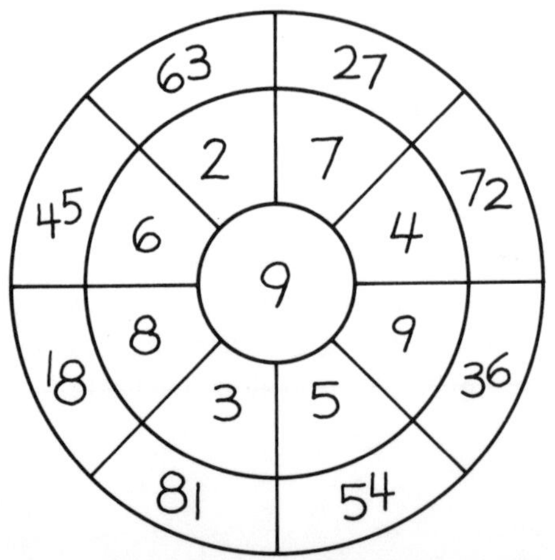

Make a chart for addition and subtraction facts so that students can check their answers quickly.

N	1	2	3	4	5	6	7	8	9
1	2	3	4	5	6	7	8	9	10
2	3	4	5	6	7	8	9	10	11
3	4	5	6	7	8	9	10	11	12
4	5	6	7	8	9	10	11	12	13
5	6	7	8	9	10	11	12	13	14
6	7	8	9	10	11	12	13	14	15
7	8	9	10	11	12	13	14	15	16
8	9	10	11	12	13	14	15	16	17
9	10	11	12	13	14	15	16	17	18

• TEE SQUARE is a good game to be used relay fashion. The first player in each team draws a TEE on the board. The Leader then calls off five numbers which are written by each player on the left side of the TEE. The Leader then calls, "Times 3" or "Plus 6" which the players must write at the top of the TEE before immediately writing the correct answer on the right side of the TEE as in these examples:

× 3	
5	15
7	21
4	12
3	9
9	27

+ 6	
6	12
2	8
9	15
5	11
8	14

• Write the numbers 1, 2, 3, 4, 5, 6, 7, 8, 9, 0 on the board, the four signs $+$, $-$, $\times$, and $\div$, and an $=$ sign. Without talking you point to number, sign, number, and then the $=$ sign. Each student must write the answer without any repetition of the problem. A checker for each row can quickly count the number of right answers for his row recording the score on the board. Use longer problems with this method just as in Mental Math.

• UP AND DOWN THE MOUNTAIN is played by forming numerals in the shape of a mountain peak as in the diagram. If the

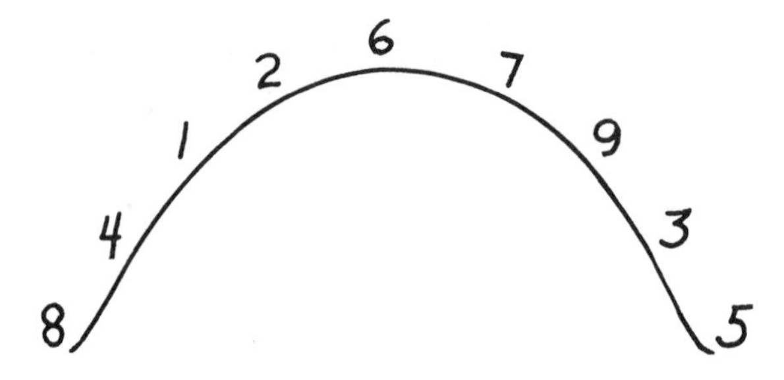

student is given Seven, he must quickly multiply each figure by Seven to see how quickly he can climb the mountain.

> **Have a club of those who know the facts in one or all of the processes. A chart can be captioned JOIN THE CLUB!**

• BEAT THE CLOCK requires each student to write a number of answers within a given time according to the abilities of the group. In 30 seconds, for example, each can try to write the multiples of eight. Or give the group numbers such as 25, 43, 92, 84, 76, and 38. At a given signal they add 15 (or another chosen number) to each given figure.

Mental math

One of the continuing favorites of both students and teachers for using arithmetic facts is MENTAL MATH which can be tucked into odd moments of the curriculum and adapted to the abilities of the students. As students increase their knowledge of mathematics, increase the difficulty of these mental gymnastics:

Take 2, add 3; subtract 1; double your answer. What's your answer? 8

Take 8; divide your answer in half; add 3. What's your answer? 7

Take 6; multiply by 7; subtract 2; divide by 5. What's your answer? 8

Take 9; divide by ⅓; add 3; multiply by 6. What's your answer? 180

> Write a group of figures on the board—6, 7, 3, 2. Immediately erase them. Who has the answer? (18)

Number sequences

• Another interesting way of focusing attention on the multiplication facts is through counting by certain groups. Have the class count aloud by eights, thus: 8, 16, 24, 32, 40, 48, 56, 64, 72. Immediately after counting in this manner ask questions about the facts involving EIGHT—How many 8's in 56? How much is 3×8? Nine times eight is how much?

• Play BUZZ, the familiar parlor game, which is usually based on Seven. Players count in turn 1, 2, 3, 4, 5, 6, BUZZ. For every multiple of Seven (7, 14, 21, and so on) or every number containing a seven (17, 27, 71, 72, and so on) the player must substitute BUZZ or drop out of the game. Use other numbers for variation and practice.

• Count in sequence for practice in addition rather than multiplication. Begin counting by four's from the number FIVE, for example—5, 9, 13, 17. . . . For practice in using subtraction reverse the process; count by 6 from eighty-one—81, 75, 69, 63, 57. . . . This MARTIAN MATH requires concentration.

Equivalents

• CAN YOU MATCH ME? is a game which two or three students can play independently at any age or ability. Encourage students to use the chalkboard for this type of activity; simple problems can also be expressed with small objects used in groups or figures placed on the flannel board. One student composes a mathematical expression which can be matched in a number of ways by other students:

Given: $\dfrac{5 + 16}{3}$

Matching Statements:

$10 - 3$ $\qquad 15 - 8$ $\qquad \dfrac{30 + 5}{5}$ $\qquad \dfrac{21 - 7}{2}$

• FIND THE MISSING FIGURES is another way of providing practice in using arithmetical facts. Here are examples:

$4 + \_\_\_\_ = 8 + \_\_\_\_$
$13 - \_\_\_\_ = 9 - \_\_\_\_$
$3 + 3 - \_\_\_\_ = 4$
$6 - 2 + \_\_\_\_ = 5$

• NUMBER FRAMES can be used in the same way to add interest to the use of these facts.

$2 + \square + \triangle = 17$
$\bigcirc + 7 \times 2 = 20$

CHARTING MULTIPLICATION

1	2	3	4	5	6	7	8	9
1	2	3	4	5	6	7	8	9
2	4	6	8	10	12	14	16	18
3	6	9	12	15	18	21	24	27
4	8	12	16	20	24	28	32	36
5	10	15	20	25	30	35	40	45
6	12	18	24	30	36	42	48	54
7	14	21	28	35	42	49	56	63
8	16	24	32	40	48	56	64	72
9	18	27	36	45	54	63	72	81

Keeping score

Many games provide excellent practice in adding scores; they also provide the motivation. Listed here are a few which may be used in school:

Shuffleboard (Indoor or Outdoors)

Ring Toss Games

Card Games (Rummy, Chinese Rum)

Bowling (Give imaginary scorings; use real bowling scoring sheets or facsimiles)

Target Games

Calendario (Drop three bottle caps on a calendar on the floor. Scores are the numbers on which caps fall.)

> **MAGIC NUMBERS:** The magic numbers are those which supply the answer to a multiplication fact. Say, "Fifty-six—what numbers do you think of?" (7 and 8) Sometimes include numbers like 23. Is this a Magic Number? Some Magic Numbers belong to more than one set of numbers (24, 36, 18).

Numbers and stories

• Write three numerals on the chalkboard—3, 7, 2. Ask the class to tell you a story about these three figures. Students might say, for example:

> Three children went walking. Four other children joined them, so there were seven children walking. Five children stopped to play which left only two walking.
>
> I had 3 cents. Mother gave me four pennies for helping her, so I had 7 cents. I bought a candy bar for a nickel which left me only 2 cents.

> **HISTORY DATES:** Use history dates to teach subtraction. How many years ago was Lincoln killed? Who was older—George Washington or Thomas Jefferson? (Use dates in the Teachers's Calendar, Chapter 1.)

• Provide a story on the board or a duplicated sheet in which all figures are omitted. Let the students supply them and find the answers to the questions as in this story:

> Nick wants to buy a ______________. The ______________ costs ______________, but Nick has only ______________. How much more money does Nick need? ______________

• Oral number stories are good ways to introduce the use of all arithmetical processes. Read the problems aloud and have students decide what process must be used. They can identify orally the key words which assist them in deciding which process to be used—difference, how much more, altogether, and so on. If students have repeated difficulty with "story problems," this method is a good one for examining the problem together. Have one student work the problem on the board after which it is erased. Then students work the same problems independently.

> **SHOPPING TRIP**
>
> "I went to the store and bought crackerjacks for 15 cents." The next child adds an item—"I went to the store and bought crackerjacks for 15 cents and an apple for 5 cents. I had spent 20 cents." The third child adds another item, thus: "I went to the store and bought crackerjacks for 15 cents, an apple for 5 cents, and a box of cookies for 20 cents. I had spent 40 cents."

Paper and pencil activities

- Give each student a duplicated copy of this number wheel. Also give each student a strip of construction paper about 2 by 5 inches (according to the size of the circle drawn). The object of this activity is to use the strip of paper to cover numerals on the wheel in such a manner that the numbers showing add to the largest possible sum. In what position can the strip of paper be placed to show the smallest possible sum?

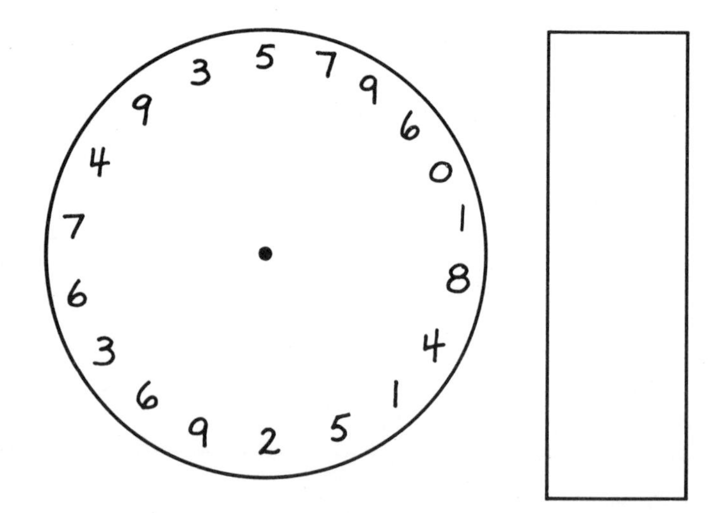

• MATHO cards can be prepared with the figures used focusing on one process such as multiplication—54, 27, 49, 35, 64, 12. For addition use 16, 9, 14, 12, 7, 18, and so on. The student covers the correct answer when the appropriate fact is read. A FREE space may be marked in the center.

• AROUND THE CLOCK IN ONE MINUTE can be played by each individual student who draws a small clock face on his paper. The Leader says, "It's FOUR O'CLOCK!" and begins watching the time while the players multiply each number on the clock times four, writing the answers outside the clock shape. At the end of one minute each student who has correctly completed the answers scores a point for his team. Another clock face is drawn, and the Leader may say, "It's EIGHT O'CLOCK!"

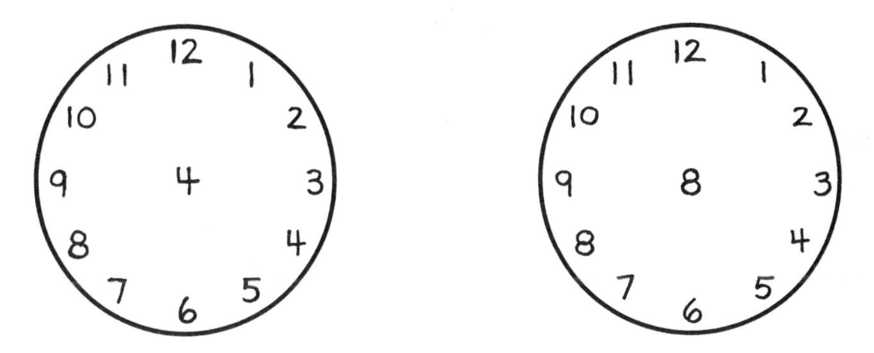

• WHEELS can be constructed by the teacher on dittoed sheets for practice in addition and subtraction. The number placed in the center of the wheel must be added and subtracted from each number around the wheel. Addition answers are placed outside the wheel; subtraction answers are written inside the circle.

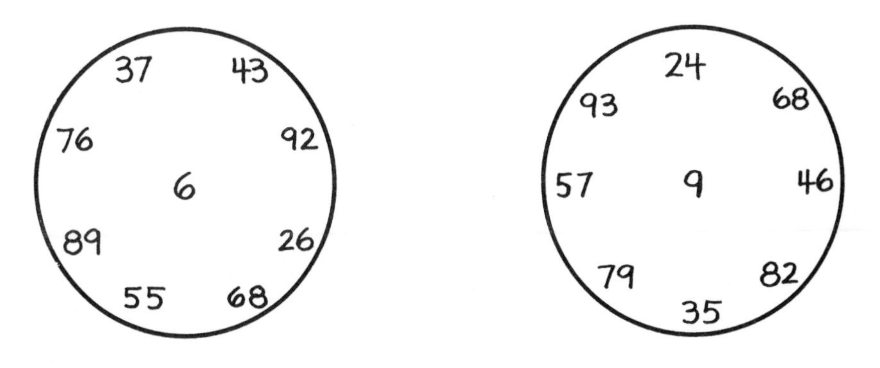

Practice that challenges the imagination

• Prepare dittoed sheets of activities which challenge the student's intellect while also providing practice. Sheets of this type provide stimulating activities for before school time and other odd moments during the day.

• TRICKY TRIANGLES are fun, but require a little thought. See how many students can solve this problem before you give the solution. The object is to fill in the numbers from 1 to 9 so that the sides of the triangle add up to 17. See if students can invent other triangles.

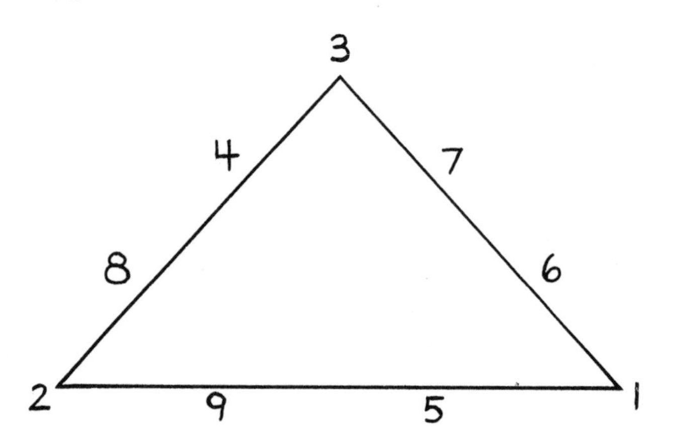

• RUSSIAN PEASANT MULTIPLICATION provides an interesting diversion while students multiply, divide, and add. Follow the example which demonstrates this method of multiplying 26 × 33.

~~26 × 33~~ 13 × 66	Halve each number on the left and double each number on the right always discarding any halves remaining.
~~6 × 132~~	Cross out any lines beginning with even numbers.
3 × 264 1 × 528	Add the numbers on the right to obtain the correct answer. Check by usual method of multiplication. Why does this work?
858	

• NUMERICAL REVERSALS are interesting to students, for when the sign is changed, the answer reverses. Duplicate these samples on a sheet of paper asking whether anyone can discover any others.

$9 + 9 = 18$	$9 \times 9 = 81$
$24 + 3 = 27$	$24 \times 3 = 72$
$47 + 2 = 49$	$47 \times 2 = 94$

• NUMBER CODES are intriguing but can also provide practice in using arithmetical processes. Have each student invent a code in which each letter is equivalent to a number; these codes can be simple or complex according to the abilities of the students as in these examples:

A = 1; B = 2; C = 3; D = 4; E = 5.
A = 26; B = 25; C = 24; D = 23; E = 22.
A = 5; B = A + 1; C = B + 2; D = C + 3; E = D + 4.
A = 4; B = 2A; C = 2B; D = 2C; E = 2D.
A = 7; B = 2A − 1; C = 2B − 1; D = 2C − 1; E = 2D − 1.

Let students challenge each other as they try to decode messages written by other students.

• FINDING FACTORS provides a challenge. Give the class a large number such as 360. Within a given time limit (5 minutes) students are to find as many factors as they can for this number. Here are a few of the numbers which divide evenly into 360:

90 4 60 6 36 2 9 40 10 18 120

• CASTING OUT NINES is a way of checking column addition which is often new to students in elementary school. Attention is focused on multiples of nine as well as addition.

6489	0
7349	5
2381	5
2515	4
18734	5

1. Add the numbers across in each figure (6489 adds to 27). Discard any whole nines, writing the remainder to the right (27 contains exactly 3 whole nines so the remainder is 0). Repeat this process for each figure including the addition answer.
2. Add the remainders which are above the addition line (14) and cast out nines (5).
3. If the latter number coincides with the remainder obtained from the addition answer, the answer can be assumed correct.

FACTS ABOUT 9

Multiples of 9 add to 9, then 18, then 27 . . .

9 = 9	99 = 18	189 = 27 (18 + 9)
18 = 9	108 = 18	198 = 27
27 = 9	117 = 18	207 = 27
36 = 9	126 = 18	216 = 27

Have students explore the nature of this progression.

• CROSS NUMBER PUZZLES encompass a wide variety of possibilities and are easily made. You can focus attention on any facts and processes which students need. Have students make puzzles like this one:

9^{a}	9^{b}	■	7^{c}	2^{d}	0	■	1^{e}	6^{f}	5^{g}	2^{h}
2^{i}	7	3^{j}	5^{k}	0	■	■	4^{l}	6	2	4
2^{m}	4	1	0	■	3^{n}	6^{o}	4	2	8	■
8^{p}	1	■	■	■	5^{q}	0	■	8^{r}	0	4^{s}
4^{t}	9	■	3^{u}	■	1^{v}	4	9^{w}	2	■	2
8^{x}	4	■	6^{y}	3^{z}	■	5^{A}	4	■	3^{B}	■
6^{C}	0	■	5^{D}	8	7	6	0	■	6^{E}	4

CROSSNUMBER PUZZLE

ACROSS

a 9 × 11
b the minutes in 12 hours
e 4 × 213 + 800
i sum of 5255, 1095, 6498, 4824, 9678
l 12 × $385\frac{1}{3}$
m 5 × 482
n 7 × 5204
p 9 × 9

DOWN

a 476 × 95 + (12 × the feet in 50 mi.) + 2000 squared, + 1,915,266
b 753 + 9, 257, 640 + (5 × 12485)
c 25 × 30
d 4 × 5
e 12 dozen
f 60 × 844 + (3 × 5214)

ACROSS

q number of states in U.S.
r $524 + (7 \times 40)$
t 7×7
v Discovery of America
x 7 dozen
y 7×9
A 6×9
C minutes in an hour
D $80 \times 567 + (4 \times 3350)$
E 8×8

DOWN

g feet in 1 mile
h hours in a day
j days in August
n $1337 - 986$
o 6×10076
s 6×7
u days in a year
w $1819 - 879$
z 3 dozen plus 2
B months in 3 years

• CATALOGS or newspaper advertisements furnish good material for practical application of arithmetic. Have students try some of the following activities:

< Students can write problems using the figures given in the catalog or advertisement. A sheet of problems is attached to the front of each catalog. These problems can then be worked in turn by various members of the class. A problem might read thus:

> Turn to page 34. Mary wishes to buy three blouses (X39642). How much will the blouses cost? How much will they weigh?

< Try to obtain duplicate copies of a grocery ad for your class. Then all students can work with the same information as they write problems which are exchanged.

> Write a shopping list on the board for which each is to compute the total.
>
> Give the students a sum of money ($20.00) which they are to spend. They can list the items purchased as they try to spend the exact sum of money.

< Study the advertisements for a sale. Figure the prices quoted at discounted rates—15%, 20%, 33%. Include the federal tax on luxury items and any local sales tax.

> **Play CASH REGISTER. Give the class the costs of a number of items for practice in column addition. Who can be first to ring up the total?**

< Compare grocery ads from different stores to determine the variation in prices asked. See how much money can be saved by shopping for the same given Shopping List (dittoed or written on the board). At which store could you save the most money?

Interesting Ways with Numbers

Often you can write a provocative question or examples of interesting facts about numbers on the chalkboard or display them on the bulletin board. These CHALLENGES serve to whet the student's enthusiasm for mathematics as well as to provide mathematical food for thought. After the Challenge has been displayed for a while discuss it with the class asking whether anyone can explain or give a solution. Here is a variety of material which can be used in this fashion.

Problems with a "catch"

These problems have a solution, but there is a "catch" in the question or the answer. Nonetheless they prove enjoyable and thought provoking. Try some of these:

★ How much dirt is there in a hole $3\frac{1}{2}$ feet by $4\frac{1}{4}$ feet wide and 24 inches deep?

(There is no dirt in a *hole*, only air.)

★ Multiply $999 \times 9 \times 0$. What's the answer?

(How many students multiplied 999×9? The answer to the problem is 0.)

★ Which is heavier—a pound of candy or a pound of printer's lead?

(A pound is a pound is a pound.)

★ Mr. Hale, an insurance salesman, drove 450 miles one day while visiting his clients. He drove 50 miles an hour for $3\frac{1}{2}$ hours and 40 miles an hour for $1\frac{1}{4}$ hours. How many miles did Mr. Hale drive in all?

(450)

★ A butcher is 33 years old, 6 feet 2 inches tall, wears a $16\frac{1}{2}$ shirt and a size 12 shoe. What does he weigh?

(Meat)

★ Can you write the number 31 using the figure 3 five times? (Let students invent some of these.)

$(3^3 + 3 + 3/3)$

★ Can you connect these nine dots by using only four straight lines? (You have to get out of that box!)

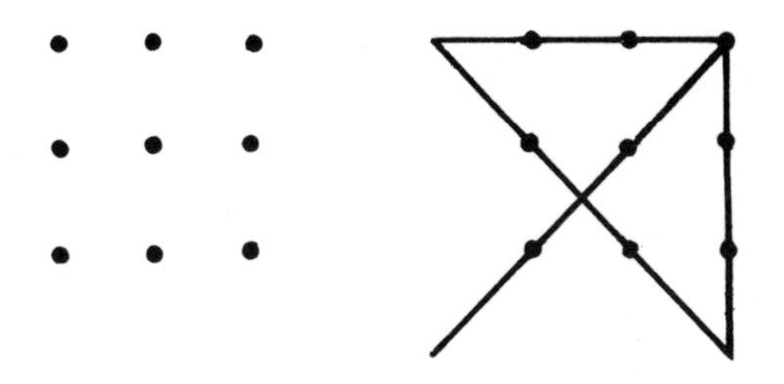

★ What figure increases its value by one-half when you turn it upside down?

(6, 66, 666, and so on)

Finding solutions

These problems have solutions although they sometimes require some time in working. Use these activities occasionally for students to work immediately on entering the room.

★ How many different ways can you express this fraction? $\frac{2}{3}$—$\frac{6}{9}$, $\frac{10}{15}$, $\frac{96}{144}$, and so on.

★ Triple this recipe for cookies.

$2\frac{1}{2}$ cups flour
$\frac{1}{2}$ cup milk
$\frac{3}{4}$ cup butter
$1\frac{1}{2}$ teaspoon vanilla
$1\frac{1}{3}$ cups sugar
$\frac{1}{2}$ cup nuts
$\frac{1}{4}$ teaspoon nutmeg

★ Figuring interest at the current rate of interest, if you deposited $1000 in the bank today, what would your account be worth when you graduate from high school?

★ Ask students to estimate the following measurements which can be checked by a committee of students during class. Who was closest to the correct answers?

The length of a window in inches.
The height of a specific chair in inches.
The length of the room in feet.
The width of the door in feet.

★ Can you complete this multiplication table?

$123456789 \times 9 = 1,111,111,101$
$123456789 \times 18 = ?$
$123456789 \times 27 = ?$
$123456789 \times 36 = ?$
$123456789 \times 45 = ?$
$123456789 \times 54 = ?$
$123456789 \times 63 = ?$
$123456789 \times 72 = ?$
$123456789 \times 81 = ?$

★ How does this Progression work out? Why?

$1 \times 9 + 1 = 10$
$12 \times 9 + 2 = 110$
$123 \times 9 + 3 = ?$
$1234 \times 9 + 4 = ?$
Continue to 123456789

★ Nineteen is a *prime number* (not divisible by numbers other than 1 or itself). How many other primes can you discover?

★ Can you complete these sequences? (Have students submit interesting sequences for this use.) Here are examples of varied difficulty:

2 3 4 5 __ __
44 45 46 __ __
9 8 7 __ __
6 12 18 __ __
52 48 24 20 10 __ __
1 3 2 4 3 5 __ __
Z Y X W __ __
B C E H L __ __
00++ 000+++ 0000++++ __ __

★ THE BIG PROBLEM! Students have fun with an occasional problem which fills the page.

123456789	5555555555	123456789
× 987654321	× 6666666666	12345678
		1234567
		123456
		12345
		1234
		123
		12
		1

★ Can you solve these problems Roman style?

MCXLVI	MMDCLXIX
× XXV	× CMXXXV

★ Multiplying by Eleven the easy way.

34	49	325
× 11	× 11	× 11
3 7 4	5 3 9	3 5 7 5
3 + 4	4 + 9	3 + 2 2 + 5

★ WHY? There is more than one possible answer to these Challenges as students supply values for Y.

$20 - Y > 8 + 7$

$\frac{1}{2} Y < 2 > 9 \div 5$

$2 \times 7 \times 3 > Y + 10$

★ NUMBER ASSOCIATIONS challenge the student to list things he associates with each number; there may be multiple suggestions.

2 (twins, pair of shoes, age of little sister)
11 (student's age, TV channel, 5 + 6, Storytime)
49 (7 × 7, Discovery of gold, price of a dozen eggs)
1492 (Discovery of America, an address)
144 (12 × 12, a gross, someone's weight)

★ Think of a geometric shape—TRIANGLE. In how many ways does this shape appear in your life? Also try CONE, CYLINDER.

Gable of roof	Letters V, W, M, N, A
Triangle (instrument)	Number 4

★ Which number does *not* belong in the group? Why?

$\frac{3}{7}$ ($\frac{4}{6}$) $\frac{2}{5}$ $\frac{4}{9}$ (can be reduced)

236 279 837 (21) (not in hundreds)

(2) 9 7 5 21 13 (not odd)

It's magic

Students like to be mystified by numerical processes which appear magical to them simply because they don't happen to know the secret formula. Here are several MYSTIFIERS.

8	Take a number from one to nine.
88	Write the same number beside it.
176	Double this number.
176 divided by 8	Divide by your original number.
Result: 22	The result is always 22. Why?

10 (October)	Write the number of your birth month.
20	Multiply by 2.
25	Add 5.
1250	Multiply by 50.
1261(11)	Add your age.
1011	Subtract 250.
	First number in the answer (10) is the month of your birth; others are your age (11).

Take any three-digit number with no repetition of numbers and no zero. Reverse the order of these digits subtracting the smaller from the larger. Then add the difference to itself in reverse.

The answer is always 1089.

$$\begin{array}{r} 976 \\ -679 \\ \hline 297 \end{array} \qquad \begin{array}{r} 297 \\ +792 \\ \hline 1089 \end{array}$$

Select a number from 1 to 9.	6
Multiply this number by 9.	54
Multiply that number × 12345679 (omit 8)	666666666

(Have several people try this to note the effects with other numbers.)

MNEMONIC DEVICES

This sentence is a humorous help in spelling ARITHMETIC.

A rat in the house might eat the ice cream.

Which is Up and which is Down—NUMERATOR or DENOMINATOR?

Numerator contains U for Up.
Denominator begins with D for Down.

Books to explore

There are numerous paperback books available which list samples of games, puzzles, and other mathematical diversions both old and new which lend spice to the teaching of mathematics to young people. Listed here is a selection of these titles:

Gardner, Martin. *The Scientific American Book of Mathematical Puzzles and Diversions.* Simon & Schuster. ($1.45)

Goddard Space Flight Center, NASA, Office of Education. *What's Up There* (Mathematics sourcebook about space and space exploration). Sup. of Documents, U.S. Govt. Printing Office, Washington, D.C. 20402. ($1.00)

Heller, Bruce & Co. *Book of Math Puzzlers.* 1 Wall Street, New York, New York 10005. (FREE)

Johnson, Donovan A. *Games for Learning Mathematics.* J. Weston Walch. ($1.00)

Is there anyone so wise as to learn by the experience of others?

—*Voltaire*

6

EXPLORING THE SOCIAL STUDIES

Described in this chapter are creative approaches to the teaching of social studies. Included are new ideas for presenting information, suggestions for motivating continued student interest, and techniques which correlate social studies with the language arts, reading, and art. The chapter has been divided into four sections—Studying History, Exploring Geography, Examining World Affairs, and Developing Citizenship.

Studying History

Whether taught as an individual subject or combined in the social studies approach, history is taught in every elementary classroom. We study the great men of our nation, the exploration of our country, and the story of the country's development. History concerns real people and events that actually happened. This in itself is sufficient to fascinate the beginning student of history. In this section we are presenting a variety of methods which many teachers have found effective in stimulating student interest in history.

Biographical time lines

The Time Line makes an excellent type of Book Review for

the biography of a figure in history. The Time Line may cover a short period in a person's life (the Civil War years for Abraham Lincoln) recording detailed events. It may, on the other hand, present the entire life of the subject from birth to death.

Encourage students to include clippings and illustrations on their Time Lines. If possible, a portrait of the person should be mounted on the paper with the Time Line. These Time Lines can be constructed in scroll form or long vertical strips of paper can be used for variety.

Writing history

Students learn much about the study of history by writing short histories about topics which interest them. Boys would be very much intrigued by the history of various sports—football, baseball, rugby, cricket, and so on. Girls could explore subjects such as the history of fashions, coiffeurs, or jewelry. Other subjects of more general interest include Libraries, Printing, your school, a building in your town, or an event of local significance. A student might write the history of your city as seen through the eyes of a landmark—an old tree, a river, or a road.

Events of the month

Each month feature a calendar which combines historical events whose anniversaries occur that month, famous birthdays, holidays, and current happenings. Here is an example:

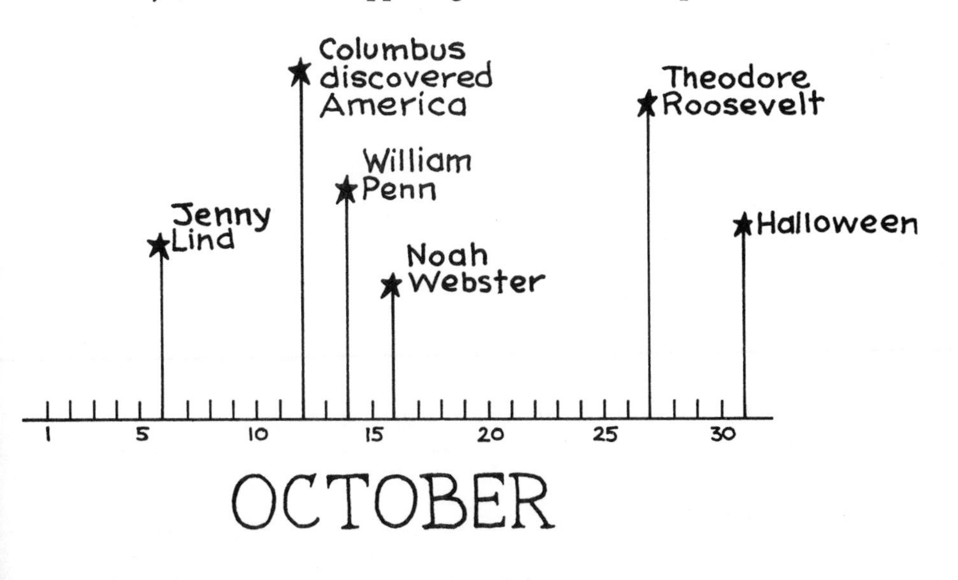

Bringing historical figures into the present

Contrast our world today with that of several hundred years ago by having students imagine that an historical figure is suddenly brought to life in the present. Each student can write a short essay on topics like the following:

What most amazed Benjamin Franklin about our city
Dolly Madison's reactions to the modern kitchen
George Washington's arrival in Washington, D.C.

Students imagine life in another time

Students will also gain much insight as they imagine themselves living in another period of history. Suggest topics like these:

I was aboard the Santa Maria.
I was the daughter of Martha Washington's best friend.
I lived next door to Paul Revere.

History quizzes

Challenge the students with a quiz about historical events. These quizzes can be made by students and can take a variety of forms. Here is one example:

FAMOUS DATES IN AMERICAN HISTORY

How many of these famous dates can you identify? If you score eight right, I predict you will be a Professor of History.

1. January 17, 1706
2. February 15, 1898
3. March 6, 1857
4. April 15, 1865
5. May 10, 1869
6. June 14, 1777
7. July 27, 1866
8. August 6, 1945
9. September 14, 1814
10. October 8, 1871

Answers:

1. Birth of Benjamin Franklin in Boston.
2. The U.S.S. Maine was blown up in Havana Harbor.
3. The Dred Scott decision of the Supreme Court (slavery could not be excluded from the territories by Congress).
4. Death of Abraham Lincoln at 7:22 on Saturday morning.
5. The Golden Spike was driven at Promontory Point, Utah.

6. The Continental Congress adopted the first official U.S. flag.
7. The Atlantic Cable completed by Cyrus W. Field.
8. The first atomic bomb was dropped on Hiroshima.
9. The "Star-Spangled Banner" written by Francis Scott Key.
10. The Chicago fire with property loss estimated $200,000,000.

Celebrate historical dates

Discussions about events of historical significance may have added meaning if they occur on the anniversary of that event. On December 15th, for example, discuss the Bill of Rights, which was signed on that date. How would our life be different without the Bill of Rights? For more information about this topic request free materials from:

National Assembly on Teaching the Principles
of the Bill of Rights
200 Park Avenue South
New York 3, New York

Other events are included in THE TEACHERS' CALENDAR at the end of Chapter 1. Have students prepare short talks on appropriate topics for significant anniversaries.

1865

An interesting bulletin board display can feature a date as a caption. Cut the numbers 1865, for example, from construction paper. Display them with facts about Abraham Lincoln or the Civil War.

Invaluable Reference: Thornton, Willis. *Almanac for Americans.* New York: Chilton Company, 1954.

History and words

Many interesting words have developed in connection with historical events and figures. Several you might wish to discuss with your class are:

Yankee—Used in the 18th century to denote the Dutch in America; corruption of *Jan,* the Dutch name for John.

Bunk or Bunkum—Derived from the name of a Congressman's county, Buncombe in North Carolina. He made a speech that was pointless but wordy, the origin of Bunk meaning foolish, untrue chatter.

Gerrymander—Governor Gerry of Massachusetts attempted to falsify electoral districts by changing their shapes. One district resembled a salamander which was called a Gerrymander.

Have each student prepare a page illustrating the interesting origin of a word to be included in a class book, WORDS IN HISTORY. Other words associated with history which students can investigate include the following:

Ballot	Assassin	Emancipation
Pilgrim	Radical	Sabotage
Propaganda	Filibuster	Civilization

There are numerous books on the origin of words for the use of both teacher and student. Here are several which we recommend:

Funk, Wilfred. *The Origin of Words and Their Romantic Stories.* Funk, 1951.

Morris, William and Mary. *Dictionary of Word and Phrase Origins.* Harper, 1962.

Weekley, Ernest. *The Romance of Words.* Dover, 1961.

Quotations of famous people

The use of quotations in teaching history assists in making the people more alive; it helps the student to understand the thinking of these men and women. Quotations can be used in the classroom in varied ways—orally as you discuss a certain person, as a provocative beginning for a discussion, or as a caption for a bulletin board display.

Paperback editions of books of quotations provide the teacher with ready material for this purpose. Listed here are three recommended titles which are inexpensive, helpful references.

Henry, Lewis C. *Best Quotations for All Occasions.* (Premier D15)

Sproul, Kathleen, ed. *The Shorter Bartlett's Familiar Quotations.* (Permabooks, M5002)

Tiedt, Sidney W. *Quotes for Teaching.* (Contemporary Press, Box 1524, San Jose, California, $1.00)

Music and history

As you study the periods of history, have students explore the music which was popular at that time to further their understanding and interest in the study. Most teachers are familiar with the Minuet and Virginia Reel associated with colonial times, but other periods, too, offer excellent songs for singing and dances which the students can learn. Here are songs which were written and sung during periods of war:

Revolutionary War: "Yankee Doodle"
War of 1812: "The Star-Spangled Banner"
Civil War: "Battle Hymn of the Republic," "When Johnny Comes Marching Home," "Tramp, Tramp, Tramp!"
World War I: "Hinky Dinky Parlee Voo," "Goodbye, Sweetheart, Goodbye."

Request a catalog from Folkways Records (121 W. 47th Street, New York 36, New York) as they offer many interesting recordings related to history.

Dramatizing episodes

Dramatization can take all forms—skits, tableaux, pantomimes, dialogues. Students will learn much by preparing the presentation of an event through any dramatic technique. Two students could, for example, play the roles of General Grant and General Lee as Lee surrenders. Original dialogue based on their reading about this event can be written.

Tableaux might be arranged around a central topic such as EXPLORING THE NEW WORLD with each tableau featuring one explorer posing before an appropriate background. Frames for tableaux can be cut from large cardboard packing boxes supported by two poles or boards nailed to the sides. Students walk behind this frame to present the scene they have prepared. Other members of the class may guess which explorer is being portrayed.

Using the sand table

The sand table (or large shallow boxes of sand) provides an excellent means for portraying historic scenes. Boys will become engrossed in depicting battle scenes after library research determines the people present and something of the topography involved. Illustrations in books often supply good information for this type of activity.

Papier-mâché can also be used to build scenes on stiff cardboard or plywood bases. Buildings can be constructed of cardboard as can other structures that are needed to complete a particular historic scene. Groups of students can work as teams or individuals can work on smaller projects.

Historical letters

Here is a suggestion for combining the writing of letters with the study of history. Have each student assume a name (real or imaginary) appropriate to the period or locale under study. Pretending to be this person each one writes a letter home to his family or a friend telling about the happenings of the Civil War, Crossing the Plains, Finding Gold in California, or whatever events are being studied.

Art and the study of history

Art can help make the study of history more attractive to many students. It provides ways for publicizing information learned as well as a means for using information. Here are several suggestions for correlating art and history:

- *Border Designs* can be made on 4 x 18 inch strips of drawing paper to frame a bulletin board or to trim a bare wall. Base repeated designs on ancient forms of writing such as hieroglyphics or cuneiform, Indian or Eskimo designs, and symbols of various periods of American history such as the pick and shovel of the prospector or the covered wagon and oxen of the pioneers.
- *Advertisements* for articles can be made on 12 x 18 inch paper. When studying the early development of our country, for example, students might advertise a Ben Franklin stove, cloth just arrived from England, bayberry candles or freshly made perfumed

May 18, 1850

Dear Mary,
We are slowly moving across Kansas. I don't know whether this letter will ever reach you, dear child, but I will write it anyway.
All of us are well although little Jenny had a fever last night. So far we have seen no Indians.
Pray for us, Mary. I miss you already.

Lovingly,
Mother

soap, and many other items which will occur to students. Color, design, and skill with printing will be emphasized as well as knowledge of the period in history.

• *Cartoons* consisting of stick figures done with pencil or pen serve to illustrate events as the student also learns to depict action with the stick figure. Captions written for the cartoon will be based on knowledge of historical information.

Using commemorative stamps

Mount commemorative stamps individually on 3 x 5 inch cards with questions about the person or scene pictured on the stamp. The familiar four-cent stamp, for example, bears Abraham Lincoln's likeness. On a card with this stamp you might include the following questions:

What's my full name?
During what years was I president?
For what act am I best known?
What books does your library have about my life?

Students can also use these cards to check each other on their knowledge about these figures of history by asking each other questions about each stamp. Stamp collectors should be encouraged to exhibit their stamp collections to add interest to this approach to history.

GET ON THE MAILING LIST!

One of the most valuable mailing lists for the social studies teacher is that of the U.S. Government Printing Office which issues frequent lists of publications.

Reproductions of the Constitution, The Bill of Rights, and the Declaration of Independence are available inexpensively as are lists of materials about periods of history such as "Facts about the Civil War." Send your request to:

Superintendent of Documents
Government Printing Office
Washington, D.C. 20402

Library research

History offers an excellent opportunity to stress the use of library research techniques as students investigate various topics of historic importance. Subjects for research will be suggested by the material being studied. Listed are a few sample topics:

The development of our alphabet
Games played by Greek and Roman children
Other calendars which have existed—Hebrew, Aztec, Chinese

A good basic rule to establish is that each student must consult at least three different sources of information. The Research

Report can be made in booklet form including illustrations, charts, and maps. Some students can report their research by preparing a bulletin board display or a large printed chart. Other topics might lend themselves to the writing of a script for a puppet show or a radio production.

History games

Games help the student to remember historical facts without painful drill which alienates interest. Here are good examples of games which supply excellent review of material read:

• WHO AM I? For this game each student has a name pinned on his back. Use names from the area or period of history you are studying. Each student comes to the front of the room, turns so that all can read "his name," and then asks questions which require YES OR NO answers. He attempts to identify his personality through these questions as quickly as possible. The number of questions that may be asked by each student may be limited so that all may have a chance to participate.

• WHAT'S THE QUESTION? Here is a reversal of the usual procedure. The Leader gives the *answer* and the Responder must supply a possible correct *question* which could have that answer. Given the answer "France" a student might, for example, supply the question, "Paris is the capital of what country?"

• ABC'S OF HISTORY This game is a paper and pencil activity which encourages students to use reference books. Each student is to list MEN OF HISTORY, PLACES IN AMERICAN HISTORY, or names in any other category. Listing men, for instance, a student might begin thus:

A—Adams
B—Benjamin Franklin
C—Cabot

Each student tries to find as many as possible (one name per letter) within a given time. Letters may be skipped and filled in out of order.

The able student in history

The gifted student is intrigued by the study of history and is usually interested in further investigation of topics related to the unit being studied by the class. Independent investigation of topics which interest the student as an individual should be encouraged. Here are several areas which are particularly suitable for the able student:

• An AMERICAN HEROES CALENDAR can be developed by one student or a team of students with each one taking certain months of the year. Listed on this calendar are the birthdates of men of literature and science, presidents, industrial leaders, explorers, patriots, etc.

• *The Literary History of Our State* can be the title of a report in booklet form which discusses the writings of authors who have lived in your state or whose stories were set in that locale. Brief biographical sketches and lists of books written by each author can be included.

• *Poetry* can be written by the able student to stimulate interest in historic events and people. Permit freedom of form and length with stress placed on the ideas expressed. (See the section on Creative Writing in Chapter 3.)

• *Essays* provide a means for expression of ideas by the able student. Supply a variety of provocative topics to stimulate his imagination such as the following WHAT IF? topics:

WHAT IF—we had not purchased Alaska?
WHAT IF—the South had won the Civil War?
WHAT IF—the United States had participated in the League of Nations?

Testing the students' knowledge

At the beginning of the year *give a pretest on historical* (or other subject area) *information to be learned* during the year. It is sometimes surprising to discover how much information students already have gained through other means and should alter your plans for developing a unit of study. Save these first tests for comparison at a later time when the students are retested.

When a unit of study has been completed, *have students compose questions which are submitted to you as possible test items.* Students can learn to construct multiple choice questions, matching questions, as well as True and False items or straight Recall questions. Select at least one item from each person's page of questions with no large number coming from any one paper. Constructing the questions serves as an excellent review, exposes students to a variety of test items, and assists you in preparing a good test. You can add a few test items yourself to cover any areas not tested by student-constructed items.

Short quizzes (perhaps 10 True-False items read aloud) on material can serve to assist students' learning of information. Give the answers immediately with each student noting the information he did not know. These scores are not recorded, but serve only to point up areas which need further study.

Extending Geographic Concepts

Young people are fascinated by the study of the map and talk of far-away places. Too, as in most cases, your own interest and enthusiasm will heighten the interest of students. Described here are varied techniques for maintaining a stimulating approach to the study of geography.

Maps in the classroom

Even the primary grades need maps of wide variety in the classroom if students are to take full advantage of opportunities to learn geographic information. The *globe* is a good type of map for teaching young students from the beginning that the world is round as they search for locations and become accustomed to the shapes and sizes of land areas.

Road maps, particularly those of your state and immediate vicinity, are especially valuable mounted on the wall. Frequently in the course of a day you can point to the map to illustrate something you are saying about a location. Students soon absorb facts about directions and the relationship of places about which they have heard.

Wall maps of the United States, North America, and the world are equally important as you begin discussing events happening in other lands. Many children have traveled to other countries and have interesting experiences to relate to classmates which introduces the concepts of distance, time, and world friendship. Even if no formal lessons are planned to teach skills of map reading, much incidental learning takes place because young students find maps fascinating; they are interested in places heard about on television programs or read about in library books.

Drawing maps for the classroom

The opaque projector will assist you in preparing large inexpensive outline maps of the United States (with or without state boundaries), North America, and the world. Any small map in a textbook can be enlarged with this projector directed toward a large sheet of mural paper or tagboard. Outline the map quickly with a pencil when the projector is turned on. Then turn off the projector while you complete the outlining of the map with a felt pen. Students can add washes of thin blue tempera paint to indicate water; other features can be added according to your needs. Print names of countries with the felt pen as you identify them with the class. Maps can be drawn on the chalkboard for temporary use.

> To assist students in drawing freehand maps direct them first to draw light lines dividing the paper into fourths, eighths, or sixteenths. By dividing the map to be reproduced into the same number of areas they can more nearly place each land mass in the correct location.

"Walk through" and "walk on" maps

Especially effective in the primary grades are maps which the children can actually experience, maps they can construct. Even kindergarteners can lay out a city street (perhaps the street corner near your school) using blocks and cardboard cartons to simulate buildings and houses. Other landmarks can be noted also such as large trees (a big circle of green construction paper laid flat on the floor or attached to the end of a dowel rod), stop signs, traffic lights, and so on.

Before developing the map have the class take a walk around the area to be mapped. After the map is begun in the classroom walk around the area again to note any corrections to be made.

Use this type of street map to teach safety practices, to present concepts of direction, to encourage role playing and creative dramatics.

Older students can construct similar maps on a smaller scale using large sheets of cardboard or plywood as a base. Buildings and other landmarks can be constructed with small boxes and construction paper. Small vehicles, people, animals, and other items can be used with this type of map. The sandbox is also useful for a map which can be manipulated.

Creative writing and geography

Foreign countries provide much provocative material to stimulate the imaginations of young writers as they begin learning about these lands and their peoples. Encourage students to write on topics of this nature:

> Write an adventure that includes yourself as you travel in a foreign city.
> What would you do if you suddenly found yourself in—South Vietnam, Cuba, Kenya?
> I would like to live in __________ because . . .
> If I could remake the world, I would . . .
> My idea of Utopia would be . . .

Compass directions

Make a large circle on the playground (or tramp a circle in the snow) with the four directions marked to play RUN THE COMPASS. Have the children number by fours and stand at the center of the circle. As you call out a number and a direction, thus: "Threes, West," all the children having the number Three must run to the West. The leader tries to catch any that are not safely at that point of the Compass. Later add the intermediate points—Southeast, Southwest, Northeast, Northwest—so that there are eight positions.

Latitude and longitude

TO THE RESCUE! provides an opportunity for students to practice the location of latitude and longitude on maps. Beside a map (of any area) on which both latitude and longitude lines are marked mount airplane shapes cut from colored construction paper. On each airplane print the latitude and longitude where that plane has been reported "down" because of engine trouble.

The problem is to locate each plane's position so that the crew can be RESCUED. Let students take turns moving each plane to its correct position on the map. For added practice students can remove the planes and locate them again. You may also print positions on both sides of each plane to double the number of items available.

HINT! Let students prepare these activities for the class whenever possible. Those preparing the activity will learn much as they work. Your time is then freed for other duties.

Geographic games

• CITY, COUNTRY, CONTINENT is an excellent game for reviewing various place names. As the leader points to a person, that student tries to answer before the leader counts to ten thus: "Anchorage—1,2,3,4,5,6,7,8,9,10!" The student must call, "City!" before the count of ten. Other classifications can be substituted in this game according to the information being studied.

• BEAN BAG TOSS is a variation of the geography quiz. As the leader asks a question, he tosses the bean bag to a person who must supply the correct answer. If he does not know the correct answer, he must go to the end of the line as each of the other players moves up one position.

• CHAIN REACTION is an interesting game which continues around the circle until someone makes a mistake. The last letter of a given place name provides the key to the next name to be added. In a Chain Reaction of Cities, for example, the Leader might name Boston, which ends with an N. The next player must name a city beginning with N, for instance, New York. The next player must now name a city beginning with K, Kansas City, and so on—Yorkville, Edinburgh, Georgetown, Nashville, Erie.

• GEOGRAPHY RELAYS can be played by several teams of students. One student serves as the leader and calls out names of locations—Peru, Kenya, Sweden, New Zealand—while team members take turns indicating the correct location. A scorekeeper keeps score for all teams on the board. As one team correctly locates the given place, he adds one point to that team's score. When a team member fails to locate the place within the time limit (sixty seconds watched by the scorekeeper), the next team in order may be given the same place to locate.

For geography games you can prepare a sheet or two of place names with which students should be familiar. Mount the sheets on the board near the world map so students can work at locating places in their spare time. The leader can use these sheets to supply a variety of names for the games.

• CARD GAMES can be constructed by a group of students. On 3 x 5 inch cards they can print names of countries (or states) and their capitals. To play the game students try to match country and capital as in Old Maid. The odd card which no one wants can be a picture of the globe (clipped from a catalog or magazine). This game can be called GLOBAL WARFARE or STATE OF THE NATION.

• JIGSAW PUZZLES can be made from maps glued firmly to tagboard or stiff cardboard. These maps will serve to increase interest in areas being studied. Students soon become familiar with cities in a state or various features of a country.

Geographic riddles

Feature riddles occasionally to make students think. You might include some of the following old favorites:

How many Portlands are in the United States? Where are they? (Portland, Oregon and Portland, Maine)
What is the biggest bus in the United States? (Colum*bus*)
Where do four states intersect in the U.S.? (Utah, New Mexico, Colorado, Arizona)
What city in Ohio has the same name as the capital of Peru? Are they pronounced the same? (Lima; No)

People-to-people school and classroom exchange

Here is an interesting source of information about other countries. Organized by a group of citizens which lists many well-known figures among its sponsors, People-to-People's *Free Service* enables students in our country to become acquainted with students in other countries through letters, pictures, tapes, and other media your class might wish to explore. The organization supplies names and addresses after which the exchange is continued independently by the participants. Application forms may be obtained from this address:

School and Classroom Program
People-to-People
2401 Grand Avenue
Kansas City 8, Missouri

Provocative place names

Let students make special studies focused on place names in your immediate vicinity or state. Some states, for example, California, have many cities, rivers, and other geographical features bearing Spanish names. Other locales have a predominance of French or Indian names. Let several students compile a booklet of names and their meanings illustrating the pages appropriately. The group can then present this material to the class leaving the book on the reading table where other students can examine it and use it as a handy reference.

You can also feature unusual place names during the year just as a matter of interest. During December, for example, ask the class how Christmas Island got its name. Post this question on a bulletin board adding the answer when a student finds it. (Christmas Island was discovered by Captain Cook on December 25, 1777.) Encourage students to contribute similar names for investigation.

Interesting commentaries on the origins of many place names can be found in:

Asimov, Isaac. *Words on the Map*. Houghton-Mifflin, 1962.

Geography crossword puzzles

To add interest to the study of geography use CROSSWORD PUZZLES which feature the names of countries and other words related to geography like this example. Crossword puzzles can be made by students for use by the rest of the class.

ACROSS

2 Geographical dictionary
8 see (past)
10 Irish (abbr.)
11 six (Roman)
12 imaginary line from pole to pole
15 Leader of Southern army in Civil War
17 European country
19 National Defense Act
21 Louisiana
22 Georgia
23 prayer ending
24 drink milk like a cat
25 land of the Angles
27 California mountain
28 grain
29 bashful
30 pig's sound
31 yes
32 German city
33 while

DOWN

1 United States
2 science of the earth
3 girl's name
4 book's name
5 opposite of false
6 evening
7 Rhode Island
9 elevated train
13 river in India
14 Scandanavian country
16 strays
17 showy
18 city in China
20 reject
23 boy's nickname
26 increase
29 South America

Acrostic puzzles

ACROSTIC PUZZLES are based on a secret word. When the correct answers are supplied, the first letters of the answers spell a word as in this example featuring SWITZERLAND:

S______	The people of this land (Swiss)
W__________	An important product (Watches)
I______	Neighbor to the South (Italy)
T__________	Biggest industry (Tourism)
Z________	Large city (Zurich)
E________	Continent located on (Europe)
R______	Inland waterway (Rhine)
L________	Peace-loving organization which met here (League of Nations)
A____	Mountains (Alps)
N__________	Position during war (Neutral)
D______	Ski center (Davos)

You can supply the first letters as shown here to reveal the theme of the puzzle or let the students discover the hidden word. Encourage students to consult maps and reference books as they search for the answers. They can also construct Acrostics.

Using reference books

Games can increase interest and knowledge of reference books. Students are amazed to discover what a wealth of fascinating information lies within the covers of the *World Almanac*. THE ABC'S OF U.S. CITIES will lead students to the almanac, gazetteer, atlas, and textbook index. Each is to supply a city (and state or country) for each letter of the alphabet insofar as possible. Lists will vary, so comparison is interesting. Here is one example:

Akron, Ohio
Boston, Mass.
Charlotte, N.C.
Denver, Colo.
Erie, Penn.
Flagstaff, Ariz.

Newark, N.J.
Omaha, Neb.
Portland, Me.
Quonset, R.I.
Reno, Nev.
Savannah, Ga.

Green Bay, Wis.	Tulsa, Okla.
Honolulu, Hawaii	Utica, N.Y.
Indianapolis, Ind.	Valley Forge, Penn.
Juneau, Alaska	Wichita, Kansas
Kalamazoo, Mich.	X (We don't know one, do you?)
Laramie, Wyo.	Yakima, Wash.
Miami, Fla.	Zanesville, Ohio

After this list is completed have students locate these cities on a United States map. They can work as teams with one leader using all their lists from which to choose cities to be located. Students can also concoct ABC quizzes themselves, for this game is adaptable to any subject area.

Collections of social studies materials

A good type of independent activity is the collection of pictures and information about topics related to social studies activities. Able students who have time will especially enjoy compiling booklets of information about worthwhile topics as they explore them in depth. Topics that may be used include the following:

Animals That Help Us
Children in Other Lands
Transportation Today and Yesterday
Winter Ways
Living in the Desert
Houses Around the World
Life in the Jungle

Writing travel brochures

Students gain much information in an interesting way as they prepare Travel Posters or Brochures tempting the tourist to visit a certain country, city, or area. Students can pretend to be Advertising Agents for the locality selected as they explore various means for advertising the desirable aspects of a visit to CANADA, NEW MEXICO, ECUADOR, OR HONOLULU. They can send for sample advertising material by writing to the Chamber of Commerce for several cities.

When studying a country, obtain copies of local NEWSPAPERS from that country by requesting sample copies directly from the largest city. Write in advance as your request may require weeks; enclosing return postage may assist the filling of this request also. Newspapers from abroad are also sometimes available in our large cities.

Reporting exploration

As your class studies the exploration of the United States, have each student select one explorer—Marquette, Clark, Champlain, DeSoto—whose explorations he will investigate. Then, assuming the identity of the explorer, each student makes a report of his experiences in the form of letters to his superiors or a daily log kept during his trips. Entries might include:

> Today for the first time I saw the broad Mississippi River. What an impressive sight! Fortunately it is low at this season. We shall be able to cross it easily tomorrow.

State studies

When studying the United States, each student may select one state of the fifty for intensive study. He can collect material for a booklet which includes a wide variety of information. Encourage students to gather factual information about the size, population, capital, economy, and geographic features as well as information about the people who have originated in that state or who have been influential in its development. Encourage students also to share sources of information and to contribute findings which may be helpful to another student's project.

Students should read fiction as well as non-fiction, incorporating in the booklet brief reports on any reading done. They can draw appropriate maps, graphs, and illustrations and include clippings from newspapers and magazines. Booklets may be made in the shape of the state by cutting paper around an outline. This same type of study can be focused on cities of the world or the United States or on nations of the world as well as specific continents such as South America.

> **The Viewmaster can be used as an excellent device for encouraging interest in geography. Let students bring their viewers and slides which can be examined by students who finish other work. The poor reader can also learn much through this means.**

Sources of additional information

Here are titles you may wish to explore for further ideas:

Huus, Helen. *Children's Books to Enrich the Social Studies for the Elementary Grades.* (#49-832). National Council for the Social Studies, Washington, D.C. 20006.

National Geographic Society. Many titles. Washington, D.C. 20006. (Write for listing of publications.)

Tiedt, Sidney and Iris. *Imaginative Social Studies Activities for the Elementary School.* Prentice-Hall Education Series, 1964. ($1.50)

Examining World Affairs

As our world grows smaller through the rapidity of transportation and communication, it must at the same time grow larger as individuals reach out to meet and understand the peoples of other lands. Our thinking, our viewpoints, must expand to encompass a larger area than the town or even the state in which we live.

Students must become aware of the significance of our relationships with other countries, the need for understanding, and our dependence on each other for existence. They need to know what is happening in this world of here and now—in the state, in the nation, and in the world.

The weekly glossary

Each week prepare on a bulletin board reserved for this purpose a GLOSSARY OF THE NEWS. As students contribute information about events and people in the news, add any names, locations, and terms which should become familiar to the students. Identify each item included in the Glossary by noting its significance in current affairs:

> Charles de Gaulle– French President, faces new crisis
> Nigeria–African country, scene of tribal uprising

Personalities in the news

A team of able students can be responsible for featuring people in the news. They should clip pictures and articles from magazines and newspapers to tell about significant contributions of men and women in the news. Each student on the team may select one person to follow such as the President of the United States or the Prime Minister of England. At the end of a period of time each student could prepare a report on the activities of the person studied. Clippings can be compiled in a book entitled PERSONALITIES IN THE NEWS which can be used as a reference by the class.

Current events crossword

A review of current events can be presented in this puzzle form. The letters down the center of the puzzle spell out a headline which has been important during the past week or month. When constructing this type of puzzle, select the headline to be used first, printing those letters in position. Then work names of people, countries, and events into the puzzle as they fit. The headline used here is fictitious as it is impossible to present a current events puzzle which will continue to be *current*. This sample, however, will serve as a guide to students who can construct these puzzles. They will learn as much through constructing them (use the same frames as those used for crossword puzzles) as they do through working them.

1 Popular singer
2 U.S. national poet
3 New York governor
4 French President
5 Star of *Cleopatra*
6 Site of World's Fair
7 49th state
8 Largest state (pop.)
9 Astronaut
10 Assassinated President
11 "Cold War" hot spot
12 Republican candidate in 1964 election

Writing letters

Students who become interested in certain aspects of the news should be encouraged to write letters requesting information or commending the actions of some person in the news. If, for example, a student has been studying the work of the Supreme Court, he might write to one of the justices regarding a decision made on a case.

Encourage students to write to their Congressmen. These representatives of the people are glad to supply information about current affairs—new bills being considered, their opinions regarding certain issues, government printed pamphlets which are highly informative, and so on. They will certainly respond in some manner to letters of inquiry.

Broadcasting the news

The preparation of a news broadcast emphasizes the importance of studying current affairs. A news broadcast can be planned for your classroom each Friday with students alternating roles so that all participate. This newscast can also be presented to other classes; you may arrange to exchange broadcasts with another room. Use the *school address system* to broadcast a school-wide presentation of the news once each week including school news along with state, national, and world coverage.

Regular reviews of current affairs

At the end of each month feature a special bulletin board captioned IT HAPPENED IN OCTOBER (or any other month). Focus attention on those events which students judge to be of lasting significance. Include pictures clipped from newspapers and magazines as well as comments and brief analyses written by students. Encourage students to compare these events with preceding happenings and to predict what will happen next month.

Debating controversial subjects

Two teams of students can prepare arguments on both sides of a current issue. Issues of more immediate interest to young students can also be used to allow youngsters to air their opinions and to develop the habit of forming an opinion. Here are two suggested topics which are suitable for this type of presentation:

All children should go to school six days a week.
Students should learn a foreign language in first grade.

Themes in current affairs

Let students select specific topics or themes to follow in the news as it develops. Civil Rights, for example, provides many new developments of interest to the student. Have two investigation teams studying different aspects of this theme with one team of students collecting clippings illustrating CIVIL RIGHTS PROTECTS THE INDIVIDUAL while the other team collects material illustrating THE VIOLATION OF CIVIL RIGHTS.

Art and current events

Students can prepare a fascinating collage of clippings, pictures, symbols of events, portions of maps, colored paper scraps (for contrast), and materials suggesting geographic areas in the news (bamboo straws near article on China, for instance). As a class project this collage can be arranged on large mural paper with all students contributing time and material.

Individual collages can center around the activities of one person or position as well as a specific theme. Reading would provide background knowledge about the person or theme to suggest symbolic items to include. A De Gaulle collage, for example, might include a piece of a map of France or Paris, a drawn replica of De Gaulle's French military uniform, parts of different pictures clipped from periodicals, his name in various types of print, and articles about him.

Enrichment activities in current affairs

• Invite *foreign students* to visit your class to tell you about their countries. If there is a college or university near you, there are usually foreign students who can be contacted through the Student Personnel Office. Churches and other local organizations can often supply names of students or adults in the community who might speak to your class.

• Hold *Man on the Street interviews* asking the people who are interviewed some question of current interest. Interview students in your own room or conduct interviews in the school hall or lunchroom if this is practicable.

• Encourage students to bring *newspapers and news magazines* to school to place on the Reading Table. Permit students to read these materials during periods designated as Free Reading or when working on World Affairs projects. Let students discuss articles which happen to excite interest of several people. Let these students lead a class discussion or seminar on the topic presented.

• Will Rogers once said, "All I know is what I read in the papers." Let students *write short essays* on this quotation bringing out the pros and cons of "Should you believe everything you read?" or "How can news in print be misleading?"

• Collect a number of short articles clipped from magazines or newspapers. Remove the headlines. Pass these numbered articles around the class letting students *suggest headlines for each article*. Compare the headlines written for each article; compare student headlines with the one actually used in the periodical.

Materials to investigate for world affairs

There are a number of *student news magazines or papers* which can be purchased in class quantities for regular use in teaching current events or a single copy can be ordered for the reading table. One series of papers (for different reading levels) is offered by *My Weekly Reader,* 1250 Fairwood Ave., Columbus 16, Ohio.

Commercial news maps provide an interesting stimulus to student understanding of events in the news. You might wish to send for a sample copy of *World News of the Week* from:

News Map of the Week, Inc.
1515 Sedgwick Street
Chicago 10, Illinois

You might also be interested in receiving a publications list from this company:

Current Affairs Press
34 East 70th Street
New York 21, New York

Developing Good Citizenship

Great emphasis is presently being placed on the development of good citizenship, for we are becoming increasingly aware that the success of a democracy lies in an informed citizenry. Described here are techniques teachers have found effective when working with young people in the classroom.

National holidays and flag days

On each Flag Day (see the Teacher's Calendar at the end of Chapter 1) discuss with the students the reason for displaying our national flag on that day. Present some of the historical background of that date and the events connected with it. On Army Day (April 6), for example, a group of boys can present a resume of the development of the United States Army listing the functions of the Army today.

Democracy in action

Have students investigate democratic practices in the school. They can list all democratic practices in evidence and also compile a list of suggested changes which might help the school to become more democratic. They can make posters to enlist the aid of students in other classrooms in keeping the school and its grounds neat. School behavior in halls, auditorium, lunchroom, and playground may also be reviewed with suggestions for improvement.

Discussions of contemporary problems

Encourage students to think about contemporary problems and to discuss possible solutions. Local town problems can be examined with various opinions aired. Critical thinking should be stimulated, and students should begin to learn respect for the opinions of others. Question their opinions as to whether they are based on fact and careful thought.

Present topics for discussion or subjects for essays. Here are several you may wish to use:

1. What are the qualities of a good leader of society?
2. How do books, magazines, and newspapers protect our liberties?
3. Can Americans be considered a *minority group?*

Holding elections

Mock elections can be held when there is a presidential election or any local election. Students should discuss the issues playing a prominent part in the election with debates held on several of the more significant issues. Students can volunteer to cover the activities of specific men and women who are running for office. They can clip articles and report on radio and television coverage. Certain students can play the roles of those individuals who are running for office. Invite a nominee to speak to your class about some specific issue or about our election system in general.

On the Tuesday of the real election hold an election (perhaps for the whole school) with duplicated ballots and booths constructed of frames hung with cloth. Have students check the voters' registration list and sign their names properly. After the polls close let a group of students count the votes, tallying the results.

Investigate the activities of the governments

Students often have only a vague concept of the workings of the city, state, and national governments. They can outline the activities of the federal government as well as those of the state government to discover the differing areas of responsibility. Have them visit local offices where possible to see what is being done.

Another way of obtaining information about government functions is to write for information from the different offices or branches of government. As mentioned previously, students can request information from their Congressmen. They can write to the head of the Peace Corps, the United States Department of Justice, the Office of Education (all addresses: Washington, D.C.). The U.S. Government Printing Office at the same address will provide a listing of publications which are very inexpensive such as "The American Ambassador" for ten cents and "The Foreign Service of the United States" for 25 cents.

Writing essays

Sometimes we take for granted words and their meanings. Do we really know what words like CITIZENSHIP and FREEDOM mean? Have students take time to think about these important words as they write essays on the following topics:

CITIZENSHIP is . . . .
FREEDOM is . . . .
DEMOCRACY is . . . .
THE UNITED STATES is . . . . . .
LIBERTY is . . . .

Words of famous men

Focus attention on the words of famous patriots of our country, men who played an important part in the development of the United States. Display these quotations on the board with the caption—WHO SAID IT AND WHEN?

He has a right to criticize who has a heart to help.

—*Abraham Lincoln*

I would rather be right than President.

—Henry Clay

Ask not what your country can do for you; ask what you can do for your country.

—John F. Kennedy

I know of no way of judging the future but by the past.

—Patrick Henry

I regret that I have but one life to lose for my country.

—Nathan Hale

Every great advance in science has issued from a new audacity of imagination.

—*John Dewey*

7

SCIENCE AND INQUIRY

Many of the scientific facts which we presently teach may soon be outmoded. It is essential, therefore, that we emphasize science as a way of knowing, a way of discovering. Described in this chapter are suggestions for encouraging the curiosity of students and stimulating the inquiring mind. Included, too, are ideas for providing specific information about the men, materials, and concepts of science.

Developing Critical Thinking

Using films

Show a science film without turning on the sound. Let students observe the demonstration of an experiment to see what they can gather by sight and their own thinking. After the film is completed have the class discuss the demonstration to see what conclusions they can draw without anyone's telling them the reasons for the outcome of the experiment. You may permit students to ask questions which require YES or NO answers. After the discussion show the film with the sound turned on so students can determine the correctness of their thinking.

"Single Concept" films are being developed especially in the science areas. These short films focus on one idea, one concept, and avoid the distractions of a more complex film subject.

Thought-provoking problems

Numerous problems in logic or clear thinking exist which intrigue students and serve to stimulate thought. Here are several familiar examples with *one plausible answer* given:

★ Three men were fishing from the bank of a river. Across the river a gun was fired. The first man saw the smoke; the second saw the bullet strike a tree before him; the third heard the report of the gun. Who first knew the bullet was fired?
(1—sight or speed of light; 2—sound; 3—bullet flight)

★ A farmer has to cross a river in a boat that can carry only 2 things at one time. He has a fox, a goose, and a sack of grain. If he leaves the fox and the goose together, the fox will eat the goose. If the goose is left with the grain, the goose will eat the grain. How can he manage to get everything safely across the river?

Trip 1: Farmer and goose .... GOOSE
Farmer returns alone.
Trip 2: Farmer and fox .... FOX
Farmer and goose return together.
Trip 3: Farmer and grain .... FOX and GRAIN
Farmer returns alone to get goose.

★ Every weekday John Dunn goes to work in a twenty-five floor office building. Each morning he gets in the elevator, presses the button marked 19, rides to the 19th floor, and then walks up the stairs to his office on the 23rd floor. At night he enters the elevator on the 23rd floor and rides down to the lobby. Why does he ride only to the 19th floor in the morning?
One Answer: John Dunn is a short man who can reach only as high as the 19th button on the operating panel of the Self-Service Elevator. At night, however, he can easily reach the button for the Lobby.

12	25
11	24
10	23
9	22
8	21
7	20
6	19
5	18
4	17
3	16
2	15
1	14
L	13

TAKE TIME TO ANSWER

As a teacher, never be afraid to say, "I don't know." Do follow this answer up, however, with the words, "Let's find out."

Accepting information without thinking

• Have students write short essays about what would happen if they accepted everything they read or heard as the TRUTH. They would follow the commands of every advertiser, accept the advice of everyone they met, and believe every superstition.

• Encourage students to question "facts" presented by other students and the teacher. Insist on facts, not just generalizations. Ask the questions, "Where is your data?" or "Can you prove that statement?" Develop the habit of "looking it up" in reliable reference books. Make students constantly aware of the usefulness of books like encyclopedias, almanacs, atlases, and dictionaries to substantiate their arguments.

• Investigate propaganda devices—begging the question, glittering generalities, colored words, and so on. Alert students to watch for examples of these devices in advertising. Have them try writing "slanted" material as they attempt to "sell" an idea or product.

Problem solving

Students can early begin to think about problem solving. They can learn to attack problems, to organize their thinking, to explore possible solutions. Young students can discuss problems which are of immediate importance to them as individuals. Present, for example, one of the following questions for discussion: "If you become separated from your mother in a large crowd, what should you do?" "Why should you go straight home from school?" "If the child across the street became very ill, how could you help?"

Older students can become conscious of problems of broader significance as they investigate some of the following broad problem areas:

Living on the Moon
Providing Food for Interspace Travel
The Replacement of Manpower by Automation
Increased Longevity
Living Peacefully with Other Nations

List on the board the many aspects of the problem to be considered. In discussing automation, for example, students might begin by a general discussion of the meaning of automation, how it affects individuals, where it occurs, how it affects society in general. They can also list possible solutions to the problems involved. Students may find that they need to read in order to discuss this problem more intelligently. Some students may investigate articles reporting their findings to the class.

Testing for learning

Test before teaching. This is a good rule at any time, for then we can begin where the children are and proceed from there. Before beginning a study of mammals, for instance, construct a brief test consisting perhaps of 15 True or False items. Check the answers to guide you in your presentation of information.

After the study has been completed give the students the same test again. Let them compare the answers they gave on the two tests. Where answers differ, ask them to write a reason for changing their answers.

Critical thinking

★ Use the following excerpt from Lewis Carroll's *Alice in Wonderland* to initiate a discussion:

> "You should say what you mean," the March Hare went on.
>
> "I do," Alice hastily replied; "at least—at least I mean what I say —that's the same thing, you know."
>
> "Not the same thing a bit!" said the Hatter. "Why, you might just as well say that 'I see what I eat' is the same as 'I eat what I see'!"

★ Write this group of statements on the board to test students' abilities in thinking:

1 All mosquitoes are insects.
2 All insects are mosquitoes.
3 Some insects are mosquitoes.
4 Some insects are not mosquitoes.

Which pair of statements may both be False, but cannot both be True? (2 is false and 4 may be, but both cannot be True.)

Which statements are True? (1, 3, 4)

Which pair of statements might both be True, but cannot both be False? (3 and 4 can be True, but both cannot be False.)

★ Write a statement on the board which was made by ancient men who "knew" they were right. Discuss the reasoning of the man who made this statement, for example: "Man will never fly."

★ Present a sealed box containing an unknown object (something a little unusual). What is in the box? Pass it around the room allowing children to shake it, weigh it, and so on. Record any guesses on the board. Then erase any guesses which are too heavy, too big, could not make the appropriate noise, and so forth. After the box is opened discuss those answers which might have been correct.

Critical reading

Students should become aware that everything they read is not necessarily true. They should realize that there are varied points of view on almost any topic—politics, religion, civil rights, and so forth. They should learn to understand, to recognize the existence of other views although they do not necessarily agree with these views. Have them read, if possible, articles or books demonstrating different viewpoints on the same subject.

As they read in science, students need also to notice the copyright date of the material read, for an old copyright date will often indicate information is out-of-date and therefore, of questionable validity. They need to know, too, that more up-to-date information can often be found in magazines and newspapers because of the slowness of the publishing process for books. Also to be considered are the qualifications of the author who is writing.

Illustrations of poor thinking

Have students write stories about the results of misguided or inaccurate thinking. Although their stories will in many cases present humorous, fictional results, these stories will focus attention on the need for more attention to details, to directions given, to the meaning of words, and to careful observation.

Collect illustrations (stories, anecdotes, clippings) of instances in which scientific thinking was not used—jumping to conclusions, refusal to accept proven data, and so forth. Items of this sort provide material for excellent discussions.

Encouraging questions

Encourage students to question results, to ask, "Why does something happen?" Maintain a QUESTION BOX in which any student can place a question. Once each week have a discussion period during which any questions in the BOX are removed and presented for class discussion and possible solution. Discuss the ways of finding required answers—books, letters to resource people, telephone calls to local experts, a reference librarian. Encourage students in their efforts to discover the answers through experimentation in school or at home.

Accuracy of reporting

Emphasize the need for careful observation in science (as well as other areas). Provide practice in observing by some of the following activities:

> Arrange on a tray a collection of many (30 or more) small articles—pin, nail, thumbtack, string, eraser, pencil, rock, card, book, rubber band, paper clip, flower, chalk, marble, and so on. Place the tray on a table around which the class can circle to look carefully at the items included. After a period of three minutes remove the tray from sight and ask each child to list every item he can. When all have completed their lists, compare the number of items listed. Then compare the lists with the contents of the tray. You may wish to repeat this activity.

Read the familiar old poem about "Six Men of Indostan" to your class to illustrate individual differences which influence our reporting ability.

The Blind Men and the Elephant

There were six men of Indostan
To learning much inclined,
Who went to see the elephant
(Though all of them were blind),
That each by observation
Might satisfy his mind.

The first approached the elephant,
And, happening to fall
Against his broad and sturdy side,
At once began to bawl,
"God bless me! but the elephant
Is very like a wall!"

The second feeling of the tusk
Cried: "Ho! what have we here
So very round and smooth and sharp?
To me 'tis mighty clear
This wonder of an elephant
Is very like a spear!"

The third approached the animal,
And, happening to take
The squirming trunk within his hands,
Thus boldly up and spake:
"I see," quoth he, "the elephant,
Is very like a snake!"

The fourth reached out his eager hand,
And felt about the knee;
"What most this wondrous beast is like
Is mighty plain," quoth he;
" 'Tis clear enough the elephant
Is very like a tree."

The fifth who chanced to touch the ear,
Said: "E'en the blindest man
Can tell what this resembles most
Deny the fact who can,
This marvel of an elephant
Is very like a fan!"

The sixth no sooner had begun
About the beast to grope,
Than, seizing on the swinging tail
That fell within his scope,
"I see," quoth he, "the elephant
Is very like a rope!"

And so these men of Indostan
Disputed loud and long,
Each in his own opinion
Exceeding stiff and strong,
Though each was partly in the right,
And all were in the wrong!

So, oft in theologic wars
The disputants, I ween,
Rail on in utter ignorance
Of what each other mean,
And prate about an elephant
Not one of them has seen!

—John G. Saxe

Scientific Activities

In this section are included a selected group of interesting activities which can be part of any classroom. The activities are those which will encourage investigation and inquiry.

Inventing

A creative approach to the teaching of science will encourage students to consider the needs of society and to invent machines to fill that need. Small models of the invention can be made or the invention can be drawn on paper. A written description should accompany the model or drawing which is presented to the class. Those students who demonstrate particular interest in this idea should be encouraged to develop it independently. Students will be intrigued, too, by hearing of inventions which never worked or ones which have long since become antiquated as other machines were invented.

A good way to introduce this activity is through the reading of Robert McCloskey's story "The Doughnut Machine" which is included in *Homer Price* (Viking). This story relates Homer's adventures revolving around a new invention which made doughnuts automatically.

The Science Center

Designate a table or a set of book shelves as the SCIENCE CENTER where materials can be displayed. Encourage students to investigate the use of magnets, to examine a collection on display, to observe the animals in a balanced aquarium and to discuss their findings or observations as well as their questions.

Feature books related to material on display or to a class study. If, for example, the class is studying birds, mount bird pictures on the nearby bulletin board and display books about birds. Let students use pictures to learn to identify the birds, particularly those common in your area. Suggest related writing activities which may be done voluntarily—poetry about birds, puzzles which describe birds, nature stories involving birds.

A small viewer for slides or a Viewmaster is an excellent addition to the Science Center. A miscroscope can also be set up so students can examine slides. A miscellany of science equipment—magnifying glass, magnets, batteries, wire—should be available for use individually or as a class. Encourage class members to share science materials they have at home.

> **To prevent breakage mount your microscope on a wide heavy piece of wood.**

The Science Fair

Motivate interest in science by initiating a SCIENCE FAIR in your school. Announce the fair several months in advance so that students who wish to enter will have ample time to plan their entries and to complete any experiments. As part of the announcement, you can explain the purpose of the fair to the parents, list any regulations regarding participation, and suggest suitable types of entries. Areas which students can explore independently for this activity include: plant growth, collections of rocks, leaves, shells, seeds, electricity, magnetism, nutrition, and so on.

Each student who wishes to enter the fair should complete (before a stated deadline) a simple form stating the type of exhibit or experiment he plans; filing this form gives the school some idea of the number of participants to expect, and it also provides impetus to the student who makes up his mind and gets started on the project.

The fair should be held on Saturday so parents can attend as there is usually much interest on the part of fathers. Each student participating should be present to demonstrate or explain his exhibit as those attending the Science Fair view it. Judges can be selected to award ribbons or certificates (every entry should receive some mark of recognition). If prizes are awarded, books in the science area might be considered.

Collections

If a student has an interesting collection of rocks, for example, ask him to bring it to school, for this type of interest can lead to a rewarding study for the entire class. Display this collection with library books on the subject. Have other students bring any samples they may have also even if it is only a single rock specimen. Have students print signs with a felt pen, identifying any objects displayed. A collection can be displayed on a table below a bulletin board which shows pictures and articles about the same subject.

The Science Club

An exciting club for intermediate students is the science club which can be named by its members—THE CATALYZERS, FUTURE SCIENTISTS, EXPERIMENTS, INC.—to add interest to the idea of a club. Meetings can be held once or twice a month after school or on Saturday with a teacher or parent as sponsor.

Each meeting can focus on a specific type of information as the group explores an area that interests them—LOCAL FLORA AND FAUNA, GEOLOGY OF OUR AREA, MAGNETISM, WEATHER, SCIENCE AROUND OUR HOME, HOW ELECTRICITY HELPS US. Local experts can be invited to share their knowledge; films and filmstrips can be used; students can experiment; field trips can be arranged. Meetings should maintain an informal atmosphere; yet, they need to be well-planned. Students should be responsible for much of the planning and organizing for a successful meeting with every student attending feeling himself a part of the group. For information about Science Clubs write:

Science Clubs of America
1719 N Street, N.W.
Washington 6, D.C.

The gifted child and science

There are a number of ways for stimulating the gifted child's interest in science. Encourage the able student to:

★ Teach the class a science lesson. He can, for example, set up an experiment to demonstrate to the class. He can explain the processes involved and answer any questions.

★ Investigate the biography of a well-known scientist. Collect clippings about the person studied. Read books and articles to prepare a booklet which the class can use as reference material in the Science Center. The booklet can include illustrations, a time line of the scientist's life, a chart explaining the discoveries of this person. There are many possibilities as subjects for this study—Henri Becquerel, Marie Curie, Hans Geiger, Harold Urey, Albert Einstein, and so on.

★ Make a sundial for the school (or other similar project). Before beginning the construction the student should read about sundials to explore the possibilities of the project. A reliable source of information on this particular project is available from:

U.S. Govt. Printing Office. Circular of the Bureau of Standards, No. 402. *Sundials.* (5 cents) Washington, D.C. 20402.

★ Scientific studies can focus on any area which interests the student. A young student might observe the movements of the sun over a period of time compiling graphs and charts to record his findings. This study might include, for instance, the measurement of the length of the shadow of the flagpole every day at a certain time. The changing position of the sun might be recorded by diagramming the position of the shadow each day. Records of sunrise and sunset times can also be included.

★ An older student might experiment with natural vegetable dyes to determine what colors can be obtained by the use of leaves, roots, bark, and so on. He can compare the results of any local plant materials such as elderberry bushes, onions, carrots, beets, pokeberry bushes. As he experiments, he can save a sample of muslin dyed with different types of juices to be mounted on pages in a report.

★ Another student interested in astronomy might develop a helpful set of 35 mm. slides showing the different constellations. Holes are pricked in used film to simulate the stars. Each constellation is studied, the slide is prepared and labeled, and a card is prepared containing the story of the constellation to accompany each slide.

Independent research

Students of all abilities can learn the techniques of scientific research. They should learn to produce a Research Outline using the correct terminology. Listed here are the essential elements of the Research Outline:

> Selection and Identification of the Problem: One sentence statement of what you plan to study.
>
> Hypothesis: Your guess of the results of your study.
>
> Collection of Data: Getting the information or facts to prove or disprove your hypothesis. What method will be used?
>
> Analysis of Data: Deciding what you have collected and what it means.
>
> Findings: Statement of the results of the study. Was the hypothesis right or wrong?
>
> Implications: What was the importance of this study?

Topics which are suitable for the young researcher are many and varied. Suggested here is a sampling:

> Speed of cars passing the school
> The most commonly planted trees in the neighborhood
> Are boys absent more than girls?

Favorite television programs
The germination periods of various seeds
Favorite colors, foods, school subjects
Opinion polls; interviews

Games featuring science

Information about science can be featured in games which use this information. Students respond to these activities with enthusiasm and learn a surprising amount of factual knowledge. Use these activities during indoor recesses or as party activities:

ANIMAL, BIRD, OR FISH is a familiar game which requires students to identify birds, animals, and fish as they are named by the leader. The leader points to one person, names, for example, GNU, and begins counting from 1 to 10. The person indicated must quickly say, ANIMAL, before the number 10 is spoken. If unsuccessful, this person becomes the Leader. Variations of this game include: ANIMAL, VEGETABLE, MINERAL.

CATEGORIES is a paper and pencil game which can be used at any time with each student finding the answers independently. A category chart may be based on the word SCIENCE.

	ANIMALS	INVENTORS	FLOWERS
S	snake		
C	cat		
I			
E			
N			
C			
E			

This activity can be varied by using a different word down the left side such as: BOTANY, ELECTRONICS, WEATHER, HEALTH,

MAGNETISM. Different categories can also be designated across the top: TREES, INVENTIONS, FOODS, FRUITS, VEGETABLES.

CARD GAMES can be developed by students who prepare sets of cards featuring science information. A card game can be prepared in sets of two with the players matching INVENTORS and INVENTIONS, pairs of ANIMALS, pairs of FISH, and so on. This game would be played like *Old Maid* with each player trying to get rid of the Odd Card.

Card games can also consist of sets of four such as four different MAMMALS, REPTILES, BIRDS, INVENTIONS, SCIENTISTS, TREES, VEGETABLES, ROCKS, and so forth. This game is played like *Fish* in which each player tries to accumulate sets of four which are then laid down. The player with the largest number of groups accumulated wins.

Science and the bulletin board

Topics in science can often be featured in bulletin board displays which stimulate the interest of students. A display of pictures and articles can serve as an effective means for introducing a new area of study. These specific suggestions will help you.

WHO HAS SEEN THE WIND? makes a good caption for a display featuring the effects of the wind—movements of trees, water, storms. Have students copy several poems such as Robert Louis Stevenson's "The Wind" and Christina Rossetti's poem which begins, "Who has seen the wind?" This topic offers students an opportunity to write original poetry and stories that illustrate wind effects.

ANIMAL, VEGETABLE, MINERAL is a caption which can accompany a group of pictures clipped from magazines—various animals, plants, and rocks plus items more difficult to identify such as a table, book, hammer, pencil, box, glass, and so on. Provide cut paper letters (A, V, M) which students can pin on each picture as they try to correctly identify the item pictured. Discuss the correct classifications.

PILOT TO NAVIGATOR focuses student attention on material about flying. Display pictures illustrating the principles of flight or a collection of pictures of different types of aircraft. Below the bulletin board feature books about this topic on a table or cart.

An excellent source of free pictures and information about flight is the following:

United Air Lines
Educational Services
5959 So. Cicero Ave.
Chicago 38, Illinois

CURRENT NEWS can introduce students to the topic of electricity. Use a length of electrical wire to form the letters of the caption and to guide the eye around the bulletin board. On a table below the board have students display electrical magnets or any other electrical connections they have learned to make.

DOWN TO EARTH is a caption for the study of planets, rocks, surface features, soil erosion, and so on. Combine pictures or reports with examples of rocks brought in by students as well as reference books from the school library.

Let students prepare displays of this nature which can be based on an article brought in by a student, a topic introduced by the science textbook, or a subject currently appearing in the news. For other suggestions on the use of the bulletin board refer to Chapter One.

Relating Science to Other Areas

Science information can be used in other curriculum areas to stimulate interest in both areas of study. Suggested here are various projects which provide for the correlation of science with another subject area.

Library research

Research can often bring together interests in the social studies with that of science as well as language arts. THE EVOLUTION OF AN INVENTION can be the topic studied as students search for information about the developments leading to jet air travel, modern photography, or the sewing machine. Students will need to read about the people involved in the development of this invention and should search for pertinent magazine articles or newspaper commentaries. Each student will develop a booklet including information collected, illustrations, charts, and a short bibliography.

SUPERSTITIONS IN OUR SOCIETY is another topic which can be studied perhaps by more able students who can conduct their research independently preparing a report for the class. Have them investigate superstitions which involve scientific information such as: "A ring around the moon at night foretells rain" or "Rain before seven; clear before eleven."

Words in science

• Words can be featured on the bulletin board or collected in a class DICTIONARY OF SCIENCE WORDS. Students can draw pictures to illustrate the definitions of words which they discover in their texts, news articles, or science magazines. Magazine clippings can be included on the page to illustrate each word. An excellent book in this area is Isaac Asimov's *Words of Science* (Houghton Mifflin).

• *Alert students to new words* which are constantly appearing in developing areas of science. Two new words in electronics, for example, include: LASER and MASER. These words derive their names from the words which define their meanings thus:

LASER: Lightwave, Amplification by, Stimulated, Emission of, Radiation

MASER: Microwave, Amplification by, Stimulated, Emission of, Radiation

• Booklets can be developed by teams of class members on words in specific areas of science. WEATHER WORDS would include such words as:

Wind Vane	Cumulus	Radiosonde
Anemometer	Nimbus	Hygrometer
Barometer	Cirrus	Humidity

Other booklets might be developed in the same way for: GEOLOGY, ELECTRICITY, ASTRONOMY, HUMAN GROWTH, FOODS, MACHINES.

• List words expressing "Scientific Feeling." Rocks, for example, can be described as rough, hard, granular, soft, smooth, slippery.

Reading and science

Encourage students to read good science fiction which can promote their general interest in scientific subjects. There are many reputable authors who are producing acceptable fiction which should be in the school library. Recommended authors are:

Ray Bradbury	H. G. Wells	Rod Serling
Andre Norton	Isaac Asimov	Poul Anderson
Robert Heinlein	Arthur C. Clarke	Alan Nourse

The reading of nonfiction in science is almost as fascinating as any fiction. Encourage this type of reading through science magazines (included in the list of sources for the teacher at the end of this chapter). When the class is studying a specific subject, bring appropriate books to the classroom for reading and for reference. Biographies of famous people in fields of science make excellent reading—Einstein, Curie, Carver, and many others.

Art and sciences

- Study the mixture of colors by shining light through combinations of cellophane. Discuss the rainbow spectrum with the use of a prism to produce this spectrum. How does the mixing of paint differ from the mixing of *light* colors?
- Focus on the identification of leaves as they are gathered in the fall. Press the brightly colored leaves until thoroughly dry; then mount each leaf on black construction paper which is cut out leaving a black edge to frame each leaf. Scatter these leaves over a bulletin board or arrange them on a paper tree shape.
- At Christmas time arrange a display of evergreen boughs to decorate the room while at the same time assisting students in learning to identify the varieties of evergreens—pines, firs, hemlock, and others typical in your locale.
- Make mobiles with each mobile featuring varied types of animals—Mammals, Fish, Birds, Extinct Animals, Insects, Reptiles, Animals from South America, Animals in Our State, Farm Animals, Animals That Give Us Food, and so on. Each student can use a combination of materials—figures clipped from magazines and mounted on stiff paper, animals drawn on stiff paper, small light-

weight animals of papier-mâché, items associated with the animals on the mobile (foods they eat, their native habitat, etc.), and other decorative additions of colored paper, plastic, or metal.

• Construct three dimensional posters about the area of science being studied—BIRDS, MACHINES, ANIMALS, FOODS, and so on. Each student selects one bird, for example, which he will feature on a poster. Using rolled paper as a base he makes a papier-mâché figure of the bird, perhaps, an oriole, painting the oriole with tempera according to colors used in a reference book. Before fastening the bird on stiff poster board the student plans an appropriate background for that particular bird—branches of a tree, a nest, and so on. He may also include some lettering—the name of the bird, a short poem about this bird, or facts about the bird's habits. To add to the three dimensional effect berries, seeds, or grains which the bird eats may be glued to the background as can grass and twigs, a real feather, or a piece of string for a nest.

• Buy blueprint paper. Cut it into squares (in a darkened room). Store the paper in a heavy manila folder until used. Arrange flowers, leaves, designs, string, and so on in a pleasing arrangement on a piece of paper. After the arrangement is planned transfer it (in darkened room) to the blueprint paper. Then expose the arrangement to the sun for approximately 5 minutes. Wash the paper twice in clear water; dry it flat under weight before framing.

Sources for the Teacher

Included in this annotated list are recommended books and other materials which we feel would be helpful to the classroom teacher in working with science. Of special interest are books of experiments which are planned for classroom use.

General books and pamphlets

Blough, Glenn O. and Paul E. Blackwood. *Teaching Elementary Science;* Suggestions for Classroom Teachers. U.S. Dept. of Health, Education, and Welfare. U.S. Govt. Printing Office, 1960. (20¢)

Helpful pamphlet discussing the teaching of science; contains bibliography of other books.

Moore, Shirley and Judith Viorst, eds. *Wonderful World of Science.* Bantam Books, 1961 (50¢)

List of free and inexpensive materials available that year.

Office of Education. *Science Books for Boys and Girls.* U.S. Govt. Printing Office.

Excellent listing of materials recommended for school purchase.

Ruchlis, H. *Discovering Scientific Method with Science Puzzle Pictures.* Harper & Row, 1963.

Varied approaches to the teaching of scientific thinking.

Science Clubs of America. *Science Projects Handbook.* 1719 N Street, N.W. Washington 6, D.C. (50¢)

Science projects and experiments.

World Almanac. New York World-Telegram and The Sun.

Annual reference available in paperback; up-to-date.

Zim, Herbert. Many titles such as *Insects, Rocks and Minerals.* Simon & Schuster.

Compact little reference books especially good for young people.

Catalogs and listings

You may wish to be placed on the mailing list of some of these groups or request their latest catalog so that you will be informed about new materials.

Allyn & Bacon, Inc. 150 Tremont Street, Boston 11, Mass.

Free Newsletter, *Science News.*

American Assn. for the Advancement of Science. 1515 Massachusetts Avenue, N.W., Washington 5, D.C.

Ask for listing of publications.

Benefic Press. 1900 N. Narragansett Ave., Chicago 39, Illinois.

Easy materials in science; publication list.

National Audubon Society, Conservation Resource Center. 2426 Bancroft Way, Berkeley 4, California.

Request listing of materials available.

National Science Teachers Association. 1201 Sixteenth Street, N.W., Washington, D.C.

Ask to be placed on mailing list for announcements and publication lists.

Science Clubs of America. 1719 N Street, N.W., Washington 6, D.C.

Request publications list.

Science Materials Center. 59 Fourth Avenue, New York, New York.
Request publications list.

U.S. Government Printing Office. Division of Public Documents. Washington, D.C. 20402.
Many inexpensive pamphlets related to science; ask to be placed on mailing list for regular listings of publications.

Experiments in science

Listed here are a number of recommended books which describe science experiments suitable for study in the elementary school. Several of these collections of experiments should be purchased for the professional library in your school or added to the school library.

Arey, Charles K. *Science Experiences for Elementary Schools.* Teachers College, Columbia University.

Baer, Marian. *Sound: an Experiment Book.* Holiday.

Freeman, Mae and Ira Freeman. *Fun with Chemistry.* Random House.

_________. *Fun with Science.* Random House.

_________. *Fun with Scientific Experiments.* Random House.

Horning, John L. and George McGinnis. *An Open Door to Chemistry.* Appleton-Century.

Milgrom, Harry. *Explorations in Science: A Book of Basic Experiments.* Dutton.

Morgan, Alfred. *First Chemistry Book for Boys and Girls.* Scribner.

Schneider, Herman and Nina Schneider. *Let's Find Out.* Scott.

Sharp, Elizabeth. *Simple Machines and How They Work.* Random House.

UNESCO. *700 Experiments for Everyone.* Doubleday.

_________. *Sourcebook for Science Teaching.* UNESCO Publications Center, 317 East 34th Street, New York, N.Y. 10016.

Yates, Raymond. *The Boy's Book of Magnetism.* Harper.

Magazines for young people

There are a number of excellent magazines which feature science topics. These magazines are recommended for your central school library or you may subscribe to several for use in your classroom *Science Center*. Listed here are addresses to assist you in requesting sample copies and subscription information.

American Forests. 919 17th St., N.W., Washington 6, D.C.
Analog. Conde Nast Publications, 420 Lexington Ave., New York 17, N.Y.
Boy's Life. New Brunswick, New Jersey.
Junior Natural History. 79th and Central Park West, New York 24, N.Y.
National Geographic. 16th and M. Sts., N.W., Washington 6, D.C.
Natural History. 79th and Central Park West, New York 24, N.Y.
Popular Mechanics Magazine. Popular Mechanics Co., 200 E. Ontario St., Chicago 11, Illinois.
Science Digest. 200 E. Ontario St., Chicago 11, Illinois.
Science Newsletter. 1719 N Street, N.W., Washington 6, D.C.
Scientific American. 415 Madison Ave., New York 17, N.Y.
Sky and Telescope. Sky Publishing Co., Harvard College Observatory, Cambridge 38, Mass.

Creation is the artist's true function. Where there is no creation, there is no art.

—*Henri Matisse*

8

CREATIVE WAYS WITH ART

Described in this chapter are suggestions for exploring the many media of art with young people as they enjoy classroom experiences with color, imagination, texture, construction, appreciation, design, and arrangement. Included, too, are many ideas for relating art to other subject areas and suggestions appropriate to the seasons and holidays.

Art techniques enhance studies in other areas of the curriculum. You can relate art to all other subject areas as you construct models, compile booklets, illustrate stories, paint murals, decorate bookmarks, make collages, and sculpture animals. By all means correlate art with language arts, with social studies, with science—*correlate, but don't squeeze the life out of the art techniques used.* To justify the term *art* the experience should consist of exciting, creative approaches to art resulting in a satisfying, artful production which in this case happens to add to the understandings in another subject area.

Exploring a Variety of Media

There is an increasing variety of media available to the amateur in art—crayons, watercolors, oil, chalk, charcoal, enamels, papers, and on and on. The surprises lie, however, in the challenging techniques used with these media. The modern artist has experimented with mixing these media to produce creative effects which can be introduced to the young artist. The joy of these techniques is that *everyone can succeed!* Every child can produce an attractive contrast or mixture of colors; every child can produce an interesting design or study in texture. All are not equally artistic in the eyes of the professional artist, but all are satisfying art experiences for the young experimenter.

In this section we shall attempt to explore a variety of media using less common techniques which are very enjoyable and effective. It is impossible to exhaust the supply of ideas along these lines, but it is our intent to suggest ideas which will in turn suggest additional ideas to you. *You experiment, too,* as we explore these media together.

Crayon

The use of crayons is nothing new to the elementary school classroom. Let us attempt, however, to discover new ways of using crayons to stimulate interest in artistic efforts.

DESIGNS are effective in crayon which produces bright glossy colors contrasted with soft blurred colors. Encourage students to use their crayons in different ways—on the side, with pecking motions, lines of color, and so on. Use these techniques in developing the following designs:

- Each student is to select three lines all of which are different; draw a variety of lines on the board from which students can choose. The student is directed to draw the three lines so that at least one line touches each edge of the paper. He then begins building on each line with colors and more lines until the entire sheet of paper is filled.
- A variation of the familiar Scribble Design is the WHIRLPOOL. Using a black crayon each student draws a whirlpool. In the crossing lines of the whirlpool the artist will see shapes which can be colored to resemble exotic tropical fish or other objects which might be caught in the whirlpool.
- Use a familiar object (canopener, pencil, spoon, cup) on

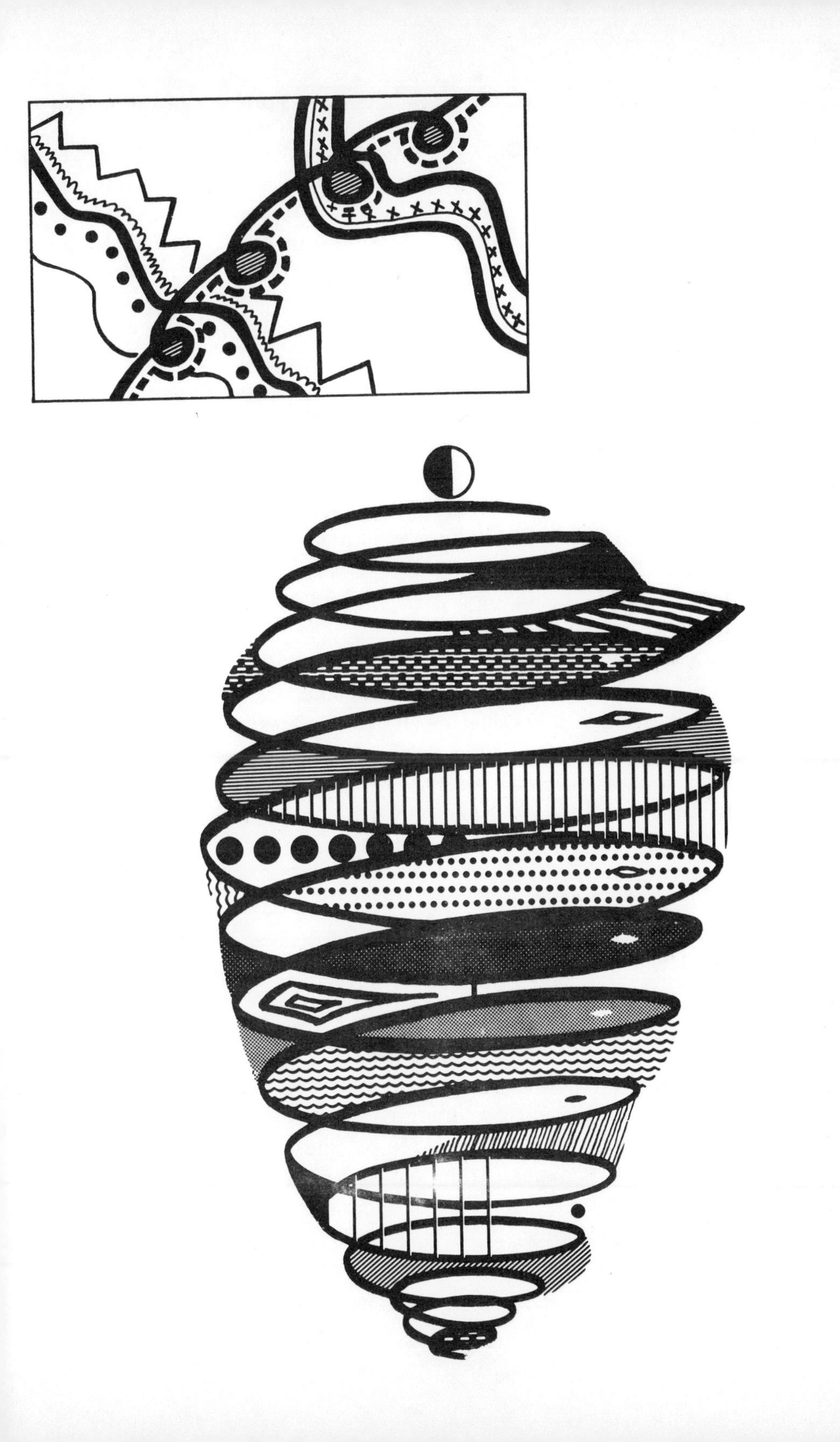

which to base a design. Draw around the object several times overlapping as desired. Develop color and decoration with crayon.

• Give each student two gummed reinforcements which he is to glue on the paper. He is to build a picture or design around these two white circles trying to produce something that no one else will produce.

> **An old window shade is a source of "canvas." Crayon a design on the shade; then paint with turpentine.**

Crayon resists are most effective. The technique calls for a picture or design made in crayon over which is painted a thin (1 part liquid tempera paint to about 5 parts water) wash of tempera. This technique is successful with any picture or design, but is especially good with the subject of an Underwater Scene. The student draws and colors with crayon a variety of animals and plantlife which might be seen under the ocean—fish, coral, octopus, seaweed, rocks, a sunken boat, a treasure. When the picture is complete, he applies a green or blue wash (or a mixture). Other subjects might be a scattering of flowers with a yellow wash, falling colored leaves with a brown wash, or a summer adventure with a blue wash.

> **Other media resistant to water paints which can be explored—rubber cement, wax or paraffin, hardened glue, varnish or shellac.**

Crayon etching is especially effective if the crayon is covered with thick black tempera. First the student's paper is covered with a coating of crayon applied in patches or streaks of color. The whole sheet of paper is then covered with the thick paint (any color can be used, but black is most common). After the paint has dried thoroughly a design or picture is produced by scratching away the painting to permit the colored crayon to show. Clown

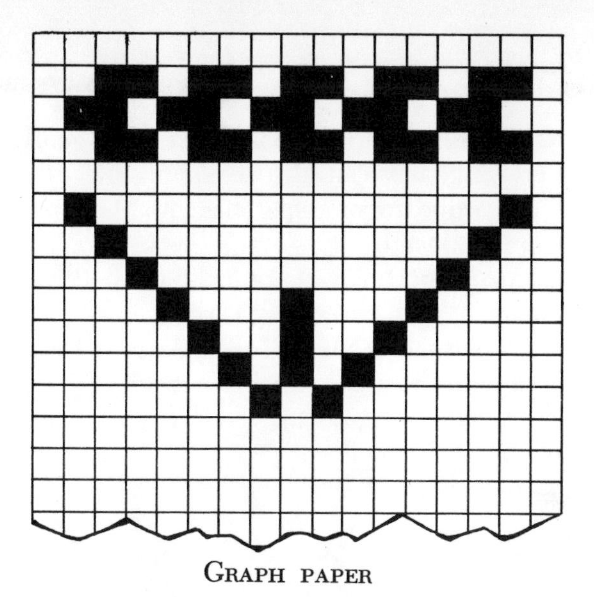

GRAPH PAPER

heads make good subjects as do large flowers, colored leaves, or toys.

BUTTERFEET are fun to make with each child tracing the outlines of his own two feet on a paper. The feet form the wings of the Butterfoot to which the artist adds a black body and antennae, and decorates the wings with bright colored designs. These insects can be cut out and mounted around the room. Decorate both sides of the wings if you wish to mount them just alighting.

GRAPH PAPER can be used to produce effects of weaving. Color blocks in patterns to simulate Indian or Mexican rugs. Color alternate blocks to produce an "over and under" design. Experiment with designs used in basketry or weaving—geometric, animals, human figures, and so on.

STAINED GLASS is made by melting bits of crayon between two layers of waxed paper. This lovely translucent paper can be used in stained glass windows or other transparencies which can be hung in the light or mounted on the window glass.

Place the crayon shavings between two large sheets of household waxed paper. Lay this paper between layers of newspaper which protect the warm iron as you press the paper to melt the crayon. Frame with black construction paper cut in teardrop shapes, large flowers, leaves, or geometric shapes.

PRINTS can be made quickly and easily by very young artists. Let students experiment as they place a sheet of paper over a variety of surfaces—screen, corrugated cardboard, burlap or other cloth, sandpaper, tile floor, corkboard—and rub gently with the side of the crayon. They can also try laying pieces of string or irregularly cut cardboard or paper beneath their papers to see what effects are produced.

STENCILS are interesting ways of making repetitive designs for greeting cards or a book cover. Begin with simple shapes appropriate to the season such as a heart for Valentine's Day. Encourage students to use both the piece which is cut out (Figure 1) and the stencil which remains (Figure 2). Overlap the shapes and vary colors to produce pleasing effects.

Figure 1 Figure 2

CRAYON ON CLOTH is an excellent method of producing designs for simple costuming or making flags for social studies units. Color heavily with the crayons and press the cloth from the reverse side to melt the crayon into the cloth. Attractive place mats, napkins, and guest towels can also be made in this way.

Water paints

Pans of inexpensive watercolors, tempera or poster paint can be utilized in many ways with striking results. Try a number of these techniques during the school year.

STRIPES OF COLOR are the result of an experiment in blending various colors. Using a very wet brush each student paints several wide stripes of paint horizontally across his paper. The paper is then turned in different ways to encourage its mixing with adjacent stripes. Water may be added by dropping it directly on the stripes.

Drops of color can be spooned on each student's paper in an irregular manner. Water should also be added to assist the color in moving freely. The student again tips the sheet in various ways to encourage the colors to mix and to produce interesting patterns and designs.

Blotto bugs come in multicolors, shapes, and sizes. Each student is given a large sheet of drawing paper. On the right half of the sheet are scattered a number of drops of paint (one color or several). The left half of the sheet is then folded over the right while the student presses the folded sheets gently to blot the paint. When the paper is unfolded (done immediately, before drying), a blotto bug will have been formed. Additional paint can be applied for a second folding, if desired. Feelers, antennae, eyes, and so on can be added.

Mixing Powder Paint: Measure 6 tbsps. water and 6 tbsps. powdered paint into small jar with lid. Cover tightly and shake.

Drawing string between folded paper produces unusual effects. Dip the cord in liquid tempera. Lay the wet string on the right side of a 12 x 18 inch piece of drawing paper. Fold the left side of the paper over the string. Holding the folded papers firmly (students may work in teams of two) withdraw the string, moving it back and forth as you pull from various angles. After the string has been removed unfold the paper. A string dipped in a different color may then be used in the same manner. This painting may be cut in half with each half in a matching frame to make a set of pictures which are reversals of each other (a very attractive gift for parents).

Wet paper and tempera combine to produce interesting blurred edges as students apply patches of color. Wet the paper (12 x 18) with a large sponge or paint brush. Limit the colors to perhaps blue and yellow, yellow and red, or red and blue. Drops of these colors are spattered from a full brush. When the sheet has tried thoroughly, India ink or black paint can be used to outline the resulting shapes. White areas can also be colored with black.

Variation 1: Make large flower shapes by blowing directly on spots of color with a straw. Stems and leaves can be added after this picture has dried.

Variation 2: After the tempera has dried thoroughly, drop India ink in several spots on the painted page letting the ink spread freely to form spider-like forms.

MARBLEIZED PAPER is made by wetting paper thoroughly and then painting it. Before the paper dries, it is crumpled and squeezed to remove excess water. Open the paper and flatten before allowing it to dry.

Variation: Crumple the paper first; then paint on it, allowing it to dry immediately. The color seeps into the cracks of the paper. These sheets can be ironed on the reverse side to smooth.

What to do with these experiments in paint?

1. Frame singly or in pairs with black construction paper.
2. Assemble on a bulletin board to form a KALEIDOSCOPE.
3. Use for booklet covers in social studies, language arts, and so on.
4. Mount side by side to form a large PATCHWORK QUILT MURAL. Cover joinings with strips of contrasting paper or colored rickrack.
5. Use as the front for greeting cards.
6. Cut the paper into strips for use as book markers.

SPONGE PAINTING is easy fun which produces interesting trees in the fall or spring. Cut out or paint a black tree shape with branching limbs to fit a background sheet of paper (pale brown for fall; blue for spring). For the brightly colored leaves of fall dip a small piece of sponge into red paint pressing the sponge over the limbs of the tree. Use another sponge to apply yellow and orange. For a blossoming tree in the spring use pink or white paint in the same way.

REFLECTIONS can be obtained by folding up one-third of the 12 x 18 inch paper while the painting is still wet. The paint will blot to form the effect of a reflection on the folded third.

SPRAYING PAINT can be done by using a small spray gun or a toothbrush which is rubbed over a piece of screen. Spray leaf shapes for an interesting collection of leaf prints which can be identified as a science project. Stencils can be sprayed to produce greeting cards or attractive booklet covers. Try a variety of materials to achieve interesting effects—screening, scattered pieces of paper, driftwood, or other objects such as bottle caps, lids, paper clips, and so on.

PAINT PRINTS enable the artist to repeat shapes to form a pleasing pattern or to duplicate the same design repeatedly. Prints can be made with a variety of materials such as the following:

Inner tubing cut in shapes, mounted on wood block
Cork mounted on wood
Sponge cut irregularly
Piece of wood carved
Potato sliced flat, then carved
Varied objects for "Gadget Printing"—bottle cap, fork, etc.
Crumpled waxed paper
Plasticene carved

Pour a small amount of thick tempera in a large lid or pie tin. Dip the block into the paint and then place it firmly on the paper to be printed. Repeat until the paint is used up; then dip the block in the paint again. Prints can be used to decorate greeting cards, personal stationery (a monogram or flower), book covers, or wrapping paper.

ORIENTAL EFFECTS can be achieved by painting on thin paper (tissue or onion skin). After the paper has dried rub a sponge dipped in turpentine over the back to produce a translucent effect. An ANTIQUING effect can be achieved by rubbing salad oil on the back of a map or picture.

Experiment with a variety of applicators:

- Brushes
- Sticks
- Nose or eye droppers
- Cotton balls
- Swabs (cotton on stick)
- Old shoe polish applicators
- Spray guns
- Squeeze bottles

ADDING SUBSTANCES TO TEMPERA will cause different effects which are interesting to try. Experiment with some of the following:

Soap flakes—smooth paint which washes out more readily
Coffee grounds or sand—adds texture to thick tempera
Varnish—bright shiny finish
Paste—1 tsp. wheat paste per cup of water to aid adherence

Chalk

Colored chalks lend a variety to the art experiences of the elementary classroom. Here are several ideas which we have found most effective:

WET PAPER eliminates the mess of work with chalk. Paint the paper with water (using a large brush or sponge). Then use colored chalk to draw a design or picture before the paper dries. If the paper dries, try dipping the chalk directly in water before applying. The effects of this technique are striking, but the chalk-dust is absent.

BLACK PAPER provides the background for a Halloween scene while white chalk makes shadowy figures bathed in moonlight. Blue paper will make a good background for snow scenes with the white chalk used to produce falling snow, snowy branches, and a snowman.

RUB CHALK heavily into a sheet of drawing paper. Over the chalk make bright patches of heavy waxed crayon. Scratch designs in the crayon which will come off the chalk readily.

An inexpensive fixative for chalk is made by mixing powdered milk with water; this is sprayed on the chalk drawing.

Fingerpaint

Fingerpainting is a bit messy, but fun. Preparing fingerpaint with this recipe including soap flakes makes the paint washable:

3 cups laundry starch in 1 cup cold water
2 qts. boiling water
3 cups soap flakes
1 cup talcum (optional)
½ cup glycerine
coloring (powered or liquid tempera)

Add the starch mixture slowly to the hot water, stirring until clear. Add the coloring and talcum. Cool; add soap flakes. Pour the mixture into jars with lids.

What can you do with fingerpaintings?

Fingerpaint movements of the sea. When dry, add foreground objects with tempera, crayon, ink, or cut paper.

Use large sheets as backgrounds for murals or bulletin board displays. Brown provides a desert background; blue, the sea; green, grass.

Use to cover boxes to make wastebaskets, storage boxes, and so on. Spray with shellac or plastic.

Fold bookcovers for library books or textbooks.

Cut butterflies, kites, flowers, or other shapes to hang as mobiles.

Cut letters (large, irregular) for bulletin board caption.

Use as Christmas wrapping paper or for a gift wrap on Mother's Day.

Use as background for dried leaf arrangements which can be framed.

Encouraging Creativity in Art

It has long been agreed that "colorbook art" and drawing around patterns is far from a creative approach to art. How, then, do we stimulate creativity in art? Suggested in this section are a number of techniques which will tend to stretch the imaginations, to encourage the thinking process, and lead to experimentation.

The warm-up period

Rather than handing each child a sheet of paper, crayons, and saying, "You may draw anything you want," it is wise to prepare for the art experience through a WARM-UP DISCUSSION. If, for example, you wish students to draw pictures of people they might see on a busy downtown street, start the thinking process with questions like these:

> "How many of you have been downtown? What kinds of people did you see?" (Have them name all kinds of people they *might possibly* have seen—newsboy, doctor, pilot, policemen, old man carrying a package, lady pushing a stroller, and so on.)
>
> "Today we're going to draw someone we might see as we walked along a downtown sidewalk." Then talk about constructing the picture—
>
> > What is the most important thing to be in the picture? What, then, will be the biggest thing in the picture? What will be drawn first?
> >
> > Does the whole person have to show? Perhaps show some pictures of people with varied portions of the head and body depicted.
>
> "Now think about the person you are going to draw while we pass out large sheets of paper."

During this discussion children have been developing ideas; they have explored possibilities. No one will be saying, "I can't think of anything to draw." They have also been given some pointers about drawing the picture, so students will not begin drawing a tiny little figure in the corner of a 12 x 18 inch sheet of drawing paper. When they receive the paper, they are ready to begin, and the results will prove far more interesting and satisfying than those produced without stimulus.

Varied topics

Children usually respond better to an art experience which has some direction but still allows for individual development and interpretation. Here are some topics which produce wonderful results:

Something that makes me smile.
What I'd like to be when I'm twenty-five.
What I think about when I'm alone.
What I want most of all.
Just suppose we all were green!
It's Picnic Weather!

> ***Have you noticed*** **that motivating art and motivating creative writing have many common elements? Refer to Chapter 3 where topics are suggested for Creative Writing. Most of these topics can also be used effectively with art activities.**

Incomplete drawings

Give each student a sheet of drawing paper on which you have drawn a line or two; all are somewhat different. Each student is to complete his drawing in anyway he wishes. Encourage the class to *think before drawing*. Here are examples of lines you might draw with a felt pen or crayon:

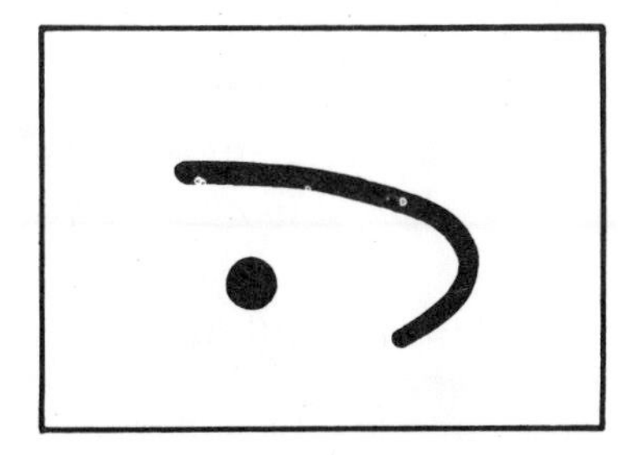

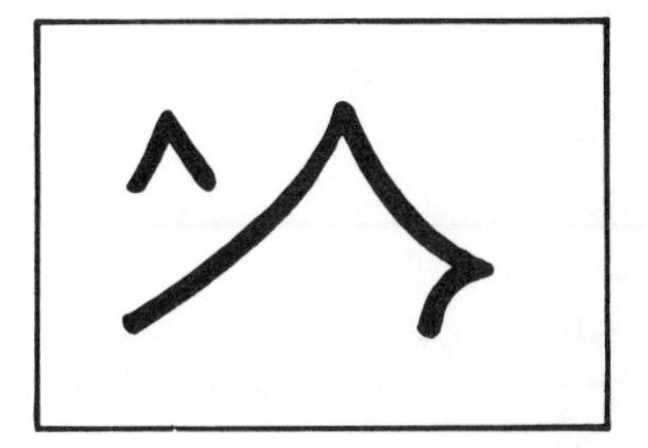

Using scrap materials

Provide each child with an assortment of scrap materials—rickrack, buttons, paper cuttings, bits of wood, and so on. Permit students to get additional scraps as needed or to exchange. Each student is to construct an imaginary animal—three dimensional or mounted on a paper backing. After the animal has been created have each person write a story about this animal, giving it a name, describing its habits, where it lives, and so forth.

Abstract nouns

Discuss with the class the meaning of an abstract noun—Sadness, Love, Happiness, Liberty, Fear. What does this word bring to their individual minds? Let many volunteers describe their concepts of this noun. After the class has thought about the selected noun have them paint pictures depicting their own feelings about this word and its meaning for them. Interesting collages can be developed around this type of theme.

Just imagine

Imaginations need periodic exercise in order to thrive. Encourage students to imagine situations or objects which can be the basis for fascinating paintings and drawings. Always have a THINKING PERIOD before using tools as you consider one of these ideas:

Imagine an ANIMAL, VEGETABLE, or MINERAL which does not exist.
What's the funniest thing you can imagine?
How does the world look to a grasshopper? (BUG'S EYE VIEW)

Relating Art to Other Areas

Art techniques add interest as well as understanding in other subject areas. In the social studies, for example, students gain much understanding of foreign lands as they study the arts of these peoples. Art enhances the enjoyment of poetry and stories. The art experience, however, must be able to stand alone as an effective art technique in order to be termed ART.

Murals

Experiment with a variety of mural ideas using different types of materials. Here are a few suggestions:

• Divide the mural paper into squares with each student assigned one square to complete. One or two students can sketch the drawing which is to be produced in mural dimensions; this drawing is also divided into squares so that each student can see what portion of the drawing will be represented in his square.

• After sketching a picture consisting of large simple shapes have students paint each shape with thin glue on which are laid pieces of torn paper. Use varied shades of one color. Add interesting materials which may produce a three-dimensional effect or contrast in texture such as curled strips of paper, straw, wood chips, dried leaves and stems, and so on.

• After a mural has been completed in crayon apply a wash of an appropriate color to fill in the background.

• Stitch a mural on burlap with each child contributing time on various figures being developed. Use a combination of appliquéd cloth cut in various shapes and stitching done with yarn, string, and other threads.

Collage

One of the most fascinating of the newer art techniques which we find to be highly versatile in the classroom is the collage. What is a collage? A collage is an abstract design which is often composed around a central theme. The design is developed by placing a variety of materials cut in different shapes and sizes on a backing (construction paper, cardboard, wood). These materials are arranged and rearranged as the student experiments with texture, color, balance, contrast, and interest. When he is satisfied with the arrangement, the elements of the collage are glued in place. Described here are a number of ways to use the collage as an art experience that is related to other areas of study:

Reading reports—A collage can be made featuring any book which has been read. A combination of original drawings and clippings from newspapers and magazines will supply materials to illustrate the theme of the book. A collage of *McElligott's Pool,* for example, would include many fish shapes made from a variety of materials. Fish could be cut from foil, sandpaper, Christmas wrappings, magazine ads, or cloth. The boy could be cut from a magazine while a thin bamboo strip could add a three dimensional fishing pole. The artist will think of other interesting elements to add—air bubbles cut from waxed paper, other underwater life, stones, and so on.

WORDS—Words can be clipped from magazines and newspapers to be arranged in a collage. The collage can be simply a collection of words that are interesting to the collector or the collection may be focused on a specific theme or study—Adjectives, French or Spanish words, Geographical words, Words of science, Number words, Words of the West, and so on. The collages developed will include cut out words trimmed in a variety of shapes as well as other pictures and materials which are appropriate to the theme of the words collected.

A collage on the theme AROUND THE WORLD WITH WORDS would include clipped words like: Rome, Africa, Singapore, London, Alaska, and so on (depending on the discoveries made) used in combination with portions of a pictured globe, maps, flags, means of transportation, newspapers (especially in foreign languages), a pair of chopsticks, and any other appropriate items.

A collage can be made as a mural with the whole class contributing to the project.

WRITING—Writing topics will often suggest collages which can be prepared to illustrate the story or essay which has been written. Or, the collage can be prepared first with the story or essay being written after the exploration of the theme through the art technique. Sample topics which might be explored in this fashion include:

My Favorite Things
Sometimes I Am Afraid
Dreaming
What I Like to Do
Summer Fun
I Am Thankful
Winter Wonderland

POETRY—Illustrate poetry by the collage technique. Let each child select one poem (original or by other poets) which appeals to him; this poem can be copied and attached to one corner of the collage or mounted on the back for reference. The student examines the elements of his selection to determine the types of pictures, materials, etc. he can use in portraying the poem.

Edward Lear's poem, "The Owl and the Pussy-Cat," for example, contains many pictorial elements—owl, cat, green boat, money, guitar, honey, Bong-tree, pig, ring, shilling, turkey, mince, spoon, sand, moon, dancing—any or all of which can be incorporated in the collage. Some can be clipped from magazine illustrations; others can be drawn. Play money, a ring of wire, a plastic spoon, sand, and so on may also be used. Students can read their poems showing the class the symbols they have used in their collage or students can first show the collage asking if anyone knows which poem is illustrated.

Paint techniques

The ideas for experimenting with watercolor described at the beginning of this chapter offer many opportunities for correlating with other subject areas. Waterpaint techniques produce excellent covers for booklets which can be used with social studies, reading, and the language arts. An attractive cover lends status to the work of the student; yet these covers require little more time than do less imaginative covers. Try these techniques (described in the foregoing pages) for book covers:

Painting stripes of color
Dropping colors which mix
Drawing string between folded paper
Tempera on wet paper
Crayon resists
Paint spraying
Prints with varied print blocks
Enamel drippings for glossy attractive designs

Varied booklet forms

The standard booklet is made by stapling together two sheets of 9 x 12 inch colored construction paper or folding a 12 x 18 inch sheet in half. You can add to the effectiveness of books constructed by your students by varying the format somewhat according to the subject of the contents.

Long, slim books for poetry (Oriental design for Haiku)
Shapes of states or countries reported on (Cover and paper inside in same shape)
Scrolls for a story or a collection of original poetry
Folders which tie as in these examples:

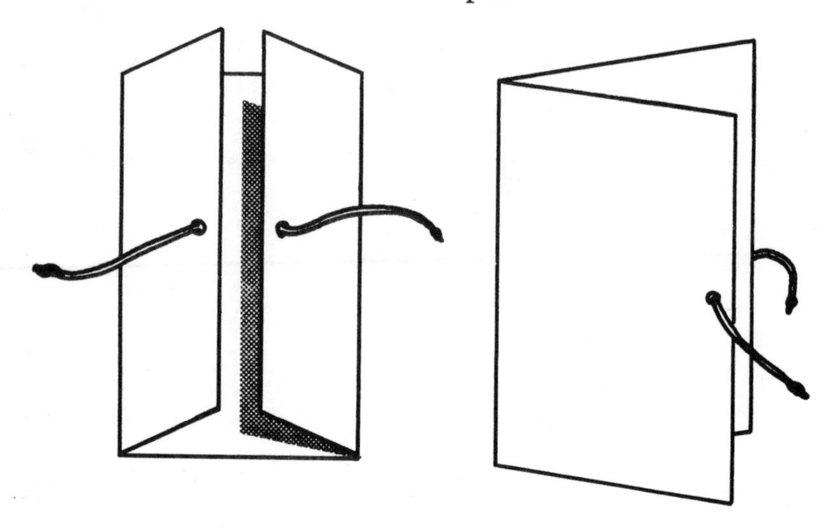

Folders made from painted paper techniques to use for writing.

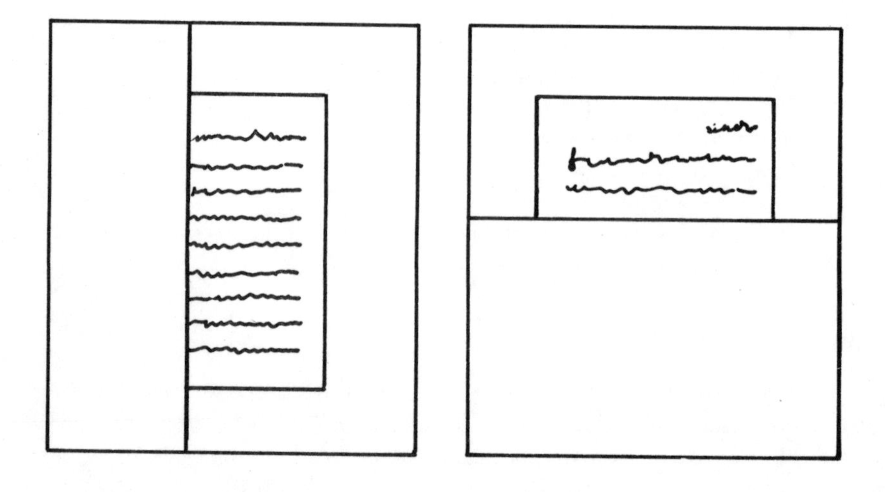

Puppetry

Puppetry can consist of the simplest of devices or it can designate the most complicated string marionette. Puppets can be used and reused in social studies scripts, sociodramas, reporting of books, and so on with only a few changes to make the puppet fit varied roles. Described here are several simple varieties of puppets which are successfully made and used in the classroom.

FINGER PUPPETS are quickly and easily made by primary students but are enjoyed by older students, too. Roll a paper into a cylinder shape which is large enough to contain the index finger (other fingers are used, too). The head for the finger puppet may be cut from a magazine or drawn by the student; it should be on stiff paper which will remain erect when attached to the cylinder. Add yarn hair, eyes, ears, hats, collars, as desired. Arms can also be attached to the cylinder.

HAND PUPPETS are equally successful and can be quickly made from cloth or paper. Using a pattern like that pictured below, cut two identical shapes from stiff paper, cotton cloth, or felt. The paper can be stapled together, but will not last as long as will the cloth which is sewn together. Eyes, hair, and simple clothing—scarves, aprons, belts, buttons—add to the fun.

INVENTING PUPPETS is another outlet for creativity as students invent new types of puppets which can be made. Have them make puppets using materials such as bottle caps (bugs with legs painted with enamel) or walnut shells (wrinkled Indian faces). Try some of these materials:

Peanuts in shells (Animals with tails, ears, legs added)
Potatoes and other vegetables (Animals suggested by shapes)
Wooden spoons (Faces painted on back of spoon)
Paper bags (Stuff with crumpled newspaper; add features)
Paper plates glued to sticks
Squares of cloth (Tie knots for head and two hands)

NO PUPPET STAGE? Puppets can be operated behind a reading table. Hang a blanket, sheet, or tablecloth over the front of the table to conceal puppeteers. Or operate puppets without a stage simply holding them up as they talk; the audience will use its imagination.

Masks

Like puppetry, masks offer a wide range of possibilities for dramatic experiences and relate well to other subject areas. They should be made simply by a method which does not require an undue length of time and effort. Try several described here:

• LARGE BALLOONS can be used to form lightweight masks. Grease the balloon adding strips of tape or newspaper dipped in wheat paste. After three or four layers of the paper have been applied and permitted to dry thoroughly, cut the sphere in half to make two masks. Features can be developed by adding papier-mâché. The masks can then be painted, and hair can be added.

• LARGE PAPER BAGS make effective masks for young students. Their heads and shoulders disappear into the bag as they speak through the openings cut for eyes, nose, and mouth.

• PAPER PLATES provide the bases for easily constructed masks which are held in front of the face as the student speaks. Hair can be sewn directly to the plate and features can be applied with crayons or paint. Three dimensional effects are achieved by adding cut paper noses, eyelashes, hair, and ears.

Use masks also as decorations when the class studies Indians or other civilizations which used the mask. The classic film, "The Loon's Necklace," can be shown to motivate interest in mask forms and to provide excellent examples of a variety of masks. Here are suggestions for developing masks as art forms:

- Cut masks from black construction paper. Working with folded paper will produce a symmetrical design. Cuts can be made to form the eyes, markings on the face, and so on which will show clearly when the mask is mounted on white paper. Older students can use razor blades for making fine cuts in the facial area of the mask.
- Use white crayon or wax to cover a sheet of white drawing paper. Cover the resistant medium with thick black tempera which is etched (scraped away) to form a mask similar to the cut paper mask.
- Develop a mask using bold, bright colors in crayon. Paint the mask and the area around it with black tempera; the entire background need not be covered as the contrasting white is effective around the black paint.

Seasonal Decor

There is a perennial need for art ideas which are appropriate to the season or the holidays which each season brings. Included in this section are ideas arranged in order from Fall through Spring. Again an attempt has been made to include less common ideas, techniques which encourage creativity rather than emphasizing the cutting of patterned decorations.

Fall

In fall we think of colored leaves, returning to school, renewing acquaintances with school books, Halloween, Thanksgiving, studies about Columbus, Pilgrims, and Indians. Let's explore ideas for art at this time of the year.

• *Leaves* can be collected and pressed between the pages of a magazine which is weighted with books. When the leaves are thoroughly dry, use these methods to focus attention on the beauty of the leaves and their identification:

Arrange brightly colored leaves between two layers of waxed paper. Press (between newspapers) with a warm iron to cause the sheets of waxed paper to adhere to the leaves and to each other. The leaves may then be cut out (leaving a wide margin of waxed paper) and hung mobile fashion from the ceiling or a tree branch. These translucent leaves can also be taped to the glass windows where the light will enhance their beauty.

Glue (classroom paste will not hold) bright leaves on black construction paper. Cut around each leaf leaving a narrow strip of black showing around the leaf. Scatter these leaves on a bulletin board or use them to decorate the cover of a booklet about leaves.

Have each student prepare a page featuring the leaves of one tree including the seed pods, if possible. Several leaves of varied size are arranged attractively on the page which is then sprayed or spattered with ink for a page of a class book on TREES WE KNOW. Each page might include (on the back) information about the growing habits of the tree identified. This same activity can be done for local plants other than trees including interesting seeds and pods.

• WHAT DID YOU DO THIS SUMMER? is a common topic for a theme or picture but children have written this same composition so frequently that it is far from inspiring. Try some varied approaches to this topic:

Let each child contribute to a class collage depicting the activities of the summer. The collage can include ideas about boating, swimming, camping, sunbathing, traveling, places visited, and so on. Collages can also be done individually on a smaller scale.

Make a CRAZY QUILT MURAL with each child drawing a picture of *The Funniest Thing That Happened to Me.* The 9 x 12 sheets of drawing paper are placed side by side to fill a large bulletin board. Use bright rickrack to cover the "seams."

Write a story or poem with an accompanying illustration

done in crayon covered by a wash of thin tempera. Use topics about summer activities like these:

A-fishin' We Will Go
I Was the Winner!
Just Imagine How I Felt!
What Would You Have Done?

• HALLOWEEN brings to mind many interesting symbols—witches, bats, black cats, jack-o-lanterns, ghosts. Here are some ideas for Halloween fun:

Torn paper ghosts are easily made by students of all ages. No scissors are allowed as bit by bit the ghost or goblin is shaped. Any size or shape is satisfactory; no two will be alike. Hang these goblins from the ceiling where they will dangle fluttering with any movement of air or mount them on windows and bulletin boards. Black cats and witches can also be made by this method.

Use orange crayon for pumpkins and white for ghostly figures against black silhouettes of trees. When the crayon work is completed, wash the picture with thin black tempera.

Paint alternate stripes of white, orange, and black paint across a piece of 12 x 18 inch paper. Turn the paper so the colors

drip into one another. When dry this sheet can be used as a folder to contain stories or poetry about Halloween. It can also serve as a background for cut paper figures of various symbols of this holiday.

• THANKSGIVING suggests many themes—Pilgrims, Indians, Thankfulness, Harvest, Turkey, Pumpkins, Full Moon. Try some of these ideas:

• Make turkeys out of varied materials:

Potatoes or apples (attach paper feathers and a head with toothpicks)

Paper plates folded in half can form the body for a handsome bird. Attach feathers at one end; cut duplicate heads from construction paper which are attached to both sides of the folded plate. Pipe cleaners make good feet.

Paper bags of varied sizes can be stuffed with paper to form plump turkey bodies. Add feathers and head cut from construction paper. Feet can be cut from corrugated cardboard.

• Have the class construct a large collage entitled WE ARE THANKFUL. The collage will depict the many things for which students in the room are grateful.

• A SCROLL written on brown wrapping paper can list the things for which the class is thankful. Have each student make an individual list with a small group of students making the class scroll which is a compilation of all the lists. Decorations illustrating the ideas expressed can be added along the margin of the scroll. For the ends of the scroll use dowel rods or rolled covers of a large magazine.

• PAPIER-MÂCHÉ FRUITS can be made over crumpled newspaper centers. When thoroughly dry, students can paint the fruit realistically. Two members of the class can construct a papier-mâché cornucopia over a frame of chicken wire or stiff paper. Fruit can then be arranged spilling from the cornucopia.

Winter

Winter reminds us of snow and winter sports, rosy cheeks and firesides. Here are art ideas focusing on winter themes:

• SNOWFLAKES can be cut so that they have eight points which is an easy fold for primary children. To obtain the more authentic six-pointed snowflake first fold the paper into fourths; then fold the square into thirds being careful to direct all folding toward the folded center, thus:

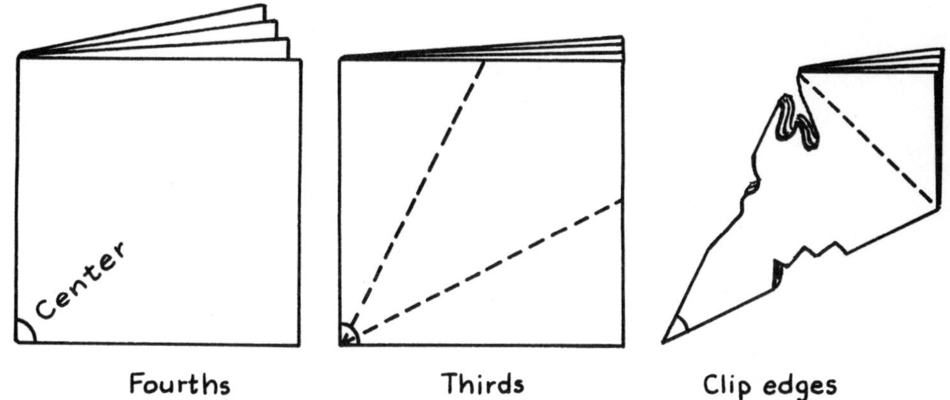

WHAT TO DO WITH SNOWFLAKES?

Scatter them over your windows attached with two or three small spots of glue. Use varied sizes of paper as some of the small snowflakes are lovely contrasted with a few huge ones.

Let each child arrange several snowflakes on a sheet of blue paper. Halves of flakes are used near the edge.

Snowflakes provide lovely patterns for spraying to make book covers or Christmas cards.

• WINTER SPORTS can be depicted in crayon with each child showing one sport—sledding, skating, skiing, hockey, iceboating, fishing through ice, making a snowman, snow sculpture, playing "fox and geese." Wash the picture with thin blue tempera. Add touches of snow with cotton, dabs of white tempera, or imitation snow in a spray can.

• CHRISTMAS is a holiday which supplies many art activities. Christmas trees can be decorated by the children with each one contributing at least one ornament.

Decorate small items such as pine cones, bottle caps, pieces of tile, and so on by dabbing spots of glue over their surface on which glitter can be sprinkled. Enamel can also be sprayed in a variety of colors to transform simple objects.

Let each child drip spots of bright tempera on a 9 x 12 inch sheet of drawing paper. The mixing colors produce lovely effects. When dry, this sheet is cut spirally beginning at one corner and continuing until the center is reached. The long strip of curved paper is wound loosely through the tree branches.

Crayon shavings pressed between waxed paper produce lovely paper for ornaments. Cut black or red paper into any irregular shapes or use the traditional bells, trees, stars, and holly leaves. Cut the center from each shape which will act as a frame. Glue this frame to the waxed paper which is then trimmed. (Two identical frames can be used together to hide the edges.) The tree lights will shine through the translucent paper with the crayon showing brightly.

• GIFTS FOR PARENTS are commonly made at Christmas time. It is our recommendation that these gifts represent something created wholly by the child. We suggest the following gifts as being worthwhile activities which represent a learning experience for the child as well as the production of a gift for his parents:

A booklet of poetry or stories written by a student over a period of several months is a treasure that most parents will really

enjoy having. Use one of the covers described earlier in this chapter to add to the attractiveness of the book. Let each child autograph his anthology appropriately.

A design or picture can be selected from individual art projects. Prints, tempera on wet paper, sponge painting, and many other techniques we have described will provide suitable art for framing as a gift. Students can experiment with framing using black construction paper which is scored and folded or cut as in these examples:

Other types of framing can be developed from thin boards or split bamboo. Wooden frames can be sprayed or covered with linen or burlap of varied colors.

Decorate *notepaper* using simple printing methods—potato, inner tube, stencils. The design can be in the upper left-hand corner or a long thin design can edge the left side of each sheet. Use varied papers such as onion skin, rice paper, or colored typing paper. The sheets of notepaper can be packaged in an attractive folder perhaps decorated with the same design as that on the paper.

Spring

Spring themes include flowers, budding trees, new grass, baby animals, and Easter. We think of light colors such as yellow, pink, and light green. Here are suggestions for spring art activities:

- *Discuss flower shapes* with the class; have them invent flowers by experimenting with crayons to produce colorful flowerlike shapes using varied lines and colors. Add stems and interesting leaves to the flowers to achieve an overall floral design. When the student has completed the flowers, paint a yellow or pale green wash over the entire sheet. Use as a booklet cover or frame in black.

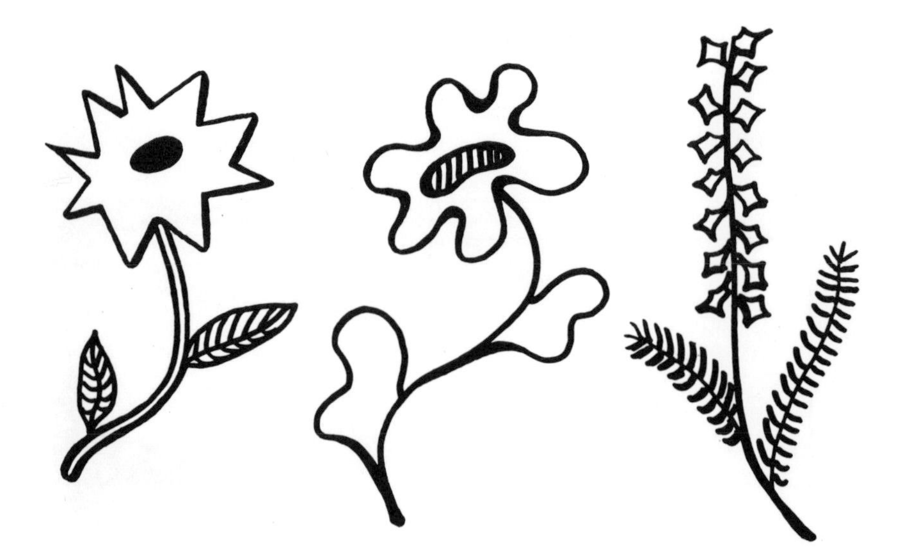

- *Stitchery* is another means of utilizing flower shapes as these designs are worked on burlap or other heavy cloth. Cut some flowers from bright cloth which is stitched to the backing. Other shapes can be developed with yarn and various threads. As a modern art form, stitchery produces attractive wall hangings and pictures which can be framed.

• Experiment with *paper weaving* cutting the paper in different ways which produce attractive results. Use spring colors to make mats which can be placed on a table or hung on the wall.

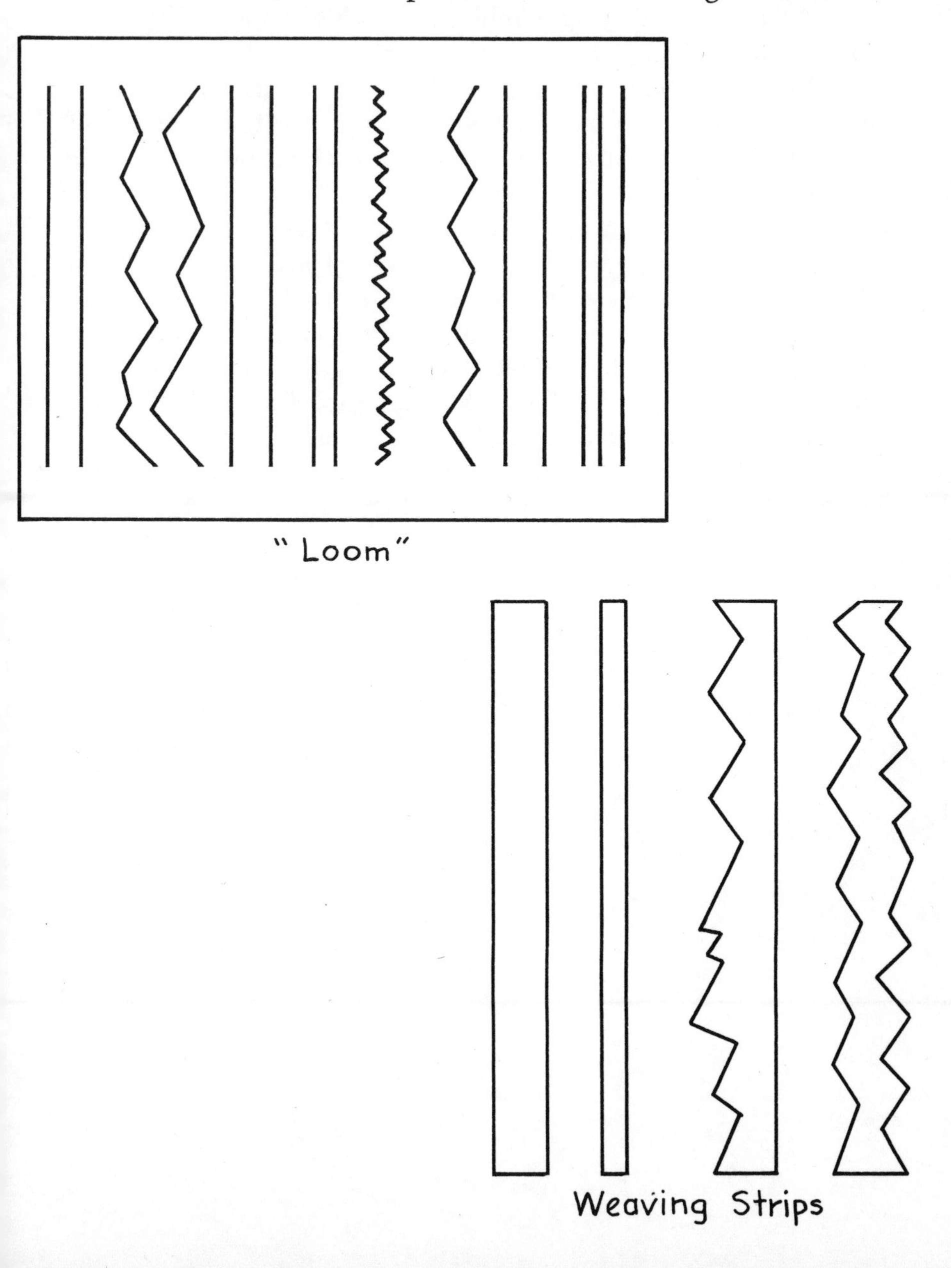

• EASTER can be featured in various media in the classroom. Young children will enjoy making large Easter eggs. On an 18 x 24 inch sheet each child crayons flower shapes, colorful lines, or geometric designs. Then the sheet is *washed* with a thin pastel tempera—pink, blue, yellow, green. When the sheet has dried, the child cuts the paper in an egg shape. These large eggs can be displayed around the room.

To make small *Easter rabbits* use white paper candy bags stuffed with crumpled newspaper which form bodies for the rabbits. White construction paper ears (lined with pink) are attached to the head as are pipe cleaner whiskers. Use a large puff of cotton as a tail. Attach two strings to each rabbit to use them as puppets in creative dramatic activities.

Older students will enjoy constructing an *egg tree* which combines the Easter and spring motifs. Have students begin "blowing eggs" early so that a number of whole shells are available (about 2 per student). The tree consists of a bare branch, big or small, which is held upright in a can of gravel. From the small branches are suspended the decorated eggs. The eggshells may be dyed with food coloring or for an unusually lovely effect dip the shells in enamel which has been dropped in small pans of water. The latter produces a beautiful marbleized effect.

Music is the universal language of mankind.
—*Henry W. Longfellow*

9

STIMULATING MUSICAL INTERESTS

All children are musical. Described in the following pages are specific suggestions for encouraging student interest in a variety of musical activities. The ideas described include both the production of music and the appreciation and enjoyment of music produced by others. Music can be incorporated in the program in many ways—exploring music of other lands, interpretation of rhythms and sounds, or as a background for art or other activities. The child's participation in the musical activities may take many forms such as the following:

Playing an instrument.
Composing original music.
Singing songs individually or in groups.
Performing for an audience.
Listening to the performance of others.
Playing musical games.

Producing Music

All children should have an opportunity to produce music—to sing, to play instruments, to compose songs. There is music in every student but it may be evidenced in different ways. It is essential, therefore, that the child have a chance to explore different aspects of music. If singing is the only type of music explored in your classroom, then you may not reach all children, for some who will not respond or participate in singing will become very much interested in playing a simple flute.

As a teacher, you do not have to be an accomplished musician to enjoy music with your class. Your interest in their musical compositions, your providing time and equipment for musical activities will clearly indicate your attitude toward music. And they will love to sing with you no matter what the quality of your voice; clear, bell-like tones are not necessary for singing "The Farmer in the Dell."

Composing music

Encourage students to compose songs or to write down tunes which they find themselves humming. They may use a xylophone, tonette, or the piano to help them produce a pleasing melody which can be written on music paper. Words can be added to these songs. Students may also be interested in writing melodies for poems which have been written for language arts—couplets, triplets, or quatrains (see Chapter 3). "The Hobo Song" is an example of a melody developed for a triplet.

Rote songs

When you are teaching the class a new song, the words and music must be repeated a number of times before the children can really sing the song. To avoid monotony and boredom many teachers vary the ways in which the song is repeated using some of the following variations:

Only the boys or only the girls sing the song.
Half the class sings at one time.
All students with blue eyes sing (or those with brown hair).
The class echoes the teacher's singing of each line.
Say the words together.
Hum the tune while thinking the words.
Small groups come to the front of the room to sing.
Each row sings a line.
All those wearing socks sing (Everyone?).

Use these techniques also for singing songs with many repetitious verses.

Singing games

Many group games involve the singing of simple songs and can be played outdoors or in the multipurpose room. The use of these types of activities furthers the concept that music is a happy experience. Here are several familiar games which include songs:

London Bridge
The Farmer in the Dell
Tisket, a Tasket
The Muffin Man
Bluebird, Bluebird
The Mulberry Bush
Jumping Rope Songs

FIND TIME FOR MUSIC

Singing can be worked into odd moments of the school day —while clearing away art supplies, while lining up or waiting for the bell to ring, as a moment of relaxation after a long period of written work, or before school begins in the morning.

Rounds

An excellent way to begin part singing is through the use of the Round. There are many familiar ones which can be used to introduce children to this type of singing:

Are You Sleeping? (Frère Jacques)
Three Blind Mice
Row, Row, Row Your Boat

Other rounds which are less well-known and, for that reason, perhaps more interesting, include the following:

White Coral Bells
We Thank Thee
Oh, How Lovely Is the Evening

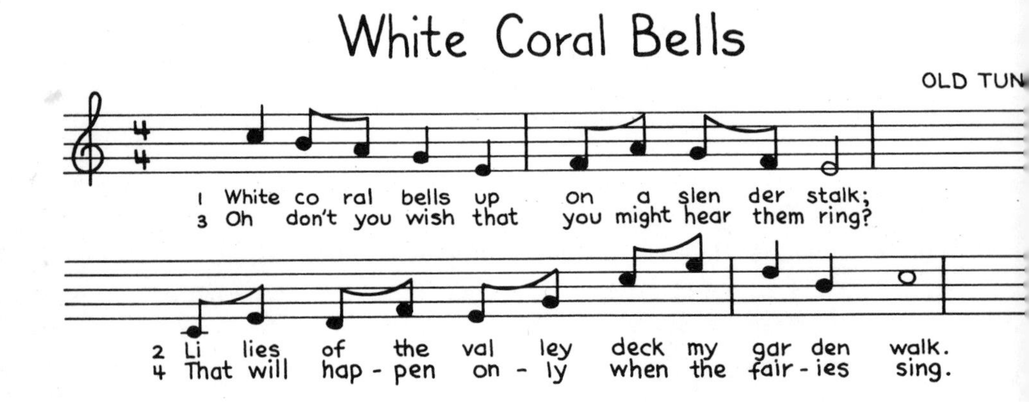

In order to sing rounds successfully students must be very much aware of the *time in which the round is written* (in most cases 4/4) and the *tempo being used* by the group. As the leader, you can set the tempo by conducting, insisting that all students pay attention to your hand as you indicate the time.

Students should also learn to *hear the other parts*, so that although each group sings different words and tune, all are aware of the completion of each phrase. Before beginning to sing any round state the number of times each group will repeat the whole song (3 times is usually enough).

Musical instruments

The making of musical instruments can lead to a Rhythm Band or provide an interesting way of exploring the folk music of a foreign country being studied in social studies. Each student can construct one type of instrument so that all participate. Here are suggestions for inexpensive types of instruments which students can make:

♪ DRUMS can be made simply by removing both ends from a two pound (or larger) coffee can. Cover both open ends with circles of inner tube rubber or linen coated heavily with shellac which can be laced with twine or cord to hold the drumheads securely in place. Drumsticks can be short pieces of doweling. The ends of some drumsticks can be padded with cloth for a different effect.

♪ RATTLES or MARACAS can be fashioned from gourds, if available. They can also be made from boxes or jars in which beans are placed. Toilet tissue tubes can also be made into attractive rattles by covering each end with heavy wrapping paper after adding beans or pebbles.

♪ STICKS are the easiest type of rhythm instrument to make. Use pieces of doweling or broomstick which are painted with bright enamel to provide simple instruments for all. Each child can use two sticks which are struck against each other or one stick can be struck against a block of wood.

♪ BELLS can be sewn on wide bands of cloth or elastic to be used as Jingle Bells. Large single bells can be struck with a stick. Small bells can be attached to painted sticks.

♪ HUMMERS provide for the production of a melody in a band. Tubes from paper supplies or combs covered with waxed paper allow the child to produce an interesting effect by humming directly against the paper.

♪ TRIANGLES can be made from a suspended piece of pipe,

metal rod, or a large spike. The suspended metal is struck by another piece of metal, a silver knife, or a small hammer.

Action songs

There are many songs to which students can add motions to increase the enjoyment of singing. After children have been sitting for a period of time have them stand up to sing "Did You Ever See a Lassie?" or "Three Blind Mice" (for which they can develop motions). "The Battle Hymn of the Republic" provides the tune for this parody for which students can write other verses:

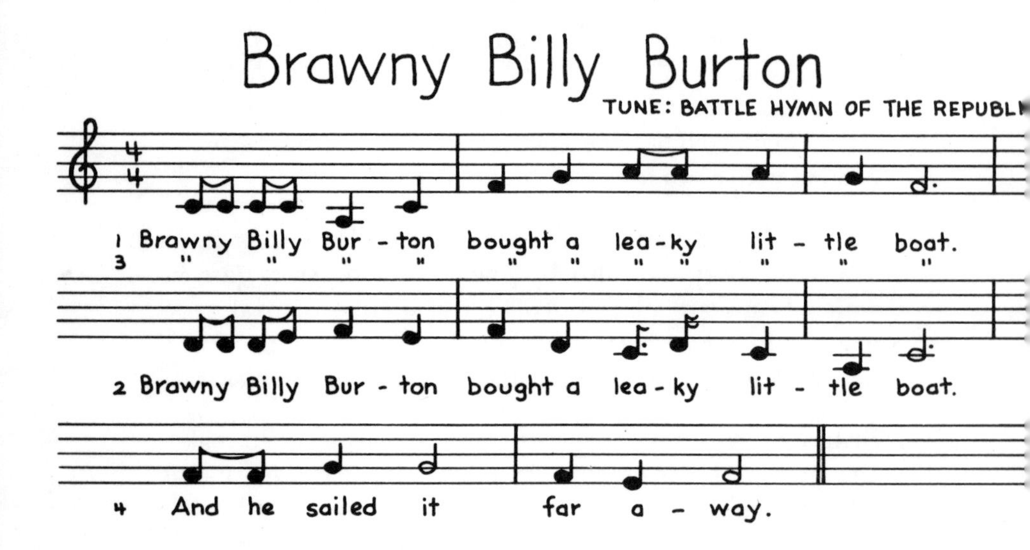

Counter melodies

Students can compose simple counter melodies to accompany familiar songs. Remember that the new melody must be in the same key and tempo as the song with which it is to be used. A simple example makes use of the song, "Twinkle, Twinkle, Little Star."

The counter melody is another way of introducing two part singing. Other songs which lend themselves to this type of singing are "Jingle Bells" and "Are You Sleeping?"

Playing music

Instruments in the classroom—piano, xylophone, tonettes—will assist students in learning to read music. They will also provide motivation for the learning of musical notation.

Colors or numbers help young students learn to play simple songs on these instruments. You may wish to make several tagboard charts for songs which can be propped on the chalk tray while students play the songs. In the music for "Mary Had a

Little Lamb" notice that the numbers (or colors) are placed on notes in their correct positions so students will be more ready to play when the number system is dropped.

Using the flannel board

The *flannel board* provides an excellent method of giving students practice in using musical notes and signs. Cut strips of black felt or paper to form the staff or use a felt pen to draw lines directly on flannel. Also cut black notes of various types, rests, and other signs as desired. Students can manipulate these materials to "write" a song which they are composing or one which they have heard. They can print words on strips of paper if they wish to add them.

> **Prepare a ditto master (can be purchased) of musical staffs. Duplicate a number of these sheets which can be cut in half for student use in composing songs and other musical activities.**

Music assemblies

Encourage students to sing by having monthly music assemblies. To build up the repertoire of the student group notify teachers ahead of time about the songs which will be sung. The assembly may be attended by the whole school or, according to the size of the group, two assemblies may be held with younger students attending one while upper grades attend the other. The division of the assemblies also allows for the selection of songs more appropriate to interests and abilities.

Include some seasonal songs, old favorites, folk tunes, popular songs, rounds, and perhaps feature one student performer playing the piano or another instrument. A first assembly might include the following:

America, the Beautiful
I've Been Working on the Railroad
Are You Sleeping? or Row, Row, Row Your Boat (Rounds)

Song prepared by one class (sung standing in place)
Polly Wolly Doodle or Oh, Susannah
The Marine's Hymn or The Battle Hymn of the Republic
Individual Student Performance (on stage)
Waltzing Matilda or Swing Low, Sweet Chariot
The Caisson Song (classes then hum this tune as they file out)

IDEA FOR OPEN HOUSE

Tape the singing of your class to be played during the parent visitation. Repeat the tape recording as needed.

School chorus

Encourage volunteers to sign up for an all school chorus which meets once each week after school in one classroom or the multipurpose room. The chorus provides an opportunity for students who are especially interested in singing to learn a wider variety of music and to further their enjoyment of music with others who are also interested.

The sponsor of this group does not have to be a music major, but she will need skill in conducting and above all, in handling a large group. The chief requisite, however, is enthusiasm. An accompanist will also be needed, preferably a student or perhaps a parent. Although many songs can be taught by rote, a set of inexpensive songbooks should be purchased for this group (at least 1 per 2 students). Here are several recommended titles any *one* of which would provide sufficient material for a year's work with a chorus of young people:

The Golden Book of Favorite Songs. Hall & McCreary Co., 434 Wabash Ave., Chicago 5, Illinois.
America Sings. Robbins Music Corp., 799 Seventh Ave., New York, New York.
Pocket Full of Songs. Informal Music Service, Delaware, Ohio.

Stress should be placed on enjoyment of music and singing, but at each meeting a few minutes can be spent on the skills of reading music, correct breathing, and singing as a group. This group can perform several times during the year to add stimulus to their interest.

Replace noise with group singing after lunch on rainy days. Duplicate song sheets if desired.

Singing songs simultaneously

An unusual type of singing which gives practice in two-part work is that of having the two halves of the class sing two different songs at the same time. Just any two songs will not work for this experience, for the songs must be matched in time and key. Here are several pairs of songs which teachers often use in this manner.

"Skip to My Lou" and "Ten Little Indians"
"A Spanish Cavalier" and "Solomon Levi"
"There's a Long, Long Trail" and "Keep the Home Fires Burning"

Developing singing skills

As children advance in their singing ability, they can be taught to read notes, to sightread songs, to sing, and to understand musical terminology. Here are several suggestions which may help develop musical skills:

♪ To assist students in being able to reproduce certain intervals which appear frequently in songs introduce these familiar tunes:

My Bonnie Lies Over the Ocean—begins with a *sixth*
Twinkle, Twinkle, Little Star—begins with a *fifth*
Yankee Doodle—begins with a *fourth*

♪ To emphasize the cutting off of consonant sounds have the students sing the sounds of N, M, or V. Demonstrate and have them try cutting this sound sharply by suddenly pressing the nostrils closed.

♪ To encourage students to sing with open throats rather than with the throat constricted direct the class to yawn and then sing *ah, oh, ee* on each note as they slowly move up the scale from C to C. Singing the syllables *loo, ah* as indicated below is also helpful.

- Stress can be placed on correct enunciation of words so that the audience can understand by having only half the class sing while the others listen critically. The tape recorder can also be used to permit the whole class to hear themselves as others hear them.

- Ask a singer (perhaps a parent of a class member) to visit your class to demonstrate correct breathing. Have the students try the recommended techniques so they can later continue them.

Featuring music on the bulletin board

Interest in music can be furthered by the use of the bulletin board. Here are several ideas you might suggest to students who can readily produce an attractive display:

- Use heavy black yarn to form a music staff. On the staff place notes for the music of a short song or just the first line of a longer song with the caption WHAT SONG IS THIS? For variety make the notes in a different shape—stars, pumpkins, leaves, bells, snowflakes, hearts, shamrocks, or flowers—according to the season or the song being displayed.

- MUSIC IN THE NEWS is the caption for a display of clippings (interspersed with cut paper notes) about music and musicians. Encourage students to bring this type of material to school as they see music news in magazines or newspapers. Several pieces of sheet music would also add to the effectiveness of this display.

Relating music to language arts

There are frequently opportunities for relating music and language arts in a meaningful and enjoyable fashion. Described here are several ideas:

- Teach young students the alphabet musically by using the familiar tune of "Twinkle, Twinkle." "The Alphabet Song" shows the phrasing for the letters.

- Develop a music dictionary for the class to use as a reference tool during the year. Have students prepare pages for the book defining terms, showing examples and meanings for musical symbols, describing the biographies of great musicians, and so forth.

- Let a small group of students work together preparing new words to familiar tunes or adding verses to songs learned. Gifted students would enjoy this type of writing.

♪ More able students can center research around music—musicians, music of a state or nation, festivals (Las Posadas—Mexico; Hanukkah—Jewish; Chinese New Year), periods of history.

Listening to Music

Children love to sing, but there are many other aspects of music to be explored as we listen to music made by others—records, tapes, and personal performances. We can think about the meaning of music, we can listen quietly without moving, and we can produce action in response to music. Here are varied suggestions for encouraging the enjoyment, understanding, and appreciation of music as students listen and respond to the music of others.

Responding to the musical rhythms

We frequently find ourselves tapping our feet in response to music. According to the music being played, students can be directed to click their fingers, cluck tongues, clap hands, stamp feet, or tap their fingers on the desks.

♪ To emphasize various types of rhythm patterns the teacher can play a pattern on the piano or tap one on the desk. Let the students immediately reproduce the pattern. Introduce patterns which will occur in a record to be played; then have the children raise their hands or tap the rhythm when they notice it.

♪ Clap the rhythm of a familiar song such as "Mary Had a Little Lamb" to see whether anyone can guess the name of the song. Have others try presenting a song in this way.

♪ Children can interpret many rhythms with a variety of movements even while remaining seated. Have them try these—tapping, stretching, bending, nodding, beating, patting, swaying, clapping, crossing arms or flexing fingers.

♪ Other rhythms can be interpreted while walking in a circle around the room. Suggest hopping, trotting, swaying, skating, whirling, stooping, reaching, stamping, bending, skipping, galloping, and marching used in varied combinations. After listening to a short song have the class select the movement to be used.

Music for listening

Even young students should be exposed to a variety of melodies—compositions by famous composers, folk tunes, popular music. Here are some recommended selections for use with young people:

Nutcracker Suite, Tchaikovsky
Peter and the Wolf, Prokofiev
Swan Lake, Tchaikovsky
Nocturnes and Waltzes, Chopin
Waltzes, Strauss
Hansel and Gretel, Humperdinck
Amahl and the Night Visitors, Menotti
The Moldau, Smetana
Jeux d'Enfants, Bizet
The Sorcerer's Apprentice, Dukas
Young Person's Guide to the Orchestra, Britten
Danse Macabre, Saint-Saëns
What Is Jazz?, Bernstein
Through Children's Eyes, Limelighters
Folk songs, Burl Ives; Peter, Paul, and Mary; Pete Seeger, and others

Sources of recorded music

Listed here are several names and addresses where the teacher can obtain catalogs of recorded materials from which to make a selection:

Children's Music Center, 2858 W. Pico Blvd., Los Angeles, Calif.
Folkways Records & Service Corp., 117 W. 46th St., New York City.
Master Record Service, Box 7111, Phoenix 11, Arizona
Rainbow Rhythms, Box 15116, Emory University, Atlanta 22, Ga.

Playing records

Play records before school as students enter quietly. While children are working with paint or crayon, put on an interesting record to be enjoyed as they work. Records can also be played quietly during reading periods when students are working independently. Repeat favorites.

For older children write the name of the composer and the composition on the board as the record is being played. Students will become accustomed to reading this information. Discuss the selection briefly as desired providing the correct pronunciation of names. Let students take turns being "disc jockey."

Conducting music

An interesting way to teach the varying rhythms of music is to show students how to conduct songs written in varied musical time. Three-four time is one of the easier times to conduct, so you may wish to begin with it. *With your back to the class* demonstrate the movement which is made by the hand; have the entire class try conducting together as they count 1, 2, 3; 1, 2, 3, etc. Play a record of a waltz to provide an opportunity for the entire class to practice this type of conducting. Teach the class a song in

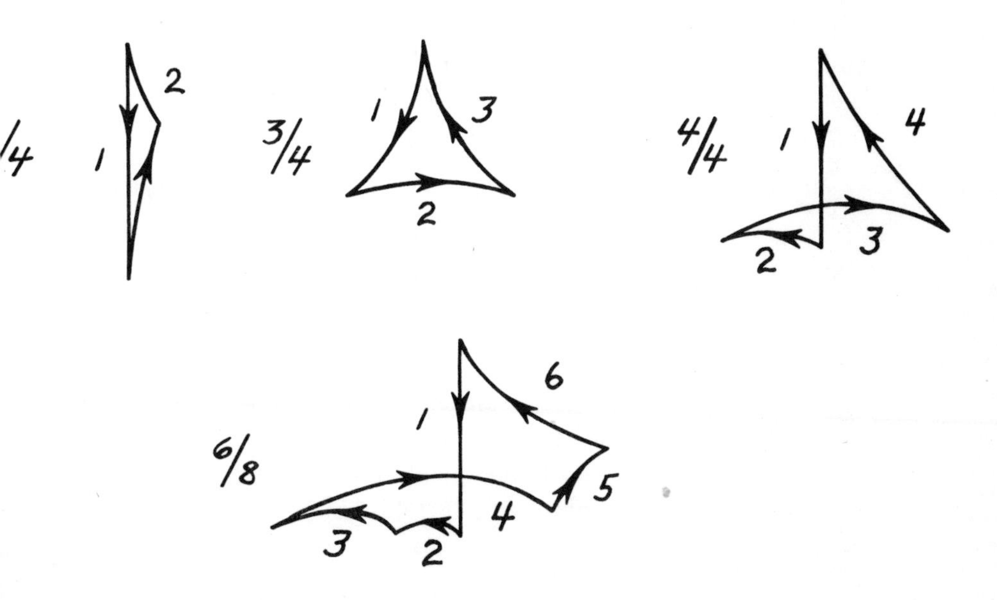

3/4 time so that individuals may take turns serving as conductors.

Suggested conducting patterns are illustrated for 2/4, 3/4, 4/4 and 6/8 time.

Listening with a purpose

There are many reasons for listening to recorded music. If students are told to listen for a specific purpose, their listening will usually be more effective than if music is played without direction. Here are several "things to listen for" in recorded music:

- ♪ Encourage children to clap the rhythm or beat of recorded music. They will soon note the differences in time and will learn to identify the time correctly.

- ♪ Students can listen for themes which are repeated several times. Play the melody of the theme or sing it before playing the record, if possible. Have students raise their hands each time this theme is heard.

- ♪ "Peter and the Wolf" is an excellent record to use as students listen for the instruments. Play the record often so students gradually learn to identify the flute, the piccolo, and so on.

- ♪ Listen to the music representative of one country. Learn something of the history of this nation and its people and discuss ways in which the music may portray the customs, feelings, and ideals of this group of people.

- ♪ Compare music played by a band with that of an orchestra. How do the instruments, the tempo, the types of music vary? What instruments appear in both band and orchestra?

- ♪ Use recorded music to stimulate creative writing. Play "The Moldau," for example, asking students what they hear or imagine as they listen. Have each one write a story about this music. Other good selections for this purpose are "Danse Macabre" and "Firebird Suite."

Repeating music

You can enlist the aid of music in accomplishing small routines of the classroom. These uses of music provide an opportunity for students to listen to music and respond. Try some of these techniques:

♪ MUSICAL ROLL CALL can require the student to echo the tune used by the teacher to call his name or a standard response can be taught for all to use as in these examples:

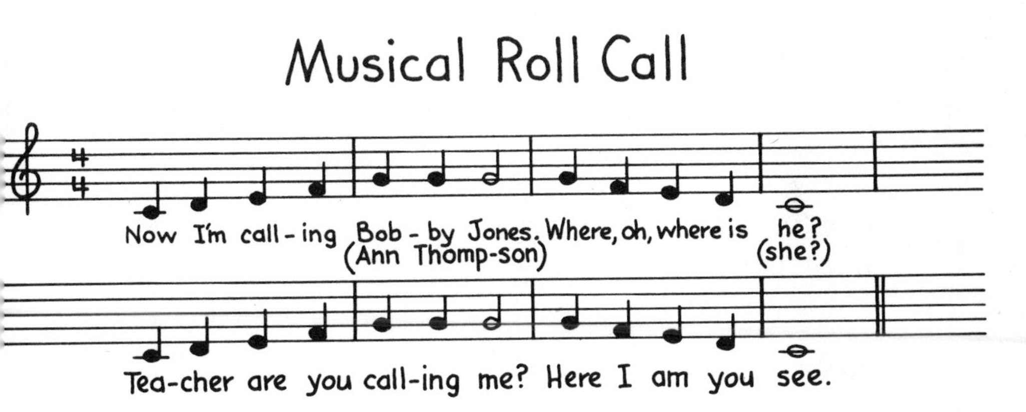

♪ MUSICAL DIRECTIONS can be directed toward one person or a row of students. When children are familiar with a Direction Song, they can take turns leading the group as with this example:

- Play a simple sequence of notes on the piano (or other musical instrument). You tell the class the first note played and see if they can reproduce the notes played on a blank musical scale as they listen for the intervals between the notes.

- Sing a melody pattern having the class repeat the pattern as an echo. Patterns can be simple at first and progressively more complex.

Patterns

Interpreting music

Encourage students to walk around the room in time to music. They will soon find themselves walking or skipping as the music moves more quickly. Let students try various movements in time to the music—swaying, hopping, turning, swinging arms. When someone discovers an especially suitable movement, draw this movement to the attention of the others who may like to try it, too.

Many types of animals can be portrayed when the music suggests the movements of an animal.

Elephant—swaying of two arms held together as student bends forward.
Camel—walking on hands and feet without bending knees.
Rabbit or Kangaroo—hopping or leaping.
Horse—galloping.
Duck—waddling slowly.

Dancing to music

Circle dances, square dances, line dances—all are easily learned by young students. These dances add to the student's enjoyment of music and can also add to his understanding of the peoples of other nations. An excellent collection of records suitable for the classroom is The World of Fun Series available from:

Methodist Publishing House
810 Broadway
Nashville 2, Tennessee

Musical programs

Music can provide the basis for an effective program to be produced by the entire school or by one or two classes. Several types of programs can include:

♪ MUSIC OF MANY LANDS can be the theme of an effective program with each participating room selecting one country to portray through music. The class can do a dance or two and sing songs or prepare a brief musical skit to demonstrate customs of that country. At Christmas this theme features national customs for celebrating the holiday and some of each nation's typical carols.

♪ THE NUTCRACKER SUITE can be interpreted by students as a form of creative dramatics using the recorded music as a background. PETER AND THE WOLF is another selection which can be interpreted very effectively by primary children who portray the various characters of the story with a minimum of props as the record is played off-stage.

♪ HANSEL AND GRETEL represents an excellent story with several songs and dances which can be portrayed through the means of puppetry. Other folk tales, nursery stories, and fairy tales can also be presented through puppet shows with a background of recorded music. Children in the class can compose short songs appropriate to the story portrayed.

𝅘𝅥𝅮 THE RHYTHM BAND, the Kitchen Orchestra, the Silent Band or other variations add fun and interest to a program. Play a recording of a march while this band marches from the stage through the audience and returns to the stage.

𝅘𝅥𝅮 BALLADS can be dramatized. Try familiar songs such as "Go Tell Aunt Rhody," "Reuben, Reuben," or "Lord Randall." Students can write modern ballads which tell a story of present day events.

The science of music

Various aspects of music can be correlated with science and mathematics as students study pitch and the production of musical tones. Here are several suggested activities:

𝅘𝅥𝅮 Obtain one or more tuning forks (or invite a tuner to speak to the class and demonstrate the process of tuning) to show students differences in pitch. Compare the pitch of the tuning fork with the pitch of the piano or another instrument.

𝅘𝅥𝅮 Compare the length and size of strings and the size of the instruments themselves with the tones produced. The string family, for example, illustrates this idea—bass, cello, viola, violin. Compare also the flute and piccolo.

𝅘𝅥𝅮 Relate the writing of music to the study of fractions as students observe that in 6/8 time there are six beats to a

measure with the eighth note receiving one beat. Care must be taken to make it clear in this case that the eighth note represents 1 part out of 6 in the measure (not 1 part out of 8). Have students make charts to illustrate various times and to compare the relative values of notes. Use the flannel board to compare these values. Begin with 4/4 time for a clear explanation.

Musical games

To promote the child's interest in music and the people who write music use musical games which require students to know something about musicians, composers, and to be able to recognize the melodies of well-known compositions.

WHO CAN NAME IT? features familiar melodies which have been introduced to the class. Each child has a half sheet of paper on which he writes the title of the selection played and the composer, if possible. After five to ten selections have been played (in part only) provide the correct answers so each can score his paper. You may keep score by rows (allowing 1 point per selection correctly named and 1 point for the correct composer and adding the scores of all in the row) for added interest. Use the tape recorder to record parts of many selections to which the children have been introduced so this game can be played easily.

WHO IS IT? requires pictures of composers (from magazines or newspapers) which are mounted on the bulletin board. At first place the name of the composer and several of his best-known works beneath each picture. Discuss these people and their music with the class perhaps playing parts of some of the works named. Another day move the names and the titles of selections around so that the children can try to identify the pictured composer replacing the names and titles correctly. Also try removing the names and titles completely having the children try to identify the composers and their works through total recall.

NAME THE TUNE is a game which children of all ages enjoy. Whistle or hum a tune that is known by the class such as "Ten Little Indians." See how quickly students can identify the song by melody alone. Use this technique for introducing a new song or one known by only a few people.

The music corner

Encourage children to explore music by developing a music corner. At certain times they can experiment with any instruments there—piano, xylophone, flutes, autoharp, rhythm instruments. Feature books and articles about music and musicians, pictures of lesser known instruments, songbooks, and sheet music. A record player and radio can also be included. Let the children contribute to this Music Center.

Live music

When planning activities for the whole school, include some programs which feature music by visiting artists. Arrange to have a concert by local talent. Usually in a community there are some good singers, either soloists or small groups, and instrumentalists. You may combine performances by several different musical talents, for example, a singer and a pianist or a singer of folk songs and a guitarist.

Invite the high school band leader to come to your school to demonstrate various instruments, both the familiar and the less known instruments. He may bring some high school students to assist him, for this helps the younger student visualize himself as a producer of music.

Work consists of whatever a body is *obliged* to do and Play consists of whatever a body is not obliged to do.

—*Mark Twain*

10

CHALLENGING PLAY ACTIVITIES

Students need periods of exercise, a change of pace from the work in which they have been engaged. These periods may take the form of an outdoor recess, an activity period in the multipurpose room, or games played in the classroom. Described in this chapter are a variety of activities to assist the teacher in planning for these periods.

In the Classroom

When weather forces the children to remain indoors during recess periods, there is a special need for good activities which will prove enjoyable yet suitable to the classroom environment. There is need, too, for classroom activities to relax students who have been working on written assignments for a period of time.

Musical activities

A number of action songs provide opportunity for children to stand as they perform active motions to a song. Usually songbooks include several which the class can learn together, and there are old favorites which children enjoy:

Did You Ever See a Lassie?
Here We Go Round the Mulberry Bush

Encourage students to write words to familiar tunes making a point of including material which calls for action. Suggest melodies such as "The Battle Hymn of the Republic," "Ten Little Indians," "The Caisson Song," "Home on the Range," and so on. For "Ten Little Indians" a student might compose the following type of song:

Hop a little, skip a little, turn all around;
Sway a little, bend a little, touch the ground.
Step a little, wave a little, jump with a bound.
Sit without a sound.

Relays

There are many variations of the relay race which work well in the classroom. These games may involve use of the chalkboard or pencil and paper or they may call for individual action. In any case the class is divided into several teams of six to eight members.

WORD BUILDING requires each child on a team to add a letter to form a word. The first may begin by writing B on the chalkboard with the second team member adding R and the next E, and so on. Each must have a longer word in mind. The letters in each completed word are counted at the end of five minutes to determine each team's score.

THE SCAVENGER HUNT is scored by one person who collects information for his team. The Leader asks questions like these:

How many people have blue eyes?
How many are wearing something yellow?
How many are girls?
How many have a red pencil?

PASS THE RING is a relay in which all remain in their seats as each team member passes a rubber canning ring (or a large jar lid) to the person behind him. The ring must not be touched by the hands but must be picked up with the student's pencil and passed to the next person's pencil without dropping. If dropped, the ring must be recovered by use of the pencil only.

CHAIN REACTION focuses attention on words with each child in turn writing a word on the board. If the first team member writes BLACK, for example, the next student must supply a word which begins with K (the last letter in BLACK). If that person writes KITE, then the next one must write a word beginning with E. The emphasis here is on speed. Score can be kept by giving 5 points to the team finishing first; 4 to the second, and so on repeating the contest several times.

FOLLOW DIRECTIONS can include a variety of actions. All students may, for instance, be requested to untie both shoes. At the word GO the first member of each team ties both his shoes and touches the shoulder of the next student, who then ties his shoes, and so on. Let students invent sets of directions like these:

1. Stand up; spell your first and last names backwards; then touch the next person's right hand.
2. Walk to the front of the room; clap your hands over your head three times; then touch the next person's shoulder.
3. Hop forward to a chair; sit down; repeat "Little Jack Horner"; hop to the last seat in your row.

WHAT'S YOUR NAME? requires the first team member to walk to the chalkboard where he writes the first and last name of some historical figure. He then passes an eraser back to the last person in the row who comes up, erases the name from the board, and writes another. The team moves back one seat each time to make room for the player who has just written so he can pass the eraser back to the student who is now at the rear of the line.

Paper and pencil games

Paper and pencil activities are diverting quiet activities which can be used for indoor recess or to fill odd moments of the day which are too short for longer activities.

ALPHABET TREASURE HUNT involves the finding of objects around the room (or in a specified book) which begin with the different letters of the alphabet. Each student prints the letters in columns on his paper. As he finds appropriate nouns, he records the words on his paper beside the correct letters: G—globe, C—

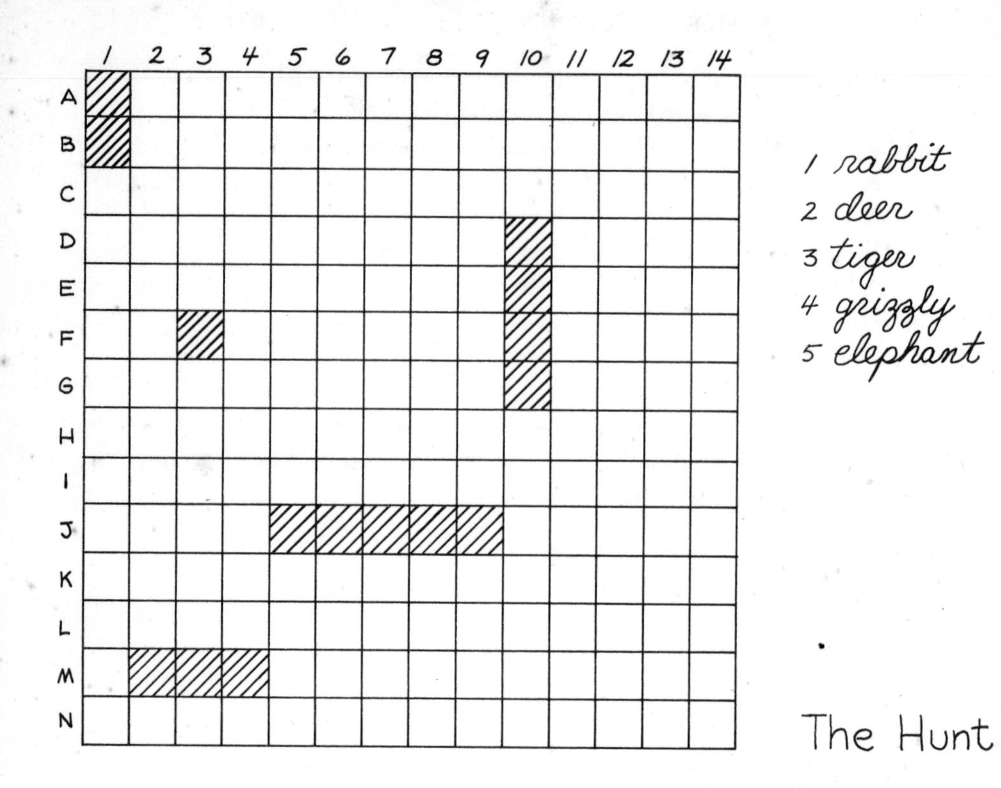

chair, W—window, and so on. At the end of the time limit the person having the greatest number of objects found is the winner.

THE HUNT is a game which is played on duplicated forms like the one shown above. Each player has one copy which represents his Forest in which he hides five animals (marked with crayon) in an effort to prevent the HUNTER from finding them. The HUNTER uses a form also on which to record his BULLETS so that he does not repeat. He might, for instance, call out: 3F, 6G, 13N. All players mark these spaces to determine whether any animals have been hit. The HUNTER sees how many animals he can bag in a given period of time. (This game can also be played by pairs of students both of whom hide animals and take turns shooting.)

WORD PUZZLES can take various forms. (See Chapter 3 for other word activities.) Here is one type of puzzle which encourages each student to find as many names of boys and girls as possible by moving one space at a time vertically, horizontally, or diagonally. A name may be started with any letter on the

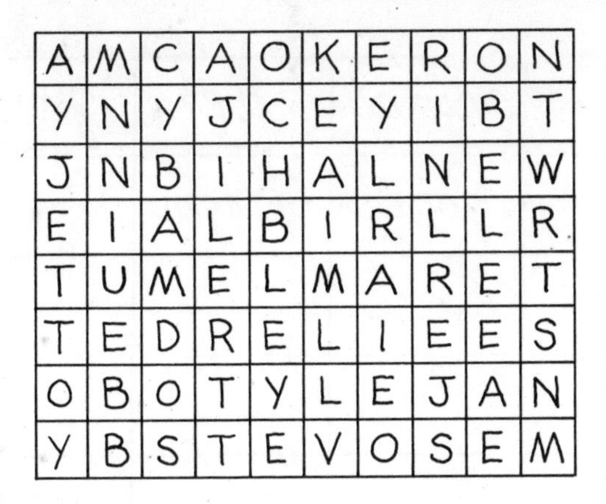

Hidden Names

chart. Starting, for example, with the A in the upper left corner one can find AMY and ANNETTE.

DIZZY QUIZ consists of a series of questions which the teacher asks to which the answer is always a number. The numbers are added to find the total score at the end of the quiz. Sample questions are:

1. How many letters are in your first name?
2. How many brothers do you have?
3. How many pencils do you have?
4. How old are you?
5. How many lines are on your paper?
6. How many stripes are on the United States flag?
7. Give yourself ten points if you are wearing something red.

REBUS are fun to concoct as well as to unscramble. This type of riddle combines pictures with letters and numbers. Duplicate several examples on a sheet of paper to acquaint students with the type of puzzle. Then encourage them to make some examples with which to challenge their classmates.

☆ + MY – ST = *defenders*

ST + ◐ – B = *horse's bedroom*

	animal	river	food
G	goat	Ganges	
H	horse		
O			
S			
T			

CATEGORIES is an excellent game which students enjoy as they search for words to complete each category. In October the key word might be GHOST.

THE SPOTTED GIRAFFE (or any other animal) requires each student to add spots on the figure of a large giraffe which you have duplicated on sheets of white ditto paper. Before the class begins you draw several large spots on one copy of the animal. Hang this copy before the class as they try to duplicate exactly the spots you have drawn (without leaving their desks). After a period of time check the exactness of the spots drawn by laying each paper in turn over your copy held against the window.

WHAT DO YOU SEE? is a test of observation. Prepare a tray containing numerous small objects. Show the class the tray letting them observe carefully for several minutes; naming the objects aloud is a good practice. Then remove the tray from sight while each student tries to write the names of as many objects as possible.

A, B, C—GEOGRAPHY! can be either an oral or written game. For each letter of the alphabet the student writes a sentence telling where he is going—LONDON—and what he plans to do there —LIFT the crown jewels. The destination and the action must begin with the same letter. In this activity begin with A but permit students to skip letters which are difficult for them; they can come back to these later.

I am going to Australia to address a group of kangaroo hunters.
I am going to Boston to browse through historic mansions.
I am going to Chicago to chastise the gangsters.

WHAT CAN I BUY? is a variation of ABC GEOGRAPHY. Here the student is given a destination such as LONDON and asked the question, "What can I buy there?" to which he answers as many items as possible all of which must in this case begin with L—lipstick, lace, lilacs, limousines, limes, lighthouses, lollipops.

Group games

The class can play a variety of games as a group with each person participating individually. Usually no score is kept.

FAMILIAR GAMES are used repeatedly across the nation and are probably known by every elementary school child. These games continue to prove enjoyable interspersed with less commonly known games. Here is a reminder list of these old favorites:

Dog, Dog, Your Bone Is Gone (Have several dogs and several bones)
Simon Says
Seven Up
I See Something
Fruit Basket Upset
Hangman
Buzz
Twenty Questions

POISON is played with a small wooden block or other object which can be passed rapidly from desk to desk. No one wants to be caught with the block as the leader counts to ten, turns around, and cries, "Poison!" The person on whose desk the block is lying at that time becomes the next leader. No one gets out of his seat except the one who acts as the Leader.

TOUCH AND TAG requires the first person to touch an object, perhaps the door, in the room and then another class member. The person tagged must then tag the door, and another object, perhaps, the wastebasket, and then a third person. That person must touch the door, the wastebasket, another object, and a fourth person, and so on.

ANIMAL, FISH, OR FOWL is a game which can be played by any number of students. The leader calls the name of a student, then says one of the categories, FISH. He then counts rapidly from 1 to 10 trying to reach ten before the designated student can name a fish.

SHERLOCK HOLMES is the child who is selected to leave the room. While he is gone, another child (or several) is selected to hide in the closet. Other children may change seats to confuse the detective. When Sherlock returns, he tries to name the person who is gone within a given limit of time.

WHO STOLE THE PEANUTS FROM THE PEANUT CAN? is a provocative game in which each student is given a number in order starting with one. Number ONE acts as the leader for the group in chanting and clapping the following rhythm:

K T O T K T O
Who stole the peanuts from the peanut can?

T K T K
Number SIX (Leader chooses any number) stole the peanuts

T K T O
from the peanut can.

T K
Who me? (Number SIX must answer without breaking the rhythm.)

T O
YES, you! (Group responds in rhythm.)

T K
Couldn't be! (SIX answers.)

T O
Then, who? (Group questions.)

T K T K
(SIX passes the chant.) Number ELEVEN stole the peanuts

T K T O
from the peanut can. (Then number ELEVEN must answer, and so on.)

K = Slap knees
T = Clap hands together
O = Throw hands out after clapping

The object of this game is to keep the chanting and clapping going without a break; each person tries not to make mistakes so that he will move toward the Number ONE position. If a student is inattentive, he will not respond quickly, and the rhythm breaks. The one making the mistake moves to the last position, and everyone else moves up one seat. ALL THE NUMBERS of those who move up will change which means that each must be alert to remember new numbers. In beginning the chant again ONE leads. This game can be played with students in rows, but it works even better if all are seated in a circle. (Have several students work out the directions for this activity which they can then teach the class. It's FUN!)

I SPY! involves the "hiding" of a small object (chalk, rubber eraser, small box) in a place where it can readily be seen without the movement of any concealing material. Five students are chosen to leave the room while one person places the object. As the five enter, they look around the room; if they spy the object, they simply sit down at their desks saying, "I Spy!" The others continue to search until all have found it. The person who hid the object may be designated to hint the location by saying, "You're cold." or "You're getting warmer." The student who first spied the object then hides it.

BLINDFOLDED ARTISTS stand before the chalkboard with chalk in hand. The leader designates something they are to draw such as a horse. As he calls out directions—Draw a body, Draw a head, Add two ears, Put on a tail—they draw a horse. The results are then admired by all.

ERASER TAG is an active game in which two persons balance an eraser on their heads while one attempts to tag the other. The two players are sometimes named CAT and MOUSE. If the eraser falls, or one player is caught, that player selects someone to take his place.

BATTY BALLOONS is a game which involves everyone actively although all remain at their desks. Several inflated balloons are batted back and forth as two teams try to get them to selected goals. Teams may consist of alternate rows with rows 1, 3, and 5 playing against 2, 4, and 6 as one group of players tries to work the balloons to the back of the room while the other tries to bat balloons toward the front.

MY UNCLE WENT TO BOMBAY and brought me back a rocking chair (begin rocking motion). The next student repeats, "My uncle went to Bombay and brought me back a rocking chair (begins rocking) and a fan (begins fanning also). The next person repeats these words and motions and adds a third. All continue the motions until someone breaks down or a new list may be started with each row of students.

CAT AND DOG FIGHT involves two students who walk rapidly in chase around the room. As the dog chases the cat, the cat can save himself only by standing at the end of a row calling, "MEOW, MEOW, MEOW!" All the students in that row move up one position with the person at the head of the row becoming the DOG. The former DOG then becomes the CAT who is being chased.

WHO AM I? is the question which each student tries to answer for himself. Pin a name of a famous personage, a known character in a book, a figure in history on the back of each student. Each in turn shows the class his name and stands before the class asking questions of specific people in the room such as, "John, am I a living American?" "Mary, was I known for writing a book?" Questions asked must require YES or NO answers. See who can identify his person through only a few questions.

Exercise

CALISTHENICS can be enjoyable and offer an excellent change of pace for students who have been working at their desks for a period of time. Standing beside the desk each student has room enough for many simple exercises.

Touching the toes
Running in place
Stretching hands out to sides or above head
Standing on tiptoe and slowly down
Knee bends, squatting position
Touching right toe with left hand and reverse

SIMON SAYS is an old favorite which provides exercise. The Leader (Simon) directs the class to perform various acts. They are to perform only when the directions are preceded by the words, "Simon says . . ." Those who do the action described at the wrong time must be seated. Let students be the Leader competing to see who can seat the most people in five minutes. In this way no one is seated very long, and several students have a chance to be the Leader.

WEATHER VANE is a good way to combine exercise with learning the directions. The Weather Man calls, "The wind is blowing from the South." All must turn so their arms point North and South like a weather vane. If he calls, "The wind is blowing from the Northeast," all must turn with arms extending Northeast-Southwest. If there is a Tornado or Hurricane, all will spin around.

BIRDS FLY, but do dogs fly or goats? When the Leader says, "Robins fly," everyone flaps his wings, but when he says, "Horses fly," they must not fly even though the Leader tries to fool them.

ON COMMAND calls for rapid moving of seats as the Leader says, "Everybody move one seat to the North." or "Move two seats to the West." The person at the outer edge in these exchanges moves to the end of the row or the opposite side of the room.

On the Playground

Children in the elementary school have limitless energy and need an opportunity to exercise and to develop skills of play. For outdoor activities it is worth a few minutes of classroom time to organize PLAYGROUND PLANS. If teams are already chosen, or several students are selected to lead certain activities, the playground time will be more rewarding and supervisors will have less difficulty with behavior.

Team games

RELAYS are probably used more than any other type of team game, both indoor and outdoor. Students will continue to enjoy them as long as ample variety is ensured. Here is a list of different activities which can be done relay fashion:

Kick a ball around a specified goal and back
Run while holding ankles

Duck waddle (squatting)
Crab walk (squatting, then tipped back with hands on ground)
Camel walk (walking on hands and feet with knees straight)
Skip, gallop, hop, walk backward
Obstacles around which to run, hurdles to jump or scale
Dribble a basketball
Hand ball over one player's head and under legs of next
Cartwheels
Three-legged race
Wheelbarrow
Elephant walk (one person atop the toes of another)
Caterpillar (hands on floor, feet inch up to meet hands)

Winter games

In cold climates there is a special need for games which require everyone to move around so that each gets exercise and keeps reasonably warm. Here are some effective activities for cold weather.

FOLLOW THE LEADER enables the whole group to participate. The Leader can invent a variety of movements to provide exercise.

Hopping, skipping, jumping, galloping
Walking backward; sliding sideward
Winding in toward the center of the circle and out again
Running around an obstacle
Walking by two's, four's
Duck waddle; camel walk
Touching toes three times
Bounce a ball three times; pass it to the next person

SNOWBALLING TARGETS especially appeals to the boys. If large cardboard targets (similar to those used in archery) are provided, students can compete individually or as teams to see who is the most accurate. Other types of targets can be used—tin cans set along a board supported by wooden horses or a large cowbell hung from an upright support. Measure off twenty feet (adjust to the group) to mark a place where each participant stands for throwing.

SNOW SCULPTURE is a challenging activity for large or small groups. All can work on one large sculptured animal or small groups can develop varied selections. Each room can work on one project with a date set for judging THE MOST BEAUTIFUL, THE MOST IMAGINATIVE, etc.

A SNOWMAN ARMY can be made in areas of heavy snow. Let students work in teams of two or three to construct snowmen in one part of the playground. See how many can be made in one recess period; add to the army as long as the snow and interest last.

FOX AND GEESE is a must after a fresh fall of snow. The game can quickly be organized if the group follows a leader who leads them in a large circle. After circling several times to tramp the path well, the leader can crisscross the circle a number of times to make more paths. A fox is then selected to chase the geese.

Group games

WALK AS I DO can best be played in circle formation. The Leader stands in the center and calls, "Walk like an old lady carrying an umbrella as she tries to avoid puddles on a rainy day," or "Walk like a boy who has a new Yo-Yo on a bright spring day." The group walks around the circle in the manner directed.

BULL IN THE PEN calls for one player, THE BULL, to be encircled by the class who lock their arms tightly. THE BULL charges and tries to break through the pen. If he succeeds in getting free, he runs away with all running after him to catch him.

RED LIGHT, GREEN LIGHT is a well known game which can be played by any number of children. The group spreads out along a line while the leader closes his eyes and counts to ten, then calls quickly, "Red Light!" Anyone caught moving against the Red Light must return to the starting point.

TAG has been a favorite game in varied form for ages. Introduce students to variations of this versatile activity which includes any number of players.

Stoop Tag (You're safe if stooping.)
Stork Tag (Safety is ensured by standing on one leg.)
Statues (The student kneels with outstretched arms for safety.)
Link Tag (Several children link arms with the two end people able to tag.)

Chinese Tag (Person tagged must hold his right hand on place tagged.)
Frozen Tag (Person tagged is frozen in position until a free player touches him.)
Hop Tag (All players hop)
Shadow Tag (IT tries to step on shadow of player.)
Ball Tag (Ball is thrown at players to catch them.)

BALLOON BREAKERS necessitates a balloon for each child. The inflated balloon is attached by string to the right ankle. Each student tries to break the balloon of another student while still protecting his own. The winner is the person who has an unbroken balloon.

KING OF THE RING is especially good for boys. A six to eight foot ring is drawn or made with a rope. All of the boys get a turn to be in the ring, but six begin. When the whistle is blown, the first six boys in the ring begin to try pushing each other out of the circle without the use of hands. Anyone stepping on the line, falling down, or moving outside the circle is eliminated and moves to the end of the line of boys. The person at the head of the line goes into the circle to replace that boy. The winner is the one who remains after all others have been eliminated.

COME WITH ME is a good game for younger children. One child skips around the outer edge of the circle. He tags someone saying, "Come skip with me." They hold hands and skip around. The first child then takes a place in the circle while the second one invites the next child to join him, "Come hop with me." The game continues in this way around the circle with each child getting a turn using varied movements.

FLYING DUTCHMAN is an active circle game in which a pair of students walks around the outer circle. Suddenly they tag the hands of two people who are next to each other and continue around the circle running fast. The tagged pair immediately begins running around the circle in the opposite direction in an effort to get back to the vacant spot before the first pair.

OLD FAVORITES still entertain the modern child. Here is a Reminder List of some of the more familiar outdoor games:

Red Rover, Red Rover, We Dare ______ to Come Over
London Bridge

Tisket-a-Tasket
Dodge Ball
Farmer in the Dell
Mother, May I?
Steal the Bacon

THREE DEEP (or Two Deep) is played with groups of three students who stand behind each other with these groups forming a circle. Two players are designated the CAT and RAT (or other titles) who chase each other. The RAT who is being chased can save himself by stepping in front of a group so that the last one of the three must leave. The displaced student must then become the CAT who chases the former CAT.

SQUIRREL IN THE CAGE is very much like Three Deep in that students are grouped in threes (or more), but in this case the center child in each group is a SQUIRREL who is safely in a tree. A student is selected to be the DOG or the HUNTER who chases one SQUIRREL (who has no tree). The SQUIRREL saves himself by hopping into a "tree" forcing that squirrel out.

Individual activities

JUMPING ROPE provides for both individual and group participation. Heavy grade rope can be purchased in quantity to cut in ten to twelve foot lengths for use in jumping activities. Encourage students to share their knowledge of verses for jumping and other activities such as Fox and Geese, High Water, and Follow the Leader. Students can also compose verses suitable for jumping activities. Here are jumping variations which can be suggested:

Touch ground with hands on alternate jumps.
Sparrow hop (jump in bent position).
Jump on all fours.
Two people hold hands and jump together.
Jump in air and touch toes with fingers.
Climb the ladder (jump toward one end and back)

ALARIA is another activity which has continued to interest girls. As the child bounces the ball, she counts thus: "1,2,3, Alaria; 4,5,6, Alaria; 7,8,9, Alaria; 10, Alaria, Postman." On the word Alaria the leg is passed over the ball. (More skilled players will use the right leg and later the left leg.) The number of times the leg is passed over increases each time with the counting continuing: "1,2,3, Alaria, Alaria," and so on. Encourage students to invent new bouncing games.

CONTESTS add to the excitement and interest of familiar activities. Competitions can be arranged with a small committee keeping scores and conducting the contest for several days. Here are suggestions for competitions:

Who can bounce the ball the most consecutive times?
Who can jump rope individually the most times without missing?
Who can throw a ball (any specified size) the farthest?
Who can run a certain distance the fastest?
Who can broad jump the farthest?

ORIENTAL PUSHUPS are fun both outdoors and in the multipurpose room. Two players sit on the floor or grass back to back with arms locked. At a signal they push against each other trying to stand up. With practice and cooperation they learn to achieve this tricky feat.

POWER TESTS are especially appealing to the boys. Two players face each other across a line drawn in the dirt. At a signal they take hold of each other's right hand and pull in an effort to pull the opponent across the line.

Play Day

In the spring students are enthusiastic participants in a Play Day which is organized by a committee of students and can include the whole school. Activities may be divided into several areas to provide for differences in physical maturity. A variety of contests and activities can be scheduled with each room being responsible for one activity. It is helpful if entrants are signed up ahead of time for all events with each child entering something and the number of entries being limited for any one individual. Listed here are some activities which might be included:

Contests—Running, jumping, throwing (Several entrants from each room)
Races—Wheelbarrow, Three-legged, Backward, Distances
Relays—(Selected team representing each room)
Scavenger Hunt—(Each room as a team)

The room amassing the most points can be awarded a prize that all can share. Make a "gold cup" by inverting a plastic bottle as pictured. Spray with gold paint and fill with wrapped candy.

In the Multipurpose Room

Many of the activities already described work equally well in the multipurpose room. Presented here are additional activities which are especially suitable for the large indoor area.

Exercises

PHYSICAL FITNESS TESTS place stress on the development of physical skill through the use of charts listing varied skills in which each student tries to achieve at least minimum ability. Include some of the following:

Running in place
Pushups (modified for girls)
Touching the toes with both hands
Turning somersaults (backwards and forwards)
Jumping rope
Ball throwing
Knee bends

Ball activities

VOLLEY BALL is an excellent indoor sport which permits the whole class to participate. Younger students succeed well with a variation which requires the catching of the ball. The person catching the ball immediately puts it back into play without the use of a special serve. Assists are permitted as needed.

KICK BALL can be played indoors. This game can also be varied with the batter catching the pitched ball and throwing it rather than kicking it. The rules are the same as those for softball.

Rules for games may be obtained from:

The Athletic Institute
209 South State Street
Chicago 4, Illinois

VARIATIONS OF BASKETBALL can be played with a mixed group. Divide the group into two teams. Each team passes the ball ten (or any specified number) times. The team possessing the ball tries to score one point by passing without interception. If they succeed, the ball is then given to the other side who tries to complete ten passes for a point.

For practice in shooting baskets divide the group according to the number of baskets available. Each group lines up before a basket. The first person bounces the ball, approaches the basket, shoots, catches the ball, bounces it to the next person, and goes to the end of the line. This shooting practice moves quickly so that each person has a number of turns.

Group games

POM POM PULLAWAY is an exciting game for a large group. Divide the group in half with each half lining up at opposite sides of the room. One group is called to advance toward the other until the Leader calls, "Pom, Pom, Pullaway." At this signal the advancing team turns to run back home. The other team runs forward to catch anybody they can; those caught join that team. Then the action reverses.

MIDNIGHT is a game in which the fox chases the sheep. The Fox's Den (there may be more than one fox) is at one corner of the room. The Sheep's Fold is located diagonally across the room. The Fox and Sheep all go out walking. The sheep repeatedly ask the fox what time it is as they advance closer. He answers, "It's five o'clock," or "It's eight o'clock." When he replies, "It's MIDNIGHT!" they run home as he tries to catch them. Those caught are taken back to the Fox's Den.

> **To distinguish one team from another or the persons who are chasing the group as in MIDNIGHT prepare a number of brightly colored sashes of inexpensive cotton cloth which can be tied on players to identify them.**

HERE WE COME, WHERE FROM?, PENNSYLVANIA, WHAT'S YOUR TRADE?, LEMONADE is a familiar chant for yet another Chase. One team advances toward the other as they begin the chant. The other team responds in turn ending with the command, "Show us!" The advancing team must then demonstrate its trade (lumberjack, surgeon, school principal, storekeeper) while the opponents try to guess what is being demonstrated. When the correct guess is made, members of the first team run toward home while those of the other team try to catch all they can.

Tumbling

Mats or inexpensive mattresses are worthwhile additions to equipment for physical education where indoor activity is essential. Students enjoy a variety of simple tumbling activities as well as gymnastics.

Forward roll from a squatting position
Forward roll from a standing position
Backward roll
Cartwheel
Headstand
Tip-up—From squatting position raise body above hands
Pyramids

INDIAN WRESTLING is started from a prone position with two persons lying side by side with their heads at opposite ends. At a signal both players raise the leg nearest the opponent and lock it around that of his opponent. Without moving from the flat position, they try to turn each other over.

Dancing and rhythms

Musical activities can be done in lines, circles, or with partners. (See Chapter 9.) At least one set of records should be purchased for use in teaching students folk dances. Select a set which includes some of the following:

Gustaf's Skoal	Schottische
Virginia Reel	Varsovienne
Oh, Johnny	Minuet
Sicilian Circle	Hansel and Gretel
Patty Cake Polka	La Raspa

Folk dancing is an excellent activity for the noon hour for the older students.

MARCHING AND DRILLING are of interest to most students. The class can begin with simple marching skills—attention, mark time, keeping time while moving. They can learn to respond to the Halt command by allowing two beats after the command and to get back in step with the group by skipping. After these basic skills are acquired you can add Right Face, Left Face, Address Right, and Address Left and students can learn to pivot while making a turn.

Have the group march around the outer edge of the room; then direct them to come down the center in two's and then in four's. (You may use this technique for readying the group for relays.) Marching is another good beginning activity for a physical education period. Lined up at attention the group can Address Right and count off to break into groups for a game.

A WORD TO THE TEACHER

How can you continue to find creative stimulating ideas to enrich your teaching? Presented here are methods which we have found helpful in searching out provocative ideas and organizing these ideas for classroom use.

The idea file

One of the most effective methods for collecting ideas we have found to be what we term an IDEA FILE. This file consists of four-by-six inch cards on which we record briefly ideas which we hear or read about. (A shoebox is a good holder for this card file.) The ideas are classified by subject or interest area. Some of the categories which we use that would be practical for any teacher include:

Addresses
Art
Books
Bulletin boards
Games
Gifted students
Listening
Mathematics
Music
Poetry
Quotations
Reading
Science
Social studies
Speaking
Writing

Since the file is meant for our personal use, we consider it unnecessary and impractical to write detailed information about every idea. We record only an explanation that is sufficient to remind us of the technique. Some ideas, of course, require the recording of more information than do others. Here are two sample cards from our file:

BB

8

$\begin{array}{r} 5 \\ +3 \\ \hline \end{array}$	$\begin{array}{r} 10 \\ -2 \\ \hline \end{array}$

$\begin{array}{r} 9 \\ -1 \\ \hline \end{array}$ $\begin{array}{r} 6 \\ +2 \\ \hline \end{array}$ $\begin{array}{r} 4 \\ +4 \\ \hline \end{array}$

Or Wr

Pass out leaf shapes in many colors.

What does this color mean to you? What do you associate with this color? Why?

Read portions of:
Hailstones & Halibut Bones, O'Neill

Sources of ideas

There are many sources for good teaching ideas. Perhaps one of the best is your colleague down the hall. Talk to other teachers about ideas for teaching; most people are quite willing to exchange ideas. Observe, too, what is going on in the classrooms you visit. You can collect many bulletin board ideas in this way as well as other types of activities.

Some magazines supply numerous suggestions for teaching. Each month try to leaf through several of the following: *Scholastic Teacher, Instructor, Grade Teacher, Elementary English, Art and Activities, Clearing House, School Arts,* and *Wilson Library Journal.* Explore back issues of these journals in college libraries. Women's magazines also provide interesting art activities especially around the holidays. Read magazines with a packet of file cards beside you so that ideas can be recorded quickly while they are fresh in your mind.

Ideas may appear in strange places. A store window decoration, an advertisement in a newspaper, a television commercial—varied sources may suggest interesting ideas for your classroom.

Books, too, can supply ideas which are new to you. Several companies are publishing booklets on a variety of topics which are of interest to classroom teachers. You can request publication lists which will describe their offerings.

Contemporary Press. Box 1524. San Jose, California.

Fearon Publishers, Inc. 828 Valencia Street, San Francisco 10, California.

Perceptive Publishing Co., 2795½ Central Blvd., Eugene, Oregon.

Teachers Practical Press. 47 Frank St., Valley Stream, Long Island, New York.

An open mind for ideas

In order to find new ideas you must be prepared to accept new ways of teaching. Too often we hear teachers remark, "That's nonsense," "It won't work," or "I've been using this method for years." No new idea will be able to penetrate this rigid wall of resistance. In order to discover new ideas, therefore, we must first of all sincerely want to find them; we must reach out to them with open minds.

Beware, too, of labels which tag a teaching technique as being for Grades Two and Three or for the Upper Grades. In this book, as you may have noticed, grade levels are seldom mentioned because we truly feel that effective teaching ideas can usually be used, at least in adapted form, in any grade. The children interpret the method at their own individual levels of ability which, as you know, vary tremendously even within one classroom.

TRY A NEW IDEA EACH WEEK. It takes courage to try new techniques, but it is also rewarding both for the student and the teacher. New ideas add sparkle to teaching!

Varying techniques

Another source of ideas lies in the techniques which you already know. A good idea can and should be repeated; a lapse of time between repetitions, however, will add immeasurably to its success.

ADAPT IDEAS so that they appear new the next time they are presented to the class. If, for example, you used a large picture to motivate student writing, the next time you may have each write about a small picture individually. If students have made time lines of events during the colonial days of our country, later you may have students construct time lines based on the life of a person. A certain familiarity with the technique is an advantage to a student as he works on a different topic.

If you have used ideas in one subject area, remember, too, that these teaching techniques are also useful in other subject areas. The game, Categories, is an excellent example of an activity which can be adapted to almost any subject area—SCIENCE, LANGUAGE, READING, HISTORY, GEOGRAPHY. Many ideas described under Creative Writing are also equally effective as oral language activities and as methods for motivating art experiences.

INVENT NEW IDEAS. Students can assist in the production of new ways for exploring subjects which are to be studied. This is an interesting method of developing creative thinking in students and in yourself as you examine the possibilities for studying a new topic. Try BRAINSTORMING with your students. This technique for producing ideas has been developed by Alex Osburn in *Applied Imagination* (Scribner's, 1957) and calls simply for the presentation of a problem to a group which begins thinking of all possible solutions. Rules for brainstorming are not complicated but must be observed carefully for successful use of this method:

1. All ideas are recorded, no matter how fantastic they seem because they may lead to other more practical ideas.
2. No ridicule or censure is permitted; it's a waste of time and inhibits the creation of ideas.
3. Adaptions of ideas already mentioned are encouraged, for this is frequently the way good ideas are produced.

Suppose, for instance, you explain to your class that the next unit of study will be focused on the Civil War and that you would like them to help you in thinking of ways the class might gain the most benefit from this study. In your own words explain to them the rules for Brainstorming and perhaps suggest several sample ideas yourself to get them started. Many common ideas will be named, but it is surprising what fresh approaches are often suggested. Too, the very thought that they helped select the methods for developing the study assists in motivating interest. Other areas for brainstorming include:

Story Starters (Titles, First Lines, Last Lines, Settings)
Beautifying the Classroom, Schoolyard, Hall
Getting Students to Read Books
Organizing Playground Activities

IN SUMMARY, then, for maintaining a continuing file of stimulating teaching ideas, we recommend that you:

Search for new teaching ideas with a receptive mind,
Record these ideas for later reference, and
Use new ideas frequently for a stimulating approach to teaching.

INDEX

INDEX

L

M

O

P

Q

R

S

T

V

W